TRANSCENDENT
MIND

-√\/\-

TRANSCENDENT MIND

RETHINKING THE SCIENCE OF CONSCIOUSNESS

IMANTS BARUŠS

JULIA MOSSBRIDGE

AMERICAN PSYCHOLOGICAL ASSOCIATION
WASHINGTON, DC

Published by
American Psychological Association
750 First Street, NE
Washington, DC 20002
www.apa.org

To order
APA Order Department
P.O. Box 92984
Washington, DC 20090-2984
Tel: (800) 374-2721; Direct: (202) 336-5510
Fax: (202) 336-5502; TDD/TTY: (202) 336-6123
Online: www.apa.org/pubs/books
E-mail: order@apa.org

In the U.K., Europe, Africa, and the Middle East, copies may be ordered from
American Psychological Association
3 Henrietta Street
Covent Garden, London
WC2E 8LU England

Typeset in Goudy by Circle Graphics, Inc., Columbia, MD

Printer: United Book Press, Baltimore, MD
Cover Designer: Beth Schlenoff Design, Bethesda, MD
Cover Art: *Mark Boccuzzi's computer-generated image #5226.* The image used on the cover was created by Mark Boccuzzi from data that he collected on a random number generator while the authors thought about the book's title. He processed the resultant numeric data using custom software, converting the output of the random number generator into the cover art. A description of this process and more examples of art created in this way can be found in his book, *Visualizing Intention: Art Informed by Science.*

The opinions and statements published are the responsibility of the authors, and such opinions and statements do not necessarily represent the policies of the American Psychological Association.

Library of Congress Cataloging-in-Publication Data

Names: Baruss, Imants, 1952- author. | Mossbridge, Julia, 1969- author.
Title: Transcendent mind : rethinking the science of consciousness / Imants Baruss and Julia Mossbridge.
Description: Washington, DC : American Psychological Association, [2017] | Includes bibliographical references and index.
Identifiers: LCCN 2016009053 | ISBN 9781433822773 | ISBN 1433822776
Subjects: LCSH: Consciousness.
Classification: LCC BF311 .B3324 2017 | DDC 153—dc23
LC record available at https://lccn.loc.gov/2016009053

British Library Cataloguing-in-Publication Data
A CIP record is available from the British Library.

Printed in the United States of America
First Edition

http://dx.doi.org/10.1037/15957-000

One does not have to wait for the advance of neuroscience to know that one has been stung by a bee!

—Max Velmans (2009, p. 46)

I'm going to describe to you how Nature is—and if you don't like it, that's going to get in the way of your understanding it. It's a problem that physicists have learned to deal with: They've learned to realize that whether they like a theory or they don't like a theory is *not* the essential question. Rather, it is whether or not the theory gives predictions that agree with experiment. It is not a question of whether a theory is philosophically delightful, or easy to understand, or perfectly reasonable from the point of view of common sense. The theory of quantum electrodynamics describes Nature as absurd from the point of view of common sense. And it agrees fully with experiment.

—Richard Feynman (1985/2006, p. 10; emphasis in original)

Not being tied to any particular school of thought, I felt at perfect liberty to see what I could learn about the subject of psychometry. I was warned by friends in the world of science that it might be very damaging to my reputation, but, having no interest in my reputation, I took no notice.

—Thomas Charles Lethbridge (1961, p. 65)

CONTENTS

ACKNOWLEDGMENTS

We thank the following reviewers for reading the prospectus or selections from the manuscript and providing us with critical comments, listed in the approximate order of their initial participation: Leslie Combs, Achim Kempf, Bruce Greyson, Antonio Calcagno, Ram Valluri, Ron Leonard, Julie Beischel, Patricia Pearson, Gerry McKeon, Rob Werstine, Dean Radin, Bryan Williams, Natalie Trent, Leanna Standish, Carlos Alvarado, Peter Bancel, John Kruth, Ed Modestino, Karen Martin, James Barrell, Zoran Josipovic, Edward Kelly, Jonathan Schooler, and Ben Goertzel. None of our readers are responsible for any errors or omissions that might remain in the book, nor do they necessarily agree with anything that we say.

Imants Barušs is grateful to King's University College at Western University Canada for a paid sabbatical leave that allowed him to work on this book without interruption. He also thanks King's University College for research grants and Medical Technology (WB) Inc. for financial support. And he appreciates the prompt and supportive response by Claire Callaghan, the Director of Libraries at King's University College, and her staff to requests for various resource materials. Finally, Imants thanks Solveiga Miezītis, who always understood the angry young poet and encouraged and mentored him through 5 decades of career development.

Julia Mossbridge is grateful to Northwestern University, specifically the support, training, and stimulating conversations offered by Satoru Suzuki, Marcia Grabowecky, and Ken Paller. She also thanks the Bial Foundation, who offered generous financial support for the work discussed in this book. Julia is grateful as well to the Institute of Noetic Sciences for their encouragement and support, as well as President and CEO Cassandra Vieten for bringing Julia into such an open, rigorous, and compassionate community of learners. Finally, Julia thanks her transcendently loving, kind, and supportive husband, Brooks Palmer; her delightful son, Joseph; her son's industrious father, Adam Mossbridge; her generous father, Edward W. Walbridge; her insightful mother, Jean Walbridge; her intuitive stepmother, Karen Martin; and her brilliant sister, Catherine Jennifer Walbridge for their ideas, encouragement, and love during the course of writing this book.

We thank our research assistant, Shannon Foskett, for unearthing, retrieving, and organizing a large amount of resource materials, providing critical feedback, and assisting with editing. We appreciate the support that we have received from everyone at APA Books in planning, writing, and producing this book, particularly Susan Reynolds, our acquisitions editor, and Tyler Aune, our development editor. Finally, we thank our students and colleagues for many insightful discussions about the material in this book. This book was written for them and for anyone else who would like to have a rational discussion at the cutting edge of consciousness research.

TRANSCENDENT
MIND

INTRODUCTION

We are in the midst of a sea change. Receding from view is materialism, whereby physical phenomena are assumed to be primary and consciousness is regarded as secondary. Approaching our sights is a complete reversal of perspective. According to this alternative view, consciousness is primary and the physical is secondary. In other words, materialism is receding and giving way to ideas about reality in which consciousness plays a key role (Barušs, 2007b; Koons & Bealer, 2010; Nagel, 2012; Pfeiffer, Mack, & Devereux, 2007; Sheldrake, 2012; Tart, 2009).

In keeping with that sea change, the purpose of this book is to explore what consciousness looks like when we do not automatically assume that consciousness must arise from the workings of matter. "Whoa!" the reader might say. "Not so fast! I like materialism. I didn't know that there was anything wrong with it!" or "I'm not dogmatic, but I want to see compelling evidence before I'm willing to become more skeptical about materialism. I'm

http://dx.doi.org/10.1037/15957-001
Transcendent Mind: Rethinking the Science of Consciousness, by I. Barušs and J. Mossbridge

willing to be convinced by some really persuasive evidence. I just haven't seen any yet." Other readers might say, "It's about time! Let's get on with it!" We begin this book by addressing the first reader's concerns. Then in later chapters, we look at research concerning anomalous aspects of consciousness—such as near-death experiences, interactions with discarnate beings, and direct mental influence on physical processes—and examine what this research tells us about the nature of consciousness and its relationship to physical phenomena.

We first examine materialism in detail in Chapter 1 ("Beyond Materialism"). There we address the problems with materialism. Then we discuss the manner in which materialism continues to dominate academia through the suppression of contrary evidence and views. We also consider a spectrum of beliefs about consciousness and reality, some of which include the notion that meaning matters and that consciousness is necessary for the occurrence of meaning.

Next we review some of the evidence for anomalous information transfer (Chapter 2, "Shared Mind"). The evidence suggests that we can sometimes know what is going on in a place that we cannot perceive with our physical senses. We discuss the possibility of a "shared mind" that allows for interconnections between ourselves, other people, and the physical universe in which we live.

We next look at time, first as it is understood in modern physics, then in neuroscience and phenomenology (Chapter 3, "Rethinking Time"). We discuss evidence for precognition of various sorts, including studies showing that we are better able to anticipate the future at nonconscious levels than conscious ones. Looking at temporality amid alterations of consciousness, we find interesting variations, including frequent reports of individuals having stepped out of time altogether. And so we consider the differences between *apparent* time, the time described by ordinary physics and our everyday experience, and *deep* time, representing whatever ordering of events exists outside the confines of apparent time.

We next examine the possibility that there could be intelligences in the universe that we cannot perceive through our ordinary senses (Chapter 4, "Interactions With Discarnate Beings"). We consider several cases in which communication with such intelligences seems to have occurred. We note that these intelligences could offer a potential for healing but could also have a less benign effect on one's life.

Can the mind exist outside of the brain? Some lines of empirical evidence, particularly from near-death studies, are suggestive of this possibility (Chapter 5, "Separation of Mind From Brain"). In fact, the evidence could be read as indicating that, in some exceptional cases, the more the brain is compromised, the greater the clarity of mental activity when it comes to perceiving information that seems normally to be hidden from the realm of our ordinary experiences.

Next we consider reports of mental control over physical processes (Chapter 6, "Direct Mental Influence"), a phenomenon that appears to be the opposite of anomalous information transfer. Although it may be possible to access information beyond that which is gained from our usual senses, it also seems as though we might be able to influence some physical processes outside of our bodies directly with our minds. The potential extent of this effect could be quite large, if cases of dramatic anomalous influencing continue to hold up to scientific scrutiny.

We then consider the psyche itself as an instrument for observing subjective phenomena in concert with third-person confirmation (Chapter 7, "Reintegrating Subjectivity Into Consciousness Research"). We discuss how the psyche needs to be properly prepared by attenuating our psychological biases and learning to think logically to critically evaluate whatever empirical evidence is available. As such preparation proceeds, anomalous ways of gaining knowledge could unfold, if they were not already present, augmenting rationality by providing additional tools for research. And continued self-transformation could lead to transcendent states of consciousness in which both existential and practical questions are resolved.

Finally, we examine models of consciousness that could help explain the empirical data we have discussed (Chapter 8, "Transcendent Mind"). We briefly consider quantum models of consciousness, then turn to filter models and a "flicker-filter" theory. Although none of these models are completely satisfactory, they each offer insights that could be incorporated into a yet-to-be developed model of consciousness. We also present some potential future research strategies and clinical applications of the material considered in the book. We conclude by giving our best guess as to the true nature of consciousness, based on the empirical evidence available to us, knowing that whatever we say will be put to the test of future research and developed accordingly.

This book is written for those who would like to rethink our understanding of consciousness. Specifically, this book is for clinical psychologists, psychoanalysts, experimental psychologists, psychiatrists, neuroscientists, and anyone else who wants to create a new way forward within the constraints of empirical data and logical analysis but without the restrictions of dogma. It is for those who want to entertain the questions "What is this stuff called *mind*? What are its properties? What does it do? What is its relationship to the brain? How can we use the mind to explore itself?" and, "How can we use it to heal ourselves and others?" So let us proceed.

1

BEYOND MATERIALISM

The idea that consciousness may be fundamental and matter secondary is gaining ground.

—Bernard Haisch (2007, p. 58)

What do we mean by *materialism* anyway? Well, that depends. We will consider different definitions of materialism as we go through this chapter to try to understand the paradigm that is disappearing. We will need to touch on physics in a bit, given that physics is the discipline whose subject matter is the study of the nature of physical reality. But perhaps the place to start is with the historical rise of materialism as an intellectual tradition in Europe. That will give us our first definition of materialism.

A VERY BRIEF HISTORY OF MATERIALISM

In the 1600s, Pierre Gassendi and Robert Boyle reintroduced the Greek notion of atomism into early modern thought. The idea was that matter is made up of continuously existent, indivisible atoms located within an absolute

http://dx.doi.org/10.1037/15957-002
Transcendent Mind: Rethinking the Science of Consciousness, by I. Baruss and J. Mossbridge

space and time (A. Chalmers, 2008; Fisher, 2014). Around 1695, Gottfried Leibniz used clockwork as a metaphor for what he believed to be a mechanistic universe (Scott, 1997; Shapin, 1981). In 1748, David Hume discussed causation in terms of the motions of billiard balls (Hume, 1748/1993). And by 1814, Pierre-Simon Laplace maintained that if we were to know all of the forces at play in the present, we would know everything that had ever transpired in the past and everything that would occur in the future (Laplace, 1814/1951). A more contemporary way of saying this would be that if we knew all of the equations governing the spatial positions of fundamental particles as a function of time, along with their initial conditions, then we would know everything that there is to know about reality (Barušs, 2010, 2014b). Let us call this the *billiard-ball version of reality*. It constitutes the historical core of materialism.

There are several things to note about this version of reality. First, it is *scalable*, in that the indivisible atoms of which everything is made are assumed to be governed by the same laws that apply to people-sized events. Second, it is *deterministic*, in that all activity is the result of predictable interactions of atoms with one another. Third, this version is *objective*, in the sense that these atoms behave as they do independently of anyone's observation of them. Fourth, it is *reductionistic*, in that people-sized events, including people, consciousness, and so on, are thought to be ultimately nothing but the activity of indivisible atoms. Fifth, it depends on an *absolute space* within which all of this activity takes place. Sixth, time is uniformly ordered from the past into the future in a *linear* manner and evolves the same way for all observers, in *absolute time*. So we have a scalable, deterministic, objective, and reductionistic model of reality that depends on the existence of absolute space and time. Each of these six prongs of historical materialism has been pretty much dismantled by now.

THE DISAPPEARANCE OF MATTER

The billiard-ball notion of matter started to unravel in the late 1800s when scientists began looking carefully at black-body radiation and the photoelectric effect. It was discovered that the amount of energy that a system of particles can contain is not continuous; it is discrete, or *quantized*. The system has a smallest value of possible energy, the *quantum*, with all other energy levels being integral multiples of that smallest amount (Daintith, 2005). This discovery led to the development of various quantum theories that, together with Albert Einstein's relativity theories, set the tone for 20th-century physics. Key aspects of these theories have held up under experimental testing while at the same time continuing to develop in response to insights gained from both theoretical progress and experimental evidence. These theories give a picture of physical reality that is incompatible with the billiard-ball metaphor (Daintith, 2014; Polkinghorne, 2002). In other words, our intuitions about the way people-sized things work do not help us to make inferences about the actual subatomic nature of matter. Let us consider this in a bit more detail for a moment.

What about scalability and determinism? Suppose that we have an empty region of space—empty in the sense that there is nothing in it. It is just space. It turns out that even if we begin with a bounded, empty region of space, as time goes by, particles will appear and disappear in it when we look. Furthermore, we cannot predict when these particles will appear and disappear; all we know is the probability of their occurrence (Kuhlmann, 2013; Srednicki, 2007). Nor should they even be called "particles," or "waves" for that matter, or anything else that stems conceptually from classical physics (Lévy-Leblond, 1988), although we will continue to use the word *particles* because that is the usual convention. So scalability is an inappropriate heuristic for understanding reality because people-sized objects do not usually appear and then disappear again, but particles apparently do. And determinism does not apply because we cannot predict when these particles will appear and disappear.

Stranger still, scalability is further undermined. There have been experiments in which the properties of particles have been spatially separated. For instance, in a recent so-called Cheshire Cat experiment, a neutron's mass went down one spatial path while another property, called its *spin*, went down a spatially separate path (Denkmayr et al., 2014). So, how would that apply to billiard balls? This would be the equivalent of striking a blue billiard ball and having the billiard ball, minus any color, go off to the right, and having the color blue go off to the left all by itself. It is difficult to conceive of detaching the color of a billiard ball from the billiard ball itself. So again, scalability is an inappropriate heuristic for understanding the nature of physical reality.

Speaking of the properties of particles, here is something else that we can consider, which will undermine objectivity and reductionism. Suppose I want to know where a billiard ball is on a billiard table and what color it is. So I look and see that it is in the left corner of the table and that it is blue. Suppose, however, that instead of wanting to know where the billiard ball is and what color it is, I wanted to know how quickly that billiard ball is travelling and what color it is. I look, and I see that it is at rest and red. Red? How does it get to be red and not blue? At the people-sized level we are used to objects having stable properties, so that the color of the billiard ball would be the same, whether I were looking for that ball's position or its speed. But not so for quantum-sized events. In quantum theory, the properties of particles either have no values until we decide which properties to measure, or the values change depending on what else we choose to measure (Gröblacher et al., 2007; Kochen & Specker, 1967). In either case, the participation of an observer is essential to the way in which reality presents itself. And quantum theory does not explain the choices made by an observer. Thus, neither objectivity nor reductionism is an actual feature of physical reality.

The notion of an absolute space also turns out to be incorrect because the space between galaxies is slowly expanding (Daintith, 2005). What this means is that in some parts of the universe, fresh space is being created moment-by-moment in between the spaces that already exist. Or perhaps those regions of space are just "elastic" and getting "stretched." In either case, space is no longer an absolute container for physical events.

By now, it is probably not a surprise that time is not absolute either. According to Einstein's special theory of relativity, when we accelerate, then time slows down. In fact, if we were to accelerate through a region of empty space, not only would time slow down, but particles would show up (Crispino, Higuchi, & Matsas, 2008). In other words, if we were to just pass through empty space at a constant speed, there would be no particles present, except as we have already considered previously; but if we were to accelerate through that same space, then there would be particles present. That does not conform to our usual intuitions about the nature of matter at the people-sized level. So, scalability, objectivity, and absolute time are not valid ways of thinking about matter at the microlevel.

More catastrophically perhaps, for many physicists, time has disappeared entirely. "Physicists and philosophers alike have long told us (and many people think) that time is the ultimate illusion" (Smolin, 2013, p. *xi*). In other words, our experience of time is "an accident of our circumstance as human beings" (Smolin, 2013, p. *xii*) and not an essential feature of reality. Some are trying to bring it back (Smolin, 2013). But none conceptualize time as an absolute framework within which physical phenomena occur. We take up some of these ideas about time in Chapter 3, "Rethinking Time." But for now, we see that we cannot depend on scalability, determinism, objectivity, reductionism, absolute space, and absolute time for understanding matter. In other words, "subatomic particles behave in very peculiar and non-mechanistic ways, which differ radically from the behavior of objects in the everyday world" (Skrbina, 2005, p. 10).

The point of bringing up these bits of physics is to make the case that historical materialism is gone as a fundamental explanation for physical reality. Nonetheless, materialism works reasonably well for our everyday experience of people-sized events (Baruš, 2010). In fact, we could argue that quantum phenomena are irrelevant to a materialist conception of reality because all we care about are people-sized events, which follow the rules of classical mechanics, chemistry, and so on. However, quantum events are not somehow encapsulated in a microdomain that has nothing to do with us. For instance, periodically uranium-238 releases an alpha particle and becomes thorium-234 (Daintith, 2005). An alpha particle is a relatively big chunk of matter that is hurled into space, where it can be detected using a magnetic α-particle spectrometer, for instance (Pommé, 2015). Such alpha decay, as it is called (Daintith, 2005), is essentially stochastic and requires quantum mechanics for its description. In fact, we will discuss later in this book the use of random event generators, which are considered to be truly random because they are based on quantum processes. As we go along, we will also encounter other examples of the "upward creep" of quantum events. The point is that not only are people-sized events just what micro-events look like at the people-sized level, but the people-sized level cannot be adequately described without reference to the microlevel when its distinctive features noticeably intrude into the people-sized level.

Nonetheless, we could argue that quantum processes somewhere out there in the world have nothing to do with us, as long as we do not require radiation therapy and no one detonates a nuclear weapon, because what matters is that our brains can be described using classical mechanics, chemistry, and so on. Actually, an adequate understanding of the brain does require quantum mechanics. For instance, a synapse is so small that electrons would be expected to cross from a postsynaptic to a presynaptic membrane through a quantum process known as *quantum mechanical tunnelling*, thereby potentially affecting the release of neurotransmitters (E. H. Walker, 1970). More generally, quantum mechanics is needed to describe various microprocesses in the brain (Korf, 2015; Meijer, 2014).

So we can find ourselves in a somewhat dissociated state. Sure, we know that according to quantum theory there is nothing really "down there" until we look at "it" (Kuhlmann, 2013; Lloyd, 2006), and we can acknowledge that there could be some "upward creep" of quantum effects, perhaps even in the brain, but we do not think that this has anything to do with our daily lives.

In a related form of dissociation, we might know intellectually that the billiard-ball version of reality is fictional, but we nonetheless use a billiard-ball schema as a way of reasoning about reality. In particular, we use prototypes as a heuristic when we think about things. So when we think about something having to do with the nature of reality, we use the prototype of bumping billiard balls, which could override whatever logical reasoning we could be using. For instance, if someone were to suggest that there is life after death, we would immediately think that that is impossible because it is incompatible with our reliance on a billiard-ball schema. If the billiard balls stop bumping into one another in the way that they do during life, then consciousness must also stop. These worldviews and schemata create biases in our thinking that are notoriously difficult to uproot (Baruša, 2013b; Tart, 2009; cf. Koltko-Rivera, 2004). To make matters worse, *bias blindness* means that we are typically unaware of the biases that we bring to making judgments about anything (Pronin & Schmidt, 2013). In fact, in one study it was found that materialists were less likely to have examined their own beliefs about reality than nonmaterialists (Baruša & Moore, 1998). So we may know intellectually that historical materialism is false, but many of us, including psychologists and neuroscientists, are still reasoning as though it were true.

VARIATIONS ON MATERIALISM

It is reasonable to argue, however, that the concept of materialism can change; it does not need to reflect an immutable historical version (Hyman, 2010). Fair enough. So let us consider something more contemporary. Perhaps we do not need to move beyond materialism entirely, if we can just bring it up-to-date. Which brings us to physicalism, our second definition of materialism.

Some would argue that materialism has evolved into *physicalism*, "the view that the world contains just those types of things that physics says it contains" (Ney, 2008, p. 1035). Well, this is a problematic definition for several reasons. The first problem is known as *Hempel's dilemma* (Ney, 2008). If the definition refers to current physics, then physicalism is false, simply because every version of physics in the past has been found to be false, and there is no reason to think that the current version is going to be an exception. Or, more precisely perhaps, every version of physical reality has given way to an updated version of reality with better goodness-of-fit to the empirical data than previous versions of reality so that any "current theory" is not a good measure of those types of things that physics says the world contains (cf. Hempel, 1980). For instance, we have just seen that the notion that matter is made up of tiny billiard balls is false and has been replaced with a more comprehensive theory in which we no longer have good metaphors for what it is that constitutes matter. If the definition refers to a future, final, and completely accurate physics, then it is meaningless because we do not know what types of things a future physics will entail. If, for instance, a completed physics posits that mental entities are a fundamental aspect of the universe, then physicalism is just another way of talking about the essential reality of mental events, the very idea from which physicalism was originally supposed to be differentiated (Ney, 2008). In fact, there are physicists who have already stated that consciousness is a fundamental building block of reality (Baruša, 1986, 2006, 2008b, 2008c, 2009, 2010; Goswami, Reed, & Goswami, 1993; Stapp, 2001, 2004, 2007; E. H. Walker, 1970, 1977, 2000, 2001). So, in this case, what is gained by calling this idea *physicalism* (Barušs, 2007b)? Here it seems that physicalism is just a poor description of the idea that consciousness is fundamental to the universe.

A second problem is that physics does not speak with a single voice. There is no clear agreement on much of physics. In a sense, contemporary physics has come apart, with tension arising between relativity and quantum theories, and considerable disagreement about the fundamental nature of physical reality (Elitzur, Dolev, & Kolenda, 2005; Kuhlmann, 2013; Smolin, 2006, 2013). So, to whom are we going to listen? How are we to define "what physics says" the world contains? As a result of these problems, physicalism probably defaults to a reliance on whatever schemata about reality a person has rather than taking into account what physical science "says." In other words, we either accept a slippery physicalism that could easily be equivalent to its opposite, or we are left with a modern-day materialism that is really the same old billiard-ball version of reality. Because of these problems, physicalism is not a good candidate for an updated version of materialism.

NEUROSCIENTISM TO THE RESCUE?

A reader could argue that our concern here is not with the nature of matter but with the nature of consciousness, so that it should not matter to us what matter is really like. According to this argument, we do not need physics. All we need is neuroscience, which tells us about the activity of neurons. We would reject reductionism whereby "for purists, the real bottom will of course belong not to neuroscience but to physics" (Churchland, 1980, p. 207) and stay away from the quantum properties of brains. We do not care about the "real bottom," to which all other phenomena can be reduced, because we believe that even though this underlying structure must exist, it cannot distort the classically described activity of neurons (Koch, 2012). It is important to note that according to this argument, we assume that it is the activity of neurons themselves that gives rise to consciousness. This position is sometimes referred to as *neuroscientism* (Tallis, 2010, p. 3). Let this be our third definition of materialism, namely, the contention that consciousness is necessarily the result of neural activity that is assumed to be isolated from quantum considerations. This is, admittedly, a sloppy definition, but it is actually a tricky matter to give a definition of materialism in this context that can do the job without being easily refuted (Koons & Bealer, 2010), so the sloppy one is about as good as any. Let us unpack this definition to see what it entails.

First, we need to decide what we mean by *consciousness*. One of the authors, Imants Barušs, identified multiple referents of consciousness by analyzing 29 definitions of consciousness in the academic literature. He found that there were essentially four main meanings of the word, which he designated as consciousness$_1$, behavioral consciousness$_2$, subjective consciousness$_2$, and consciousness$_3$. *Consciousness$_1$* is the capacity of an appropriate organism or machine to discriminate stimuli in its environment and to act in a goal-directed manner. There are several things to note about this definition. First, it is a definition "from the outside" in that a judgment about the presence of consciousness$_1$ can be made through observation of a functioning system. Second, the notion of consciousness entails both input and output modes, so that consciousness is not just equivalent to "awareness." This feature also implies that a conscious system that has no control over its actions in the world would not be considered to have consciousness$_1$. Third, consciousness$_1$ is clearly a variable, in that there are organisms, such as various microorganisms, whose capacity to behave in this manner could be less complex than those of others, such as human beings. This means that someone using the word *consciousness* should indicate whether she has a threshold of complexity in mind and, if so, where that threshold occurs (Barušs, 1987, 2008a).

However, most of us who use the word *consciousness* want to refer to phenomena that are not available "from the outside" but only "from the inside" (Barušs, 1990; Toulmin, 1982). Thus, *subjective consciousness$_2$* refers to the contents of experience that occur subjectively for a person within the privacy of her own mind. This is a problem for conventional science given that observations are supposed to be made of events that are publicly accessible. Private experience, by its nature, is not publicly accessible and, therefore, not directly amenable to scientific investigation. Historically, subjective consciousness$_2$ was operationalized by adding the capacity for self-reference to consciousness$_1$, thereby resulting in the behavioral demonstration of metacognition as an operational definition of consciousness (Barušs, 1987, 2008a). Thus, we can define *behavioral consciousness$_2$* as an organism's or machine's ability to explicitly demonstrate knowledge of its situation or internal states (Barušs, 1987, 2008a). Now, of course, the operational version of consciousness$_2$ is clearly not logically equivalent to the subjective version because one could build a machine that appears to demonstrate consciousness but is not subjectively conscious. But this definition may be as close as we can get when attempting to look at a conscious system from the outside. And that gap, between the inside and the outside, will turn out to be lethal to materialism.

The fourth common referent of the word *consciousness* is also "from the inside." Whereas subjective consciousness$_2$ refers to the contents of experience, *consciousness$_3$* refers to the sense of existence that a person has for herself. Existence is occurring, and for many people, it is apparently experienced as occurring (Barušs, 1987, 2008a; Helminiak, 1984). We will adopt the term *qualia*, which refers to the "raw feels" of perceptions (Price & Barrell, 2012; Rosenberg, 2004) and use the expression *existential qualia* to refer to the subjective feelings that anything is going on at all. Thus, the word *consciousness* has also been used to refer to the presence of existential qualia. For the purposes of this book, unless we specify otherwise, when we use the word *consciousness* we will be referring to a combination of subjective consciousness$_2$ and consciousness$_3$. In other words, for us, consciousness refers to subjective events suffused with existential qualia that occur privately for a person.

Related to the notion of consciousness is that of mind. For the purposes of this book we define *mind* as the aspect of the psyche that embodies consciousness along with all nonconscious cognitive processes. We will add descriptors to both consciousness and mind as we engage with the material in this book. For instance, *transcendent mind* refers to the notion that mind is "transcendent" in nature, in that it cannot be adequately characterized in physical terms.

Embedded within our third definition of materialism, neuroscientism, is the contention that, in particular, existential qualia are necessarily the result of neural activity. Well, we clearly have a problem. Existential qualia do not seem anything like the neurons of which they are supposed to be made. Hence, we have an *explanatory gap*. To put it bluntly, qualia are a nuisance for mechanistic versions of the universe. According to one variation on Gottfried Leibniz's *principle of sufficient reason*, "there must be a rational reason for every apparent choice made in the construction of the universe. Every query of the form, 'Why is the universe like X rather than Y?' must have an answer" (Smolin, 2013, p. *xxvii*). If it is true that there is a reason for everything, then we can ask why existential qualia exist, rather than there just being a universe that runs "in the dark" without the "light" of consciousness (Haisch, 2007; Rosenberg, 2004; Seager & Allen-Hermanson, 2013). This is related to the *hard problem of consciousness* (D. J. Chalmers, 1995): How do we get existential qualia out of neurons?

THE FALSE PROMISE OF COMPUTATIONALISM

Working with neuroscientism as our definition of materialism, let us move forward and see what happens when we attempt to address the question "What is the process by which neurons produce existential qualia?" In general, there are two approaches that have been taken to answer this question—*emergentism* and *panpsychism* (Seager & Allen-Hermanson, 2013)—so let us take a quick look at those, starting with emergentism, which in this case refers to the notion that existential qualia naturally arise from brains or computational systems of the right sort.

Perhaps the place is start is with Alan Turing's *imitation game*, which is now usually referred to as the *Turing test*. In the course of the development of artificial intelligence we can ask at what point we should attribute intelligence to a machine. Turing suggested a game in which there is a computer, a person playing the role of "witness," and a person playing the role of "interrogator." The computer and witness are isolated from, but in communication with, the interrogator, who does not know which is the computer and which is the witness. The interrogator asks questions of each in turn to identify which is which. The object of the game is for the computer to get the interrogator to identify it as the witness and for the witness to assist the interrogator in making a correct identification. The point at which an interrogator makes an incorrect identification is the point at which we can say that a computer has passed the test for intelligence (Barušs, 1990; Turing, 1950).

The Turing test was conceived as a test of machine intelligence but has subsequently been extended to become a test for the presence of subjective consciousness$_2$ (Harnad, 1987). How? Using the terminology that we introduced previously, passing the Turing test requires a certain degree of behavioral consciousness$_2$. The idea is that we make judgments about the presence of subjective consciousness$_2$ in other people as a matter of course based on our observation of their behavioral consciousness$_2$, and so the right degree of behavioral consciousness$_2$ should be all that is required to infer the presence of subjective consciousness$_2$. Such a position is

> just the acknowledgment that observable behavior is all that psychologists will ever have by way of objective data, that the only case in which one can know there are subjective experiences going on for sure is one's own, and that the only ground for imputing them to anyone else is behavior indistinguishable from one's own. (Harnad, 1987)

So, we operationalized subjective consciousness$_2$ to get behavioral consciousness$_2$, and now we use the Turing test to take the reverse path by insisting that whenever we see behavioral consciousness$_2$, then subjective consciousness$_2$ must necessarily be present (cf. Dennett, 1978, 1982, 1988). Incidentally, such a position has consequences for the ethical treatment of animals (Koch, 2012) and machines whose feelings would thereby need to be taken into account. "What moral rights would an intermediate or marginally intelligent machine have?" (Lycan, 1987, p. 127).

The problem with this reverse path is that it is undermined by a flaw in logical thinking. It is like saying that because Sheila always brings a rain jacket to work on Thursdays, and she brought her rain jacket today, then today must be Thursday. Just because it *appears* that subjective consciousness$_2$ is required for the presence of behavioral consciousness$_2$ does not mean that it actually *is* required for the occurrence of behavioral consciousness$_2$. In other words, a system with behavioral consciousness$_2$ does not necessarily possess subjective consciousness$_2$ as well. The notion that behavioral consciousness$_2$ implies the presence of subjective consciousness$_2$ is a statement of faith. It is not logically necessary, nor is there any empirical evidence for it, nor *can* there be any empirical evidence for it given that no objective measure of subjective consciousness$_2$ is possible using conventional scientific methods. All we can do is make a leap of inference on the basis of what is objectively observable. For instance, as one neuroscientist argued, in the case of animal consciousness "[the] cornucopia of behavior and the numerous structural and molecular similarities between the canine and the human brain lead me to conclude that dogs have phenomenal feelings" (Koch, 2012, p. 116). All we are doing when we apply the Turing test for consciousness is asserting a belief that existential qualia must be present whenever the "right kind" of wiring produces the "right kind" of behavior. This does not move us toward understanding how consciousness emerges from neural activity. It moves us instead toward erroneously thinking that we understand how to determine whether consciousness is present.

Neuroscientism includes the contention that consciousness is necessarily the result of neural activity. Does this activity need to be neuronal? The argument as presented previously is an argument in the context of *computationalism* (Fodor, 2000; Horst, 2011), the notion that what determines cognition, emotions, consciousness, and so on is not the material of which some computing device is made but the calculations that the device carries out. In other words, existential qualia emerge from sufficiently complex calculations in a device that has the right causal connections to its environment (Barušs, 1990). Alternatively, we can restrict ourselves to only considering neurons and, more broadly, physical bodies, a move that makes consciousness *embedded cognition* (Horst, 2011). Or we might insist, as John Searle (1983) did, that consciousness is necessarily a biological process:

> On my view mental phenomena are biologically based: they are both caused by the operations of the brain and realized in the structure of the brain. On this view, consciousness and Intentionality are as much a part of human biology as digestion or the circulation of the blood. It is an *objective* fact about the world that it contains certain systems, viz., brains, with *subjective* mental states, and it is a *physical* fact about such systems that they have *mental* features. (p. ix; emphases in original)

So we see that there is a range of options for emergentism. Let us consider that consciousness could arise from computation, computation in neurons, or something else having to do with neurons. But let us, for the moment, specifically consider computation in neurons.

THE FAILURE OF EMERGENTISM

An *emergent property* is a property of a physical system that is not necessarily expressed by its constituent parts. The analogy that is usually used in this context is to say that existential qualia are just what it feels like when neurons do their thing in the same way that the wetness of water is just what it feels like when water molecules do their thing. Thus, existential qualia are an emergent property of neural activity in the same way that the wetness of liquid water is an emergent property of the activity of large collections of water molecules. However, "wetness" is an instance of a quale, and it is not clear how we can get qualia of any kind out of water molecules, so this is just an example of the original problem.

What we need to do is to rephrase this analogy in terms of objectively observable properties of water. So what we can say is that existential qualia are an emergent property of neural activity in the same way that the properties of water that we objectively identify as wetness are an emergent property of the activity of large collections of water molecules. But there is no reason why this analogy should hold. In one case we have the properties of water emerging from the properties of water molecules interacting with one another, and in the other case we have existential qualia emerging from the activity of neurons interacting with one another. The problem is that neurons do not appear to be constituent parts of qualia in the same way that water molecules are constituent parts of water. The analogy fails. But rather than engaging in these various heuristics, what we need is an actual logical argument, based on empirical evidence, that takes us from neural activity to existential qualia. "The endpoint . . . must be a theory that explains how and why the physical world is capable of generating phenomenal experience. Such a theory can't just be vague, airy-fairy, but must be concrete, quantifiable, and testable" (Koch, 2012, pp. 114–115).

Many consciousness researchers have spent a good chunk of their careers carefully running experiments and analyzing arguments trying to bridge this explanatory gap. So how is this effort going? Well, Jerry Fodor (2000), one of the originators of computationalism, said that he "would have thought that the last forty or fifty years have demonstrated pretty clearly that there are aspects of higher mental processes into which the current armamentarium of computational models, theories, and experimental techniques offers vanishingly little insight" (p. 2). In other words, the computational program appears to have run out of gas. In fact, it is not clear how any argument could work. "Once you assume that the brain operates by physical laws, qualia have no place in this operation" (Elitzur, 2006, p. 18) given that physical laws are all about mindless physical events, and qualia are anything but mindless.

> Under the standard physicalist view, there are no relevant properties
> in matter that would allow mind to emerge. . . . In fact precisely the
> opposite: matter is *explicitly* devoid of mind and experience, we are told.
> Hence the emergence of true mind becomes an inexplicable miracle.
> (Skrbina, 2009, p. *xiii*; emphasis in original)

To say this another way, "Subjectivity is too radically different from anything physical for it to be an emergent phenomenon" (Koch, 2012, p. 119). It is not at all clear how qualia could be an emergent property of neurons, so the analogy of existential qualia with the wetness of water breaks down (Koch, 2012; cf. BonJour, 2010; Siewert, 2010; Skrbina, 2009; Wallace, 2007).

It might be instructive to look at what happened in one effort to bridge the explanatory gap. To solve the problem of the existence of qualia, William Lycan (1987) proposed that qualia are already properties of the physical world. He decided to "identify greenness in particular with some complex microphysical property exemplified by green physical objects" (Lycan, 1987, p. 91). As Lycan acknowledged, there are "undeniable difficulties" with his view (p. 91). One obvious difficulty is that no such microphysical properties have ever been found. Lycan was aware of being in the position of telling physicists what they must find. He backed out of this problem by saying that

> It is not our place to second-guess the physicists. If we are good Scientific
> Realists, we will not tie the physicists' hands by taking it upon ourselves
> to tell them what they may or may not posit as their theories develop
> and flower in response to encounters with new and even zanier micro-
> phenomena. (Lycan, 1987, pp. 99–100)

Rather, according to Lycan, "the best way . . . is to understand it, not as handing out orders, but as simply *predicting* what physicists will in fact end up positing in their final account of nature" (p. 100). So, this is the final-account version of physicalism with a twist. Physicists do not know what the final account of nature will look like, but apparently some philosophers do. This version of materialism has also been called *promissory materialism*, in that it promises that someday everything will be properly explained in appropriately physical terms (Popper & Eccles, 1981, p. 96; D. E. Watson & Williams, 2003). According to Lycan, those physical terms apparently will also include mental properties. So the explanatory gap is bridged by promising that the explanatory gap will be bridged in the future. Clearly, this is not a sturdy bridge.

It appears that after failing to finesse qualia out of computations, neuronal or otherwise, a computationalist simply gives up and fixes the explanatory gap by turning qualia into a fundamental feature of all matter (Gabora, 2002; Tallis, 2010), or maybe just "living" matter: "I believe that consciousness is a fundamental, an elementary, property of living matter. It can't be derived from anything else" (Koch, 2012, p. 119). The position, known as *panpsychism*, is "the view that all things have mind or a mind-like quality" (Skrbina, 2005, p. 2) or, more precisely, that "all objects, or systems of objects, possess a singular inner experience of the world around them" (Skrbina, 2005, p. 16). There is no single panpsychist position, and it is not clear how many of them, if any, would qualify as materialism under some definition of materialism (cf. Schmitt, 2007; Skrbina, 2005; Tegmark, 2014). However, to the extent that existential qualia are acknowledged to be an ontologically fundamental aspect of reality, such panpsychism is no longer a materialist position by any of the definitions of materialism that we have entertained previously. At the same time that materialism is on its way out (Koons & Bealer, 2010), it appears that panpsychism is on its way in or, at least, is an "active player" in speculations about the fundamental nature of the world (Seager & Allen-Hermanson, 2013).

ANOMALOUS PHENOMENA

We find ourselves in a situation in which the dominant paradigm, materialism, is in a state of flux. Into these shifting waters comes the recognition that if materialism is not a correct theory for understanding consciousness, then the phenomena that pose a serious challenge to materialism should be examined more carefully, as they may have been unfairly rejected under materialism. We will call phenomena related to consciousness that are incongruent with materialism *anomalous phenomena* (Cardeña, 2014).

> Discovery commences with the awareness of anomaly, i.e., with the recognition that nature has somehow violated the paradigm-induced expectations that govern normal science. It then continues with a more or less extended exploration of the area of anomaly. And it closes only when the paradigm theory has been adjusted so that the anomalous has become the expected. (Kuhn, 1970, pp. 52–53)

Anomalous phenomena include *remote viewing*, the ability to know something that is happening at a distance without the use of the physical senses (discussed in Chapter 2, "Shared Mind"), and *remote influencing*, the apparent ability to alter physical manifestation in an intended direction without a chain of physically causal events (Chapter 6, "Direct Mental Influence"). These can be temporally displaced, as in the case of *precognitive dreams*, in which a person dreams about events that occur in the future (Chapter 3, "Rethinking Time"). These types of phenomena have sometimes collectively also been labelled as *psi* or *psi phenomena*. There are also other phenomena associated with consciousness that can have implications for the *survival hypothesis*, the hypothesis that consciousness continues after physical death (Chapter 4, "Interactions With Discarnate Beings," and Chapter 5, "Separation of Mind From Brain"). The existence of all of these phenomena seriously challenges materialism by any of the definitions we have considered. Thus, they have been called "anomalous" not because they occur rarely or because there are no data to support their existence, but because, from a materialist point of view, they should not exist.

What is the evidence for the occurrence of these phenomena? Well, there is empirical evidence that has been gathered and analyzed using the standard methods of scientific investigation. Indeed, much of the rest of this book is a presentation of the empirical evidence for anomalous phenomena and a discussion of the implications of the occurrence of such phenomena for an understanding of consciousness. But there is a second source of information about anomalous phenomena, and this comprises the personal experiences that a person can sometimes have that are sufficient to convince her of their existence (Baruš, 1996; Fontana, 2005; Irwin, 2014; cf. Bering, 2014). Perhaps the prototypical case is that of someone who has had a near-death experience and has been thereby convinced that her consciousness will continue after the death of her body (Baruš, 2003a, 2007b).

"Wait!" the reader might say, "You can't expect me to buy into that sort of woo. I was taught that this kind of thing is not science; that it's pseudoscience!" That is a reasonable response given that most of us were educated under a materialist assumption. Here, we consider some of the frequently used strategies for approaching this research, from the more superficial to the more substantive. In the book chapters, we discuss the details of the evidence for anomalous phenomena of various sorts and address specific criticisms that have been raised about them.

First, a global strategy is sometimes used to denigrate research examining anomalous phenomena by calling such research "pseudoscience," "junk science," "woo," and so on, to discourage others from taking it seriously. The point of such a strategy is to push whole areas of scientific evidence off-limits to scientific exploration so that there would never be any need to actually evaluate the evidence (cf. Braude, 2014; Cardeña, 2014). This strategy is clearly inappropriate and has nothing to do with science. Science is an empirical investigation of whatever one wishes, regardless of how strange one's subject matter may seem at the outset.

Second, the results of research concerning anomalous phenomena are often unjustly treated. Criticisms of such research are sometimes uninformed (Braude, 2014), and papers in which the occurrence of anomalous phenomena are reported are sometimes rejected for publication in mainstream journals irrespective of their quality. "Whilst critics continue to launch uninformed but widely publicized attacks, editors of mainstream journals have admitted to stick to the rule of rejecting papers reporting positive psi effects irrespective of the quality of submitted manuscripts" (Sommer, 2014, p. 43). One way of getting rid of papers about anomalous phenomena is to reject them on the basis of methodological failures. This can be a sound argument against any form of research, and methodological lapses are present in any field of scientific endeavor, so that failures of method are not specific to the examination of anomalous phenomena. In fact, there has been increasing acknowledgment that the results of research into uncontroversial phenomena are not nearly as robust as they are assumed to be and are, actually, frequently false (Ioannidis, 2005). Arguably, research concerning anomalies has been carried out more carefully than research in other areas of investigation precisely because of the degree to which it has been scrutinized. "The work of the psi researchers is often more rigorous methodologically than that of scientists in less controversial fields" (Goertzel & Goertzel, 2015, p. 295). There needs to be a level playing field so that research concerning anomalous phenomena is treated with the same professionalism as research in other areas of scientific endeavor. That includes providing knowledgeable criticisms and publishing papers of sufficient quality in mainstream journals (cf. Cardeña, 2014).

Third, researchers, or the "psychic" individuals they are studying, are sometimes accused of fraud. Cases of prevarication and dishonesty have been uncovered in the past, not only by those supporting the existence of anomalous phenomena (Carter, 2007/2012a) but also by its critics (Child, 1985; Goertzel & Goertzel, 2015; Storr, 2014). Such behavior, by anyone, has no place in science. Also, appealing to hoax as an explanation by imagining some way in which a phenomenon could have been the result of a hoax is not sufficient to conclude that a hoax is the best explanation for it. One also needs to show actual evidence that a hoax has been perpetrated (Baruss, 2003a).

Fourth, the objection has sometimes been made that any unusual experience can be fully explained as a hallucination, delusion, wishful thinking, and so on (Wilson, 2013). This can be used as an argument to focus only on the results of laboratory experiments, rather than on carefully examining credible anecdotal reports. When attempting to use mental aberrations to explain anecdotal reports, one requires actual evidence that such aberrations are the best explanation for any such experience. And this is a knife that cuts both ways. We can equally deceive ourselves that nothing extraordinary ever happens (Radin, 1997a). For instance, in research about anomalous phenomena experienced during athletic performances, participants who initially described extraordinary events that had occurred in the course of competition sometimes subsequently insisted that nothing unusual had happened (Murphy & White, 1978). How many of those are instances of psychological maneuvering to deny the existence of unusual events?

The fifth objection has serious consequences for public health. The argument is that anyone who thinks that anomalous phenomena actually exist is mentally ill. In fact, belief in the existence of the occurrence of some types of anomalous phenomena is formally a symptom of schizotypal personality disorder (American Psychiatric Association, 2013). What this means is that those who have had extraordinary experiences occur for them could be afraid to speak up because they are afraid of being regarded as crazy (Barušs, 2014b). This is not to say that there cannot also be overlap between the occurrence of anomalous experiences and psychopathology, given that trauma associated with psychopathology appears to sometimes open up the occurrence of such experiences (Barušs, 2003b), but the two are not the same. A competent mental health professional can tell the difference between exceptional functioning and psychopathology (cf. Irwin, 2014). However, a client who is otherwise psychologically healthy could still need assistance integrating any exceptional abilities that she might be manifesting into the dynamics of her psyche. To the extent that we deny the existence of anomalous phenomena and regard belief in their occurrence as a mental disorder, we fail to serve the needs of those who have these abilities, and in some cases, we could cause unnecessary psychological damage. This is a serious ethical issue that we will take up again in Chapter 8, "Transcendent Mind."

A sixth objection is the argument that anomalous phenomena are impossible because they violate the known laws of physics. This objection is just an application of the definition of *anomalous* if the known laws of physics are taken to be some version of materialism. Anomalous phenomena do not fit easily with a billiard-ball version of reality, but they are compatible with contemporary physics (Broderick & Goertzel, 2015b), which, as we have already seen, has painted a radically different picture of reality from that of classical physics. In any case, theories need to fit the empirical evidence, not the other way round, so if there were to be a disparity between observation and theory, then it is the theory that would need to be rewritten.

A seventh objection is that extraordinary claims require extraordinary evidence. But a claim is only "extraordinary" in light of human understanding. For nature, there is no extraordinary—there just is. What at one time seemed extraordinary to us was often later shown to reflect just another day in the life of the natural world. Furthermore, there is no clear criterion for what "extraordinary evidence" should be. How shall we quantify extraordinary? This is a nonscientific rule. In science, one takes the theory with the best goodness-of-fit to the data and gets rid of whatever theory has poor goodness-of-fit (Goertzel & Goertzel, 2015).

The eighth objection is simply the false insistence that there is no evidence. This objection brings us outside the realm of science and into the social psychology of science. Scientists are human beings and, as such, will each have had different experiences that condition her understanding of reality. In particular, just as all human beings use various irrational judgmental heuristics, scientists do as well. In fact, it requires considerable discipline to dispassionately reason logically without interference from judgmental heuristics. In the course of their training, scientists are seldom led through a process of self-development whereby they can identify and neutralize the various distorting mechanisms. We take this up again in Chapter 7, "Reintegrating Subjectivity Into Consciousness Research." However, as a result, two scientists can look at the same data and reach different conclusions because of differences in the ways in which they make judgments (H. L. Friedman & Krippner, 2010). One way to approach this is to say that each person has a *boggle threshold*, namely, the degree to which a person is willing to deviate from normative beliefs (Braude, 2007; Brennan, 2013). For some people, any anomalous phenomenon is too mind-boggling, whereas for others, what seems impossible in one decade ends up becoming understandable in the next (Baruš, 2013a). Taken together, all of these objections suggest a more serious issue.

MATERIALISM AS DOGMA

The problem is that materialism, and its offspring neuroscientism, are not just theories. We have already seen that they can function as worldviews and schemata. But they can also function as dogma (Baruš, 1996; Bowie, 2014; Eccles, 1976; Sandelands, 2006; Tallis, 2010). Once an ideology becomes dogmatic, it is held in place by the usual mechanisms of social compliance acting within academic, scientific, and political institutions.

> Modern western science regards consciousness as an epiphenomenon that cannot be anything but a byproduct of the neurology and biochemistry of the brain. . . . While this perspective is viewed within modern science as a fact, it is in reality far stronger than a mere fact: it is a dogma. Facts can be overturned by evidence, whereas dogma is impervious to mere evidence. (Haisch, 2007, p. 53)

Dogma distorts science so that it no longer functions properly but devolves into *scientism*, an inauthentic version of science with materialism as its central tenet. Thus, *groupthink* replaces critical thinking, so that everyone is required to say the right things or risk being left unheard or, worse, persecuted for failing to conform (Janis, 1971; Whyte, 1952/2012). This has led to a politics of science in which it can be dangerous to challenge materialism (Baruš, 2007b, 2014b).

Psychoanalyst Ruth Rosenbaum (2011) proposed an explanation of the academic silence surrounding the evidence for anomalous phenomena, particularly telepathy. She asserted that the minimization of anomalous phenomena has evolved from the minimization of the maternal experience of shared body space. She argued that at least part of the power behind the present-day scientific dogma of materialism and determinism is an attempt to not acknowledge the overwhelming power of the space we all shared with our mothers when we were in the womb.

> The phrase "women's intuition" has often connoted a kind of marginalized, "cute," childlike capacity, not anything to be taken seriously as a valid mode of information gathering. And stories of mother-infant telepathy, where a mother might know from a distance that her baby is in danger, and rush to save the baby just in time, seem to be more easily accepted than other instances of telepathy, possibly because they are neatly bracketed. As long as psi stays within the nursery, and we can say that such uncanny symbiotic moments are just for babies and mothers, the threat to the secure boundaries of adult identity is diminished. (Rosenbaum, 2011, p. 81)

She also argued that what has been validated continuously in the Western scientific tradition has been what is "seen"—physical objects for which there is evidence. The "unseen," but experienced, has been marginalized. Rosenbaum pointed out that there may be a parallel here to the emphasis on the phallus—the more visible genitalia of the two sexes. To focus on the unseen would be unseemly. These arguments may shed some light on the strength of the dogma surrounding materialism.

As a result of studying anomalous phenomena or challenging materialism, scientists may have been ridiculed for doing their work, been prohibited from supervising student theses, been unable to obtain funding from traditional funding sources, been unable to get papers published in mainstream journals, had their teaching censored, been barred from promotions, and been threatened with removal from tenured positions. Students have reported being afraid to be associated with research into anomalous phenomena for fear of jeopardizing their academic careers. Other students have reported explicit reprisals for questioning materialism, and so on (Barušs, 2014b; P. L. Berger, 1970; H. L. Friedman & Krippner, 2010; Hess, 1992; Rossman & Utts, 2014; Sommer, 2014; cf. Chargaff, 1977; Jahn, 2001; Siler, Lee, & Bero, 2015).

Prior outstanding accomplishment in other areas of endeavor has not protected faculty from persecution. The following is an account by Brian Josephson, a Nobel laureate in physics:

> My transition into believing that mind has to be taken seriously as an entity in its own right proved also to be a transition into an environment that was hostile where previously it had been very supportive. The scientific community has its own belief systems that it is dangerous to challenge. . . . Being a Nobel Laureate protects one from the worst pressures, but not from curiosities such as this letter relating to a conference to which I had previously been given an invitation and even been asked how long I wished to speak:
> "It has come to my attention that one of your principal research interests is the paranormal . . . in my view, it would not be appropriate for someone with such research interests to attend a scientific conference."

> I learned from subsequent correspondence that it was feared that
> my very presence at the meeting might damage the career prospects of
> students who attended, even if I did not touch on the paranormal in my
> talk. (Josephson, 2012, p. 261, italics in original)

Such dogmatic behavior, to the extent to which it exists in the academy, is unacceptable. There needs to be an open atmosphere in which research that challenges any view and seeks to understand the nature of reality is supported, especially when it provides evidence that the mainstream view is not correct (Barušs, 2014b; Cardeña, 2014).

A final issue that arises as a result of these sorts of objections is the question of who has the right to set the agenda. Those who study anomalous phenomena have spent considerable time and resources responding to counterarguments (e.g., Barušs, 1993, 1996, 2010; Cardeña, 2014; S. A. Schwartz, 2010; Tart, 2009). One could spend a good chunk of one's career mired in this debate. At some point, it is appropriate to develop a positive program rather than just continue to respond to criticism (Goertzel & Goertzel, 2015). The purpose of this book is explicitly not to get mired in the debate but to move forward with a positive program by looking at empirical evidence concerning consciousness without a materialist bias.

It seems to us that materialism is like a dyke holding back the water of knowledge. There are lots of holes in the dyke, and to do "the right thing" we are supposed to hold our fingers in the holes to support materialism. But what if we were to be proactive instead? If all of us were to take our fingers out of the dyke at once, then materialism would collapse on its own. The analogy of the dyke suggests that not every scientist is a materialist in the first place. In fact, there have been lots of academics who have entertained other versions of reality all along. Let us look at what some of those versions of reality are.

BELIEFS ABOUT CONSCIOUSNESS AND REALITY

One of the authors of this book, Imants Barušs, and Robert Moore were interested in the relationship between ideas about consciousness and the personal beliefs about reality held by consciousness researchers. To that end they conducted a survey in 1986 with 334 participants who either had written or who could potentially write about consciousness in the academic literature. Using various multivariate statistical analyses, a single dimension was revealed to underlie beliefs about reality. In the following description, the terminology comes from the wording of the questionnaire items and could well be inconsistent with wording in philosophy or other disciplines. In addition, the following descriptions are based on statistical averaging and need not represent a given individual's actual beliefs (Barušs, 1990, 2008a, 2012).

Baruš and Moore identified three positions along what they called a *material-transcendent* dimension: materialism, conservative transcendence, and extraordinary transcendence. On this scale, those tending toward *materialism* believe that the world is a physical place governed by determinism, that the mind is a product of the brain, and that science is the way to acquire knowledge. They also do not have any religious affiliation. This gives us the final definition of materialism that we will use in this book, namely, that materialism is whatever constellation of beliefs attaches to the "material" pole of the material-transcendent dimension as revealed through statistical analyses of survey data. The *conservatively transcendent* position is a midscale position with two main characteristics: endorsement of conventional religious ideas and the notion that meaning is an important aspect of reality. Those who hold this position are dualists, believing that both mind and body are real. They think that the proper way to acquire knowledge is through an examination of the meaning of human discourse. And they tend to be Christian or Judaic. The *extraordinarily transcendent* pole of the scale is characterized by the endorsement of belief in the occurrence of anomalous phenomena and the importance of inner self-development. Those tending toward this position believe that they have had experiences that science cannot explain, that physical manifestation is a by-product of the mental, and that anomalous means of acquiring knowledge exist. For "religious affiliation" they were likely to have checked off a box labelled "own beliefs" (Baruš, 1990, 2008a, 2012).

Baruš and Moore found that ideas about the nature of consciousness are closely tied to beliefs about reality. Thus, materialists regard consciousness as an emergent property of neural activity or as information in an information-processing system and tend to emphasize the behavioral and objective aspects of consciousness. For them, consciousness is an incidental aspect of reality. Those tending toward conservative transcendence endorse the subjective definitions of consciousness, believe that consciousness gives meaning to reality, and that it is evidence of a spiritual dimension within people. Consciousness is a significant aspect of reality. Those tending toward the extraordinarily transcendent position prefer definitions of consciousness that emphasize the significance of altered states of consciousness. For them, consciousness is the ultimate reality that can only be known through a process of psychological change. Consciousness is all that exists (Baruš, 1990, 2008a, 2012).

Supporting the idea that worldviews can entail schemata, it turned out that notions of consciousness were tightly correlated with beliefs about consciousness, so that the distinction between the two was dropped, and they were collectively designated as "beliefs about consciousness and reality." A subset of items from the original survey was developed into the Beliefs About Consciousness and Reality Questionnaire (BACARQ), which was then used in further research (Baruš, 1990; Baruš & Moore, 1989, 1992).

Several studies have since been carried out using the BACARQ. In a study with 75 volunteer university students, the personality trait of "understanding" turned out to be correlated with transcendent beliefs. Understanding is characterized by qualities such as curiosity, intellect, logic, rationality, and inquisitiveness (Jackson, 1999). In other words, participants who tended toward more transcendent beliefs were more likely to have a rational approach to reality than participants tending toward materialism. Also, scoring higher on transcendence was negatively correlated with social recognition, so that those who tended toward transcendence were less likely to care what others thought about them, suggesting that these results were not simply due to compliance (Jewkes & Baruŝs, 2000).

Understanding is a facet of the personality trait of "openness," which has been shown to have small but positive correlations with intelligence, so it is worth asking whether transcendence is correlated with intelligence. In a study with 39 university students from a participant pool, all of the statistically significant correlations between transcendence and intelligence were in the positive direction, so that higher scores on transcendence were correlated with higher scores on intelligence. In addition, there was a strong negative correlation of $r = -.48$ ($p = .002$) between the questionnaire item "There is no reality other than the physical universe" and Full Scale IQ as measured by Jackson's Multidimensional Aptitude Battery—II. For this small student sample, those who rejected materialism were also the most intelligent (Lukey & Baruŝs, 2005).

Finally, in a study of 212 respondents to the BACARQ who attended the 1996 "Toward a Science of Consciousness" conference in Tucson, Arizona, one third thought that anomalous phenomena do not occur, another third thought that these phenomena occur but could in principle be explained in physical terms, and another third thought not only that anomalous phenomena occur but also that consciousness is primary (Baruŝs & Moore, 1998). Although this study has questionable generalizability to academics more broadly, it does suggest that acceptance of the existence of anomalous phenomena could be a majority position. It also suggests that there are healthy numbers of academics who reject materialism and think that consciousness is primary (Baruŝs, 2014b).

Putting the materialist viewpoint aside may be difficult for some readers. But in so doing, we allow ourselves to follow the evidence where it leads, which is the essence of the scientific method. We now proceed to explore the nature of consciousness in an open-minded but rigorous fashion, unencumbered by the materialist assumption.

2

SHARED MIND

Out of my experience, such as it is (and it is limited enough) one fixed
conclusion dogmatically emerges, and that is this, that we with our lives
are like islands in the sea, or like trees in the forest. The maple and the
pine may whisper to each other with their leaves. . . . But the trees also
commingle their roots in the darkness underground, and the islands also
hang together through the ocean's bottom. Just so there is a continuum
of cosmic consciousness, against which our individuality builds but accidental fences, and into which our several minds plunge as into a mother-
sea or reservoir.

—William James (1909, p. 589)

We are just beginning to emerge from a paradigm in which clinical and
experimental psychologists have been trained to ignore or discount any experience suggesting that there is access to information outside of the usual sensory
modalities. We are not out of the woods yet. The most recent version of the
Diagnostic and Statistical Manual of Mental Disorders cites "belief in clairvoyance,
telepathy, or 'sixth sense'" as a symptom of schizotypal personality disorder
(American Psychiatric Association, 2013, pp. 655–659). Meanwhile, in the
lab, some experimental psychologists find themselves making bizarre excuses
to explain away their own positive laboratory results supporting telepathy
(Delgado-Romero & Howard, 2005; Radin, 2007). Nevertheless, two types
of *shared mind* experiences are being discussed quietly but seriously among
clinical and experimental psychologists. These experiences are, first, *telepathy*,
which we will temporarily define as *seeming* communication between minds
without using the usual sensory modalities and, second, *clairvoyance*, temporarily

http://dx.doi.org/10.1037/15957-003
Transcendent Mind: Rethinking the Science of Consciousness, by I. Baruš and J. Mossbridge

defined as *seeming* direct reception of information about a situation or object without an apparent human "sender" and without accessing the usual sensory modalities (Radin, 2013). Toward this serious discussion of shared mind, which is quietly occurring within a swiftly evolving and increasingly postmaterialist paradigm, we direct the focus of this chapter.

SHARED MIND IN PSYCHOLOGY

Telepathy and clairvoyance are usually dangerous to discuss in the current climate of experimental psychology because we fear that we will be labelled unstable or credulous for even suggesting that there might be a possibility that these phenomena should be taken seriously. Thus, to maintain our respect in the field, it is reasonable to suppose that many of us stay silent, despite our personal experiences, beliefs, and even our data. This fear-of-losing-status problem could explain why experimental psychologists are less likely than any other natural science faculty surveyed (e.g., zoologists, mathematicians, physicists) to admit to belief in psychic phenomena (Otis & Alcock, 1982) and why professors in the social sciences in general are more likely than those in the humanities to state that they believe that extrasensory perception or ESP is an impossibility (Wagner & Monnet, 1979). However, another reasonable explanation for this same result is that social scientists are all too aware of the very human tendency to ascribe incorrect meanings to events after they occur (Nickerson, 1998).

A brief history of Sigmund Freud's progress in dealing with his understanding of shared mind is potentially instructive for our own process here. Freud struggled with his own growing acceptance of the reality of shared mind. His struggle was likely magnified relative to ours because he was the de facto voice of psychoanalysis. As we shall see, it appears he was afraid of dooming the whole operation of psychoanalysis before it could even take hold. Yet it also appears that he worked through these fears to eventually speak openly about shared mind—at least a shared unconscious mind or minds.

The course of Freud's change of heart in relation to telepathy has been described by psychoanalyst Claudie Massicotte (2014; see also commentaries by de Peyer, 2014, and Hewitt, 2014). Let us consider a few highlights here. In an early paper titled "Dreams and Telepathy," Freud described in considerable detail two seemingly telepathic experiences relayed to him by his correspondents. After spending much of the paper communicating these two experiences to his audience, he ended his paper with these seemingly disingenuous words:

> Have I given you the impression that I am secretly inclined to support the reality of telepathy in the occult sense? If so, I should very much

regret that it is so difficult to avoid giving such an impression. For in reality I have been anxious to be strictly impartial. I have every reason to be so, since I have no opinion on the matter and know nothing about it. (S. Freud, 1922/1962a, p. 220)

One year before this confusing pronouncement, in his paper "Psychoanalysis and Telepathy," Freud outlined the struggle facing psychoanalysis and wondered whether a collaboration with those interested in telepathy could potentially be useful:

It does not follow as a matter of course that an intensified interest in occultism must involve a danger to psycho-analysis. We should, on the contrary, be prepared to find reciprocal sympathy between them. They have both experienced the same contemptuous and arrogant treatment by official science. To this day psycho-analysis is regarded as savoring of mysticism, and its unconscious is looked upon as one of the things between heaven and earth which philosophy refuses to dream of. The numerous suggestions made to us by occultists that we should cooperate with them show that they would like to treat us as half belonging to them and that they count on our support against the pressure of exact authority. Nor, on the other hand, has psycho-analysis any interest in going out of its way to defend that authority, for it itself stands in opposition to everything that is conventionally restricted, well established, and generally accepted. (S. Freud, 1921/1962b, p. 178)

Even though his public face was one of open skepticism, in 1921 Freud privately wrote to the founder of the short-lived American Psychical Institute, "If I were at the beginning rather than at the end of a scientific career, as I am today, I might possibly choose just this field of research, in spite of all difficulties" (E. L. Freud, 1961, p. 334). Later Freud apparently denied writing this, but the letter had been saved (Massicotte, 2014). Freud's public confusion and denial about his thoughts on telepathy are not without precedent in other areas (e.g., Masson, 1985). However, in the case of telepathy, Freud eventually showed a stronger backbone. He made a clear public pronouncement in 1925 in "The Occult Significance of Dreams" that he believed telepathy represents actual thought transference through nonordinary means:

On the basis of a number of experiences I am inclined to draw the conclusion that thought-transference of this kind comes about particularly easily at the moment at which an idea emerges from the unconscious, or, in theoretical terms, as it passes over from the 'primary process' to the 'secondary process.' In spite of the caution which is prescribed by the importance, novelty and obscurity of the subject, I feel that I should not be justified in holding back any longer these considerations upon the problem of telepathy. All of this has only this much to do with dreams: if there are such things as telepathic messages, the possibility cannot be dismissed of their reaching someone during sleep and coming to his knowledge in a dream. . . . It would be satisfactory if with the help of psycho-analysis we could obtain further and better authenticated knowledge of telepathy. (S. Freud, 1925/1961, p. 138)

One way to explain the timing of this pronouncement is to say that Freud had finally come to the conclusion that psychoanalysis was better accepted than it had been previously and could not be threatened much by his views on telepathy; another is that he realized that he had become so venerable that his reputation was unlikely to be tarnished. If the latter explanation is correct, then we can see that perhaps although he may have struggled with how his decision to admit his belief in shared mind might influence the reputation of psychoanalysis, a larger part of the struggle might have been closer to home. Most of us do not want to lose status or be personally marginalized.

The experiences that convinced Freud that individual minds can communicate with one another are similar to those that have arisen in modern-day offices of clinical psychologists and psychoanalysts. Clients and therapists have dreams that are uncannily related to one another's lives, or they use words that eerily resemble the words in the therapist's mind at that moment. More than one clinical psychologist has put aside fears of a tarnished reputation to report phenomenally coincidental if not verifiably telepathic occurrences. A therapist who never called his patients in the middle of the night reported that he risked violating his patient's trust by calling him at midnight, only to find his patient had secretly gone to his father's house to get a rifle and was at that moment contemplating suicide (Carpenter, 2014). Another psychoanalyst wrote a paper that was only to be published after his death, in which he described a client's dream about an older man falling through a pane of glass without knowing that the therapist himself had fallen through a pane of glass that weekend (Mayer, 2001). Finally, the inventor of electroencephalography (EEG), Hans Berger, was motivated to try to understand the electrical fields produced by the brain partially because of a seemingly telepathic experience that his sister had. Berger was almost run over by a horse pulling a cannon, and when he got home, he received a concerned telegram from his father sent at the request of his sister (who lived miles away), inquiring about Berger's health. His family had never previously sent him a telegram (Millett, 2001). "It was a case of spontaneous telepathy in which at a time of mortal danger, and as I contemplated certain death, I transmitted my thoughts, while my sister, who was particularly close to me, acted as the receiver" (J. Berger, 1940, p. 6). It is possible that if telepathy and clairvoyance actually occur more often during crisis situations, they could be considered useful adaptations that could potentially mean the difference between life and death.

Early on, Freud (1922/1962a) made his readers aware that these experiences cannot be used as evidence of any form of communication or reception of information by means other than the ordinary ones. In noncontrolled environments, there could always be an unconscious memory or forgotten piece of information that had been previously transmitted that could eventually explain an experience that had seemed to be telepathic, and statistically rare coincidences do sometimes occur. However, laboratory scientists would be remiss to dismiss these anecdotal claims without examining whether they represent some form of communication that could be especially useful when survival is threatened. But they have not been remiss in this way; for example, in the 1930s, J. B. Rhine began running laboratory experiments using simple symbols on cards that participants would attempt to guess (Rhine, 1934). It turns out that the results from well-controlled laboratory experiments are compelling.

LABORATORY EVIDENCE OF SHARED MIND

Remember the original definitions of clairvoyance and telepathy with which we started this chapter? We temporarily defined telepathy as *seeming* communication between minds without using known forms of communication, and we temporarily defined clairvoyance as the *seeming* reception of information from a nonconscious source without using known sensory means. The purpose of this section is to point out that on the basis of results from experiments with sound experimental designs, we might consider altering our definitions so that they more strongly assert that mechanisms other than the usual sensory ones are at play. However, for now it is worth withholding judgment while we examine how controlled studies can shed light on clairvoyance and telepathy. Instead of giving a history of controlled studies of telepathy and clairvoyance, here we outline results from a few innovative protocols, then discuss meta-analyses that bring together data from multiple similar studies to determine whether, overall, there is good support for these effects (for more comprehensive reviews, see Baptista, Derakhshani, & Tressoldi, 2015; Broderick & Goertzel, 2015a; Radin, 2013). Finally, we speculate a bit about mechanisms underlying shared mind phenomena.

We will start with a unique experiment designed by a clinical psychologist who also does experimental research. Jim Carpenter (2002) attempted to create a controlled situation in which he could examine clairvoyance after he had observed that telepathic and clairvoyant experiences seemed to occur during group therapy sessions. He performed a group therapy experiment in which the participants agreed to use a role-playing type of therapy. At the same time as they were doing role-playing sessions, a sealed envelope containing a target picture and three other pictures that were unknown to anyone had been blindly selected by the experimenter from a prearranged group of envelopes and sat waiting in another room. After each therapy session, the group would open the sealed envelope and compare each of the four images in the envelope with the emotional issues that arose in the session, ranking each image according to its similarity to the therapy session. When the group did this ranking, no one knew which of the images had been selected by a computer as the target image. So this protocol was designed to test for clairvoyance rather than telepathy, because no human knew which image was the target. Once the rankings were completed, the computer software was consulted, and the target image was announced to the group. After performing 385 sessions, Carpenter calculated that the correct target image was ranked as the first- or second-highest match 58% of the time, with odds against chance of 1 in 1,000 (Carpenter, 2002). This is not overwhelming evidence for anything, of course, but we describe it here to give a flavor of one of several protocols that have been developed to examine shared mind.

Decades earlier, Carpenter (1991) had developed another novel paradigm to show that shared mind phenomena could be applied in a useful way, such as communicating a code word. Carpenter knew that previous data supported the existence of an apparent information channel outside normal forms of communication. He also appreciated that such a "channel" has two characteristics that would make it difficult to use for applied purposes: (a) it is noisy and therefore not always accurate, and (b) it can be influenced by expectations that often disrupt the quality of the information. These characteristics of the channel had already been established from results of previous work using remote viewing (Puthoff & Targ, 1976), which we discuss later in this chapter. Carpenter set up three relatively complex experiments in which participants tried to receive words and numbers from a hidden target, and he kept these two characteristics of the channel in mind.

Carpenter (1991) followed in the footsteps of several other researchers in the field who had realized that when any information channel is inconsistent, repeating the signal is helpful (Fisk & West, 1957; Ryzl, 1966). In other words, if the connection is noisy, repeat yourself and you will have a better chance of being heard. Experimentally, Carpenter translated this idea into asking 110 "receivers" to get repeated impressions of the same targets. These guesses were tallied using a "majority-wins" rule, in which the guess that had the most number of participants reporting it was considered the official guess for that particular target.

In an attempt to avoid intrusion from conscious expectations, instead of asking participants to receive the letters and numbers in the actual signal, Carpenter (1991) asked them to determine the presence of a "0" or "+" symbol. Then, according to the majority-wins rule, in a particular instance if

40 participants reported that they received "+" and 70 reported they received "0," the symbol "0" could be translated into its coded letter or number. We say "could" because Carpenter also used a complex analysis of receivers' moods, so the translation relied on both the number of votes and self-reported mood. Note that this analysis was preplanned, in that Carpenter determined what it would be before each experiment began. We say this because if he had performed this analysis after looking at the data, he easily could have made the analysis give whatever result he liked. Using this unique method, Carpenter was able to send the word *PEACE* correctly and was able to almost send a second word, *INFO*—except the O was turned into a G through the process. Signals made from numbers did not fare as well (e.g., 0625 was received as 5655).

Again, this outcome could support the existence of telepathy (in that at least one person knew the correct target when the participants were attempting to guess the symbols) or clairvoyance (in that the correct target was written down in a sealed envelope that could conceivably be accessed clairvoyantly). Either way, Carpenter's (1991) use of multiple mood scales to determine which votes to include in the majority-rule procedure made the study simultaneously innovative and also difficult for others to replicate. These results, while hardly convincing alone, support other research suggesting that telepathy and clairvoyance may potentially be used for useful purposes (Broderick, 2015).

REMOTE VIEWING

An applied approach that seems more straightforward is what has become known as *remote viewing*. In most remote-viewing experiments, a "viewer" is asked to draw and describe in words a target location or image. For example, the target could be a building site in Mongolia, or it could be Van Gogh's painting "Starry Night." The viewer attempts to access the target, knowing nothing about the target that could exactly specify it (e.g., "the target is coded as a number," "the target is within 30 miles of us," or "the target is underground"), and draws and writes words describing her experiences as she attempts to access it. Sometimes this is done in complete isolation, and sometimes the viewer works with a "monitor," also unaware of the target, who asks the viewer questions about what she perceives. In the protocols producing the results we briefly describe here, no one interacting with the viewer knew what the target was at the time of the viewing. There are many applications of this kind of procedure, including locating lost children, finding valuable stolen items, and gathering intelligence from remote and dangerous locations without risking lives. The latter motivation is what led the United States' Central Intelligence Agency, among other governmental agencies, to fund initial investigations into the usefulness of remote viewing for intelligence purposes, which they did via operations from 1972 to 1995 (Puthoff, 1996). Thousands of remote-viewing trials have been recorded (for comprehensive reviews, see May & Marwaha, 2014; Puthoff, 1996; S. Schwartz, 2015; Targ, 2004). Here, we briefly summarize the evidence.

Multiple statistical analyses of thousands of remote-viewing trials have revealed that trained remote viewers describe the target location or image significantly more often than nontargets. The similarity of a remote-viewer's sketch to the target is analyzed by asking judges who are not aware of the target (i.e., they are "blind" to the target) to rank the similarity of each sketch to each in a group of possible targets, one of which is the real one. Readers will recognize this strategy from Carpenter's (2002) group therapy study; it is one used throughout psi research because it allows for a nonbiased judging process. So in this case, if there were four dummy targets and one actual target to be judged, a judge would have a chance of one in five of choosing the actual target as the one matching the sketch if the judge were just randomly picking. The actual results, however, are significantly above this level expected by chance.

One report in an influential journal included illustrated sketches and their corresponding target photos by a single gifted remote viewer who had been placed in a shielded room, away from anyone who knew anything about the targets. His detailed drawings showed correspondences so numerous that it is difficult to imagine that they occurred by chance. However, statistics were nonetheless calculated on the basis of blind judges' scores of similarity between the targets and the photos. This analysis revealed that the odds that the remote viewer sketched the target by chance were calculated as less than 1 in 3.5 million (Targ & Puthoff, 1974). In another examination of 653 trials obtained over 25 years from multiple remote viewers (Dunne & Jahn, 2003), we conservatively calculated the odds that the results were obtained by chance as less than 1 in 17 million. Another examination using a slightly different scoring method included 50 trials by "expert" participants—remote viewers who had been screened for their ability to receive and report this kind of information—gave 32 correct matches to targets (May, 2014), which we calculate conservatively as representing odds against chance of greater than 75,000 to 1.

Statistician Jessica Utts was contracted by a government agency to examine a subset of the remote-viewing evidence, obtained from 1,215 government-funded, remote-viewing trials performed at the Stanford Research Institute (SRI) and Science Applications International Corporation (SAIC) from 1973 to 1995. Like many others at the time, she used the word *psychic* to refer to telepathy and clairvoyance phenomena. She concluded,

> Using the standards applied to any other area of science, it is concluded
> that psychic functioning has been well established. The statistical results

of the studies examined are far beyond what is expected by chance. Arguments that these results could be due to methodological flaws in the experiments are soundly refuted. Effects of similar magnitude to those found in government-sponsored research at SRI and SAIC have been replicated at a number of laboratories across the world. Such consistency cannot be readily explained by claims of flaws or fraud. (Utts, 1996, p. 3)

We would like to highlight that in her analysis, Utts (1996) also noted that the use of "expert" participants—remote viewers who had been screened for their ability to receive and report this kind of information—may have been key to the success of these experiments. The value of prescreening for participants who are already talented in the skill to be measured is underscored by results from other studies that we discuss later.

One example of the power of expert or "gifted" participants is the case of Sean Harribance, who was asked by researchers at the Psychical Research Foundation at Duke University to perform 15 photo-card guessing experiments between 1969 and 1971 (B. J. Williams, 2015). As the experiments went on, they became progressively more methodologically controlled to avoid the possibility of information about the cards being inadvertently revealed to Harribance. In each one, Harribance's task was essentially the same: Name the contents of a series of photographic cards that were laid out under a blanket, piece of cardboard, or other such shield. In five of these studies, Harribance was located in a separate room entirely from the cards, in an attempt to rule out any subtle sensory cues from the cards. Of these five, two were performed under a clairvoyance assumption in which no one knew the order of the photo cards, and the other three were performed under a telepathy assumption in which the experimenter knew the order. Harribance did not perform any better than would be expected by chance in one of the clairvoyance experiments, performed remarkably better than chance in the other clairvoyance experiment, and performed remarkably better than chance in all three telepathy experiments (B. J. Williams, 2015). Here, by "remarkably better than chance," we mean that by our conservative estimate, in each of the four studies, there was less than one chance in 1 million that Harribance could have named the order of the photo cards correctly by chance. Though Harribance, like every other expert, likely had "on" and "off" days, the odds of having such remarkable performance on four out of five well-controlled experiments by chance are extremely low. The conclusion is that this particular expert was tapping into some kind of information that is possible to be accessed remotely, consistently, and with relative accuracy. Other anomalous means could have been used to obtain this information (in particular, precognition, which we discuss in Chapter 3). But for now we are focused on clairvoyance and telepathy.

TELEPHONE TELEPATHY

Beyond gifted participants, another approach to pinpointing evidence for shared mind is to find opportune times that minds are most likely to be shared. For example, one might think that telepathy could occur naturally when one person has an intention of contacting another person. Experiments investigating this idea, sometimes called "telephone telepathy" experiments, were originally designed by Rupert Sheldrake in response to the commonly reported experience of thinking about someone just before that person calls on the phone. Although these kinds of telephone-telepathy experiences have been reported by approximately 40% to 70% of the population queried (Brown & Sheldrake, 2001; Sheldrake, 2000), it is reasonable to consider that these anecdotes can be explained by unconscious awareness of contact patterns. Some nonconscious part of your mind may know that your Aunt Ann calls every 6 months, even if you are not consciously aware of that regularity. Other telephone-telepathy events could potentially be explained by a form of selective awareness called *confirmation bias* (Nickerson, 1998). It is likely that if we think we might have an ability to know who is calling, we are impressed with our ability, and therefore we keep better track of the number of times we think about someone and they contact us, compared with the number of times we think about someone and they *do not* contact us. An alternative explanation is that it is likely we think about many people throughout our days but do not remember all of these thoughts, so the likelihood of coincidence of these thoughts and receiving contact from them is greater than we assume.

Beyond these explanations, Sheldrake's (2000) hypothesis was that some form of telepathy underlies at least some synchronistic contact phenomena. To test this hypothesis, he designed and performed a series of experiments to determine whether, under controlled conditions, recipients of calls would be able to guess which person was contacting them before they actually received the call. What were these controlled conditions? The protocols became more carefully controlled as the studies progressed, but we describe the most tightly controlled protocol here. In this protocol, all senders and receivers of calls were videotaped, and these videos were scored to determine whether there were times that either the receivers or the senders could have surreptitiously sent a message via cell phone or another device. Receivers of calls, or "receivers," were asked to choose from a list of possible callers *before* picking up the phone, and trials in which they did not choose from the list of callers before picking up the phone were discarded. Callers and receivers were in different buildings a kilometer apart, with the callers in a room in a bar and the receiver in a hotel room. Four potential callers sat at the same table and a die was used to determine which caller would be the one to call the receiver next. Videographers for the news outlet 20/20, who were unrelated to the study team, recorded all proceedings, which occurred on a single day. In this particular protocol, but not in most other telephone-telepathy protocols, the callers were all sisters of the receiver.

The receiver would have guessed, on average, one out of four calls correctly, so that 25% of the guesses would have been correct, but the receiver was correct a statistically significant 42% of the time (Sheldrake, Godwin, & Rockell, 2004). Another similar protocol without the 20/20 videographers (but with continuous videotaping and scoring) produced similar performance, around 45% correct over 271 trials, giving odds of 1 in 1 trillion that these results were obtained by chance (Sheldrake & Smart, 2003). One problem with interpreting the results from these two studies is what is known as the *file-drawer problem*. Specifically, we do not know how many studies were performed that did not give such impressive results. We will discuss this problem in more depth below. Another problem with interpreting the data from these experiments is that even outside the experimenters' knowledge, the videographers and call recipients could have agreed on some sort of signaling system. Although this is unlikely, it is of course possible. Thus, it is important to ensure that no one involved in a telepathy experiment can possibly collude to pass information from the sender to the receiver using conventional means.

NEUROPHYSIOLOGICAL MEASURES OF TELEPATHY

One attempt at circumventing the concern about collusion in telepathy experiments is to use the receiver's brain activity as the dependent measure, so that no one reports anything—brain activity does the reporting. The idea is that if brain activity in a receiver is reliably different between times when a remote sender is attempting to send information to that receiver and when the sender is not trying to send any information, this result would be considered by some to be good evidence for telepathy. However, this is not a true circumvention of the problem. There is a widespread but unwarranted bias that if a researcher includes neuroscientific measures in a study, that study is of higher quality or is more rigorous (Weisberg, Keil, Goodstein, Rawson, & Gray, 2008). There is no reason why a lab assistant who is determined to get a positive result could not whisper to a participant in a brain scanner that "now" is the time that a sender is attempting to send a signal. Or, more likely, the lead experimenter could unintentionally change her behavior during the sending times if she knows exactly when these times are. If either such intentional or unintentional collusion occurred, the brain activity after the whisper or following the experimenter's change in behavior could be different from the brain activity not during that time period. There would be a clear difference related to the receiver's expectation and desire to receive a message during that time, but it would have nothing to do with telepathy.

Even barring such collusion, it is easy to find statistically significant differences in neural activity in a brain-imaging experiment in which there are no anomalous effects, because there are so many measures that can be taken and there are so many places to take those measures. Rigorous researchers take this into account when they statistically analyze their results. Finally, there are normal physiological oscillations to consider—regular changes in activity that repeat over time. This is a problem in terms of brain-imaging experiments investigating telepathy only if an experimenter asks senders to "send" information during times with intervals equal to "nonsending" or rest periods. The problem here is that without using time intervals of different durations, or "jittering" the time periods or the epochs between them, it is easy to find a difference in brain activity between, for instance, every other 5-second period. This is because the brain is changing in a repeated way continuously over time, producing oscillating physiological changes (Cohen, 2014). For neurophysiological experiments not using jittered time periods, conclusions about brain activity in the receiver that occurs during sending periods have to be considered tentative because this correlation between sender and receiver could be due to ongoing oscillations in the receiver. However, if the times used for sending and nonsending periods are jittered so that they are not always following one after the other in predictable intervals, any consistent brain activity changes in the receiver during sending times are more impressive. Fortunately, some experimenters have taken these concerns into account by using jittered (random) time periods (e.g., Achterberg et al., 2005; T. L. Richards, Kozak, Johnson, & Standish, 2005; Standish, Johnson, Kozak, & Richards, 2003).

In other words, if neuroscientific evidence of telepathy is desired, what is needed is a well-controlled brain-imaging experiment that (a) safeguards against accidental or intentional collusion, (b) confirms previous results indicating that the current results are less likely to occur by chance, and (c) includes methods of avoiding the pitfall of mistaking ongoing oscillations for telepathy. If an experiment meets all these requirements, its results are easier to interpret.

Taking into account these concerns and others, exactly this experiment has been performed. A pair of people who had been participants in a previous electroencephalography (EEG or "brainwave") experiment were asked to participate in an experiment using two measures: EEG and blood oxygenation related to functional magnetic resonance imaging (fMRI). Previously, one of the two had significant EEG changes when the other was "sending" versus "not sending" a visual image (Standish, Kozak, Johnson, & Richards, 2004), although design flaws in the study precluded drawing strong conclusions. The presently discussed EEG/fMRI study was performed to fix these flaws and determine if either EEG- or fMRI-related measures in the receiver differed reliably between sending and nonsending periods (T. L. Richards et al., 2005). The study had two identical sessions, the second being used to double-check the results of the first. In terms of the EEG measure, the pretested pair of participants produced a significant EEG effect once, but not the second time. Meanwhile, the results from the fMRI-related measure were consistent across both sessions of the study.

What was demonstrated via the fMRI-related measure in the two separate sessions was a significant difference in activity in the visual areas of the receiver's brain when compared between the sending and nonsending times. That the change in activity was in the visual areas makes sense in this case, as the stimulus the sender was receiving was a visual stimulus. The experimenters established that no one dealing with the receiver knew when the sending and receiving periods were, ensured there was no auditory or visual leakage of information between the sender and receiver, used statistical methods to account for the multiple comparisons that can be made across the brain, jittered the times of the sending/nonsending periods, and replicated the original functional-imaging result (T. L. Richards et al., 2005). Taken together with the remainder of the experiments discussed thus far, we might consider it reasonable to come to the conclusion that telepathy and clairvoyance may be more than "apparent."

STATISTICAL EVALUATION OF CUMULATIVE LABORATORY EVIDENCE

These results are intriguing, but it is important to consider that they could be explained by so-called "questionable research practices" (QRPs). For instance, any researcher could perform an experiment and only report the results if they are in line with her hypothesis. Such "selective reporting"— the root of the file-drawer problem—is officially frowned on, although it is implicitly encouraged by psychology journals that refuse to publish reports of nonsignificant effects or replications of previous experiments (e.g., Greenwald, 1975). Other common QRPs include dropping participants from analyses on the basis of decisions made after analyzing the data (e.g., "Well, she didn't do a great job, but she did say she was stressed that day"), and "optional stopping" with no preplanned number of participants in the experiment (e.g., "We have a nice effect now—let's not gather any more data that might mess it up"; John, Loewenstein, & Prelec, 2012).

The first step in detecting whether such QRPs can explain a given effect is to perform a "meta-analysis"—a statistical analysis of a group of experiments from different laboratories that all use similar protocols. Such an analysis allows researchers to consider all the data resulting from similar experiments to determine the size and statistical significance of any overall effect. Once the data are gathered, statistical and mathematical modeling tools can be used to estimate how often QRPs may be occurring and whether they could account for all of the positive results. However, it is worth noting here that the prevalence of QRPs increases with the funding available for research in a field (Ioannidis, 2005). On the other hand, psi research has been relatively poorly funded, with one researcher calculating the total worldwide expenditure on psi since 1882 as equivalent to less than 2 months of spending on conventional psychology research (Schouten, 1993). By this measure, psi research is not likely to be rife with QRPs.

Here we focus on two areas of continuing research that have become topics for meta-analyses: telepathy during dreams and telepathy in what is called a *Ganzfeld* state. Note that although the experiments included in these meta-analyses were largely designed to investigate telepathy, we cannot rule out that participants could have used clairvoyance to access information that was being "sent" by another person.

The most famous experiments designed to examine dream telepathy are the 13 formal studies and three pilot studies that were carried out at the Maimonides Medical Center in New York from 1962 to 1978, seven of which were attempts at testing the idea that telepathic messages can be sent to a dreaming receiver and successfully received (Child, 1985). During the night, a receiver was monitored for the occurrence of rapid eye movement (REM) sleep, which is usually associated with dreaming, and when REM sleep began, a sender was notified with a buzzer. At this point, the sender attempted to send the contents of a randomly selected image to the dreaming receiver. This image was unknown to the experimenter working with the receiver or the receiver herself, and there was no communication between the sender and either the experimenter or the receiver until after the receiver had reported all of her dreams. At the end of the REM sleep period, the receiver was awakened and asked to report any dreams. As in the judging of remotely viewed targets, a similarity ranking was assigned by independent judges who compared dream transcripts and each image in a pool of images, one of which was the target image (although, of course, the judges did not know which one this was). Receivers also judged the images and selected the target that they felt was closest to their dream, but in general their guesses at the target were not as accurate as those of the independent judges (Child, 1985).

We analyzed judges' rankings of dream content across all 130 dream-telepathy trials following this protocol in the Maimonides studies. Overall, they produced 38 incorrect judgments (i.e., the dream was judged to be similar to a nontarget image) and 92 correct judgments (i.e., the dream was judged to be similar to the target image), which, given a 50% chance of a correct judgment, conservatively gives odds of greater than 410,000 to 1 that this effect was not produced by chance. However, all 130 trials were performed in the same laboratory, so there is always a concern with such data that the results could have been derived from a problem that is replicated throughout the laboratory.

Many clinical and research psychologists know something about the Maimonides studies, but unfortunately most of us have heard about these studies from sources that did not correctly report the details of the original experiments. This problem was described by Irvin Child, who pointed out that the researchers published their work in journals that were not among those normally accessed by mainstream researchers. A bigger part of the problem, Child suggested, is the inherent bias among mainstream researchers against research into anomalous human capabilities or *parapsychology* research. This bias existed in both research and clinical psychology. Child stated that it resulted in inappropriately rejecting and misrepresenting the controversial work arising from the Maimonides Medical Center. In his summarizing abstract, he stated,

> Books by psychologists purporting to offer critical reviews of research in parapsychology do not use the scientific standards of discourse prevalent in psychology. Experiments at Maimonides Medical Center on possible extrasensory perception (ESP) in dreams are used to illustrate this point. The experiments have received little or no mention in some reviews to which they are clearly pertinent. In others, they have been so severely distorted as to give an entirely erroneous impression of how they were conducted. Insofar as psychologists are guided by these reviews, they are prevented from gaining accurate information about research that, as surveys show, would be of wide interest to psychologists as well as to others. (Child, 1985, p. 1219)

In addition, updated meta-analyses examining experiments performed in multiple laboratories and designed to test psi hypotheses provide compounding evidence that the dream state is one in which shared mind can be accessed (Sherwood & Roe, 2003). However, the variety of methods used in these studies makes it difficult to examine the possibility that QRPs could have produced the significant results arising from dream-telepathy studies.

To determine whether QRPs might be responsible for at least some of the positive results obtained to date in shared-mind research, it is useful to turn to a set of experiments performed in multiple laboratories using established and relatively consistent methods. The *Ganzfeld telepathy experiments* are such a set. They are named after the German word *Ganzfeld*, which means "whole field." Ganzfeld is a sensory-management method using soft, undifferentiated lightning; halved ping-pong balls covering the eyes to provide diffuse light; and unpatterned sounds to create homogenous sensory stimulation for a receiver while a sender attempts to send an image to the receiver (Storm, Tressoldi, & DiRisio, 2010). This method has been thought to be helpful for inducing a state of reception in a receiver because participants lose interest in the uniformed stimulation, and therefore such stimulation is thought to reduce sensory and cognitive noise that could compete with what is conceptualized as an incoming "signal."

A procedure whereby a computer randomly selects and presents an image or video clip to be sent by the sender is called *autoganzfeld* procedure. The automation of the original protocol was made in the early 1980s, after the collaborative effort between telepathy researcher Charles Honorton and psychologist Ray Hyman, the latter of whom was skeptical of previously statistically significant positive results obtained in a meta-analysis of Ganzfeld studies (Hyman & Honorton, 1986). In autoganzfeld experiments, the sender is in a soundproofed room alone with the computer monitor, so there is no other person apart from the sender who has normal sensory access to the target image. Further, the computer controls judging of a pool of randomized images and video clips containing the target, which in this case are judged by the receiver herself as to their similarity to the experiences she had when she was in the Ganzfeld condition. The autoganzfeld procedure was examined by two professional magicians to determine whether it could be breached using trickery; they both agreed that the method provided no clear opportunity for cheating (Bem & Honorton, 1994).

A meta-analysis of 11 autoganzfeld studies, consisting of 354 trials, all performed in the same laboratory by eight different principal experimenters, found a correct-judgment or "hit" rate of 32.2%, when a rate of 25% would be expected by chance (selection of one target among three decoys). The investigators insisted there were no unreported sessions. These results were obtained after removing a study that produced very impressive results but did not follow the same protocol as the other 10 studies. That study used "optional stopping," one of the QRPs that should be avoided. Bem and Honorton (1994) showed that the results across the remaining 10 studies provided statistically significant evidence for a form of anomalous communication—in other words, telepathy or clairvoyance.

This meta-analysis was followed by one conducted by Milton and Wiseman in 1999, which included another 30 autoganzfeld studies performed between 1987 and 1994. This new meta-analysis did not provide evidence for telepathy—the hit rate of 27.55% was not beyond the 25% chance level (Milton & Wiseman, 1999). However, even skeptics of telepathy have noted that if the proper statistical analyses had been used—specifically, weighting each study according to sample size—the effect would have been twice as big (Delgado-Romero & Howard, 2005). Further, in understanding this apparent failure to replicate, it is important to keep in mind that many previous

Ganzfeld studies used preselected receivers. Experimenters in those studies only admitted participants who exhibited traits that were believed to be conducive to being a telepathic receiver, including training in meditation, belief in psi, previous apparent psi experiences, and creative output (Baptista et al., 2015). However, a reanalysis of the database of articles used in the Milton and Wiseman meta-analysis of autoganzfeld studies indicated that only three of the 30 studies used preselected receivers, whereas almost 100% of the receivers in the Bem and Honorton (1994) autoganzfeld meta-analysis had been preselected (Baptista & Derakhshani, 2014; Baptista et al., 2015).

Thus, it has been pointed out that a more exact replication of the Bem and Honorton (1994) meta-analysis would only include the three studies in the Milton and Wiseman (1999) database that used preselected participants, and for these studies combined, the hit rate was a significant 34.2% (Baptista et al., 2015). In addition, the Milton and Wiseman meta-analysis was followed by an extensive meta-analysis of 30 additional Ganzfeld and autoganzfeld studies performed in multiple laboratories between 1997 and 2008, 47% of which used preselected participants (Baptista et al., 2015). One study was removed from this meta-analysis because its results were so remarkably positive that the authors felt that it was not representative of the general body of evidence. Note that excluding this outlying study increases the homogeneity of the data set and therefore makes the overall effect size more representative of the bulk of the studies, but it also reduces the statistical significance of the overall data set. Regardless, the remaining 29 studies revealed a hit rate of 32.2%, with a likelihood of less than 1 in 47 million that the results were obtained by chance (Storm et al., 2010).

Were researchers failing to report Ganzfeld studies that did not show a significant effect? In this meta-analysis, the authors performed a calculation to determine whether such a file-drawer effect could explain the results. They calculated that 86 unpublished studies that showed results opposing the direction of the original results could have been hidden away and still the significant outcome of the meta-analysis would hold (Storm et al., 2010). Overall, it appears that Ganzfeld and autoganzfeld procedures using participants preselected for previous training in meditation, belief in psi, and previous psi experience have produced significant effects with a hit rate a little above 30%, where 25% would be expected by chance. Suggesting that there is some kind of consistent effect, this same hit rate of about 32% seems to keep cropping up through multiple meta-analyses of Ganzfeld data across decades of research.

In fact, there is general agreement that these effects signify something that is remarkably consistent. The question is, of course, what? One possibility is that there is some sort of telepathy or clairvoyance that Ganzfeld studies reveal at a significant rate beyond what one would expect by chance. Another is that these studies are revealing consistent use of QRPs, like those we discussed earlier. Two skeptical researchers assumed that the latter was the proper explanation, so they performed eight of their own Ganzfeld studies and, to their surprise, found a significant overall hit rate of 32% (Delgado-Romero & Howard, 2005). In their conclusions, they stated, "So, for the moment, even the evidence against humans possessing psychic powers is precariously close to demonstrating humans do have psychic powers" (Delgado-Romero & Howard, 2005, p. 298). However, they did not stop there, and it is difficult for us not to wonder whether they did not stop because they were concerned about the strength of the evidence they had already obtained. They then performed one more experiment using a novel design, which resulted in psi-missing: receivers reporting the target correctly significantly *less often* than would be expected by chance (Delgado-Romero & Howard, 2005). One wonders whether the clearly stated fear of being "precariously close to demonstrating . . . psychic powers" (Delgado-Romero & Howard, 2005, p. 298) may have been somehow transmitted to the participants in this final experiment, potentially producing a psi-missing effect.

Delgado-Romero and Howard (2005) then concluded that the apparent consistency of previously reported Ganzfeld results might be explained by selective reporting, even though their own results, which apparently were not leaving anything out, did not support this conclusion. Despite the confusing way that Delgado-Romero and Howard went about drawing conclusions from their research, it is not unreasonable to think that selective reporting or other QRPs could explain the significant Ganzfeld and autoganzfeld results. However, ignoring previous examinations of data that had already attempted to address this concern is also not reasonable, and it appears that Delgado-Romero and Howard had done exactly that.

Another way of addressing concerns about research practices is to model what the data would be if certain QRPs could be assumed at the rate they are reported in conventional psychology research. One research group did just this, using modeling to examine the potential influence of QRPs on the overall significance of the Ganzfeld and autoganzfeld data sets. Their conclusion was that, assuming QRPs were present in these studies at the same levels as suspected in conventional psychology research, these practices could potentially explain around 60% of the significant results. After taking into account such practices, the results of the Ganzfeld studies remained statistically significant and therefore suggestive of a truly anomalous effect (Bierman, Spottiswoode, & Bijl, 2015). Finally, a different group of researchers examined the rate at which Ganzfeld telepathy results are replicated across multiple labs. Successful replication across multiple labs suggests that QRPs cannot easily explain an effect as long as we make the assumption that only some labs use these practices.

This group found the replication rate to be about 35%, which is slightly above that of conventional psychology results (Baptista & Derakhshani, 2014). Thus, it appears that Ganzfeld telepathy should be taken as seriously as other successfully replicated phenomena.

The results of these careful analyses justify our dropping the hedge words used in our initial definitions of telepathy and clairvoyance. For the remainder of this book, we will define *telepathy* as apparent communication between minds without using usual sensory means, and *clairvoyance* as apparently anomalous reception of information without an apparent sender or without using usual sensory means. The reader may have noted that we have just replaced the word *seeming* in our initial definitions with *apparent*. It does not appear that we have backed off the hedge words at all! Well, that is because we cannot, not yet. Though the data supporting telepathy and clairvoyance are relatively clear, the mechanisms are not. Just because it appears that telepathy results from mind-to-mind communication does not mean that a signal is actually sent. And just because clairvoyance appears to not involve another mind, this does not mean that no other mind is involved. The point is that we do not understand the mechanisms of either phenomenon, and both are anomalous. Next we explore what we *do* know about them.

WHAT UNDERLIES SHARED-MIND PHENOMENA?

Native American Iroquois refer to the *long body*—comprising the current tribe members, ancestors, tribal land, the objects belonging to the tribe—all of which can be accessed to receive information that helps guide the tribe (Roll, 2008). The results of the telephone-telepathy experiments we discussed earlier, in which participants were able to guess which of their friends or family were about to contact them at a rate beyond chance, support the intuition that telepathy occurs with other minds in our immediate social and family circles. However, there are scant data to support the idea that we have fewer verifiable telepathic experiences with individuals outside of our social and family circles. Further, as we already briefly mentioned, the idea that telepathy represents a link between two or more minds, or the idea that clairvoyance occurs when there is a lack of a link between minds, may both be incorrect. However, the idea of the long body is also consistent with other ways of thinking about telepathy, including those that involve less of an individual-mind-to-individual-mind communication model and more of an individual-mind-to-long-body-mind information-access model.

Another way to think about both telepathy and clairvoyance is that with these skills we are sharing minds, but not necessarily with other individual people. The idea here is that we could be sharing access to a larger pool of information, like a unified, larger mind. Because most of us on a day-to-day basis do not have omniscience even when we want it, we can conclude that although our access to this information source may be influenced by our desire to access it, it is also controlled by some additional rules that we do not understand. These rules would govern parameters like what gets accessed, by whom, and when. However, it is clear that intention must be involved at least in some cases—otherwise, there would be no consistent significant results in any telepathy or clairvoyance experiment because arbitrary pieces of information would come to a participant rather than the desired information about a target. According to this view, which we introduce here as the *information-access view*, there is no signal sent and received between two people or between an object and a person (E. H. Walker, 1975). Instead, in the case of telepathy, there is a simultaneous and mutual access of information from a third source. In one person, whom we have previously called the sender, the information arrives via sensory means (like a perception of an image on a computer monitor), and in the other person, whom we have previously called the receiver, the information seems to have arrived by an idea, image, feeling, or dream. According to the information-access view, both individuals are accessing some kind of well-informed source. In the case of clairvoyance, there may also be simultaneous and mutual access of the same information by multiple people, but only one is aware of accessing the information.

This information-access view is speculative. Yet it normalizes psi skills such as telepathy and clairvoyance as being just two among many ways of accessing a continually existing source of information, including non-anomalous access methods such as memories, sensory perceptions, and feelings. This information-access view could find support in the results of a set of "wisdom of the inner crowd" studies showing that when one asks each member of a group of people to make an estimate (e.g., "What is the weight of this cow?") without any person being aware of any other's estimate, the mean result converges on essentially the same correct answer as asking a single person to make the same estimate multiple times (Herzog & Hertwig, 2014). This result could be interpreted to mean that we are all drawing on a single information source, and our ability to access that source varies across people (during a single time) and across time (within a single person). In the case of this study (Herzog & Hertwig, 2014), the information source does not have to be anomalous—but in the information-access view, all information is coming from a single source, which we think of as anomalous in some situations and not in others. Such a source of information could be considered to be analogous to the long body, or Carl Jung's (1936/1969) collective unconscious.

Regardless of the mechanisms underlying telepathy and clairvoyance, it appears that individuals who are good at these skills have certain characteristics. For instance, brain activity in the alpha range (oscillations between

8 and 13 cycles per second) in the apparently gifted psychic Sean Harribance was measured in two studies to be significantly higher during runs of clairvoyant card guessing in which he scored better than chance versus runs in the same study that were no better than chance (B. J. Williams, 2015). This result suggests that successful clairvoyance could be related to alpha activity, although there is a caveat to this idea based on two other clairvoyance studies in which Harribance did not score significantly above chance. In these two studies, trials on which his guess was incorrect had greater alpha activity (B. J. Williams, 2015). One possible interpretation of all four results is that Harribance was using some kind of internal cue linked to high alpha activity to tell him what his guess should be. In studies for which high alpha activity was generally associated with the correct response, he would score above chance, and in studies for which high alpha activity was either inconsistent or linked to the incorrect response, he would still follow his alpha cue and score at or below chance.

The idea of any relationship between alpha activity and clairvoyance is interesting, especially in light of the discovery that a high level of alpha EEG activity in visual areas has been associated with reducing visual perception of the outside world (Mathewson, Gratton, Fabiani, Beck, & Ro, 2009). Further, alpha EEG activity has been found to increase significantly just before people discover an insight leading to a solution of a problem—for example, just prior to the "aha!" experience that comes with solving a word problem (Kounios et al., 2006). Potentially, alpha activity is related to the process of "looking inward" and retrieving an answer.

THE CREATIVITY LINK

People who manifest musical and artistic ability seem to perform better as receivers in Ganzfeld telepathy tasks than nonselected participants. Specifically, the effect sizes of studies in which receivers were musicians and artists are significantly higher than those studies in which receivers were not preselected, even though both groups of studies produced results significantly beyond chance (Baptista & Derakhshani, 2014). This finding supports the idea that although each of us may have some access to information that is not normally available to the usual senses, some of us may be either more gifted or more motivated to access this source of information in a way that also may help with creativity, or some of us may have been trained or have trained ourselves inadvertently to access this information in the course of doing creative work (Carpenter, 2005).

In an in-depth discussion of the mechanisms underlying genius, Ed Kelly and coauthors (E. W. Kelly, Greyson, & Kelly, 2010) noted that the steps to the creative process described by creativity researchers Graham Wallas (1926) and Eliot Hutchinson (1939) are similar to the steps in the process that psi researcher Rhea White believed were necessary for success in telepathy or clairvoyance experiments:

> Her resulting "recipe" for psi success strikingly parallels the Wallas/ Hutchinson model of the creative process: Specifically, following an initial period of sensory isolation and relaxation, it prescribes a deliberate demand for the needed information (preparation) followed by waiting and release of effort (incubation), spontaneous emergence of information into consciousness (inspiration, usually in the form of involuntary visual or auditory imagery), and evaluation or elaboration of the information so retrieved (verification). White's analysis was one of the main influences leading to . . . the large body of successful psi research using "Ganzfeld" procedures. (E. F. Kelly & Grosso, 2010a, p. 484)

This may seem all well and good—we may be willing to admit that creative people have more access to some kind of information, or be better at picking up "signals," than people with lower levels of expressed creativity. Maybe this kind of information sometimes, or even always, acts as the source of their creativity.

UNDERSTANDING ACCESS TO ANOMALOUS INFORMATION

But *how*, really, does such access work? We speculate about this in the last chapter of the book. Along the way we will offer some ideas. Some food for thought that we provide briefly here is that our waking conscious experience is all we can know about reality, so everything we know about reality is mental and therefore not physical in the usual sense. The boundaries we normally draw between people's individual conscious experiences are meant to be analogous to what we infer to be separate bodies in a physical reality. However, the boundary between individuals breaks down when we recognize that our primary, and indeed only, direct experience is mental. Then, perhaps this inferred physical boundary we see "out there" does not apply to mental phenomena "in here."

We do not necessarily have to abandon the idea that there is a physical world outside of our individual experiential realities, nor do we need to abandon that we have personal conscious experiences that do not always seem to be shared. However, we do need to consider that our individual experiential realities may not be bounded in the same way as we infer the physical world to be. Indeed, it is possible that our individual experiences are connected to one another as well as to other sources of information of which we are not necessarily conscious. "Just so there is a continuum of cosmic consciousness, against which our individuality builds but accidental fences, and into which our several minds plunge as into a mother-sea or reservoir" (James, 1909, p. 589).

If this were to be the case, then to understand consciousness, we must attempt to understand the natural laws that describe the behavior of the mental, experiential reality we each inhabit, and we must keep in mind that there is no reason these laws should have anything to do with the laws we use to describe the inferred physical reality. These natural laws of the mind must include laws related to time, so it is the question of time that we address next.

3

RETHINKING TIME

The study of time is not just that—it is the study of everything.
—Julian Barbour (2000, p. 17)

We usually think that we know what *time* is. Time is whatever it is that moves uniformly from the past through the present into the future, carrying us with it. We can detect its passage with a clock. In fact, we can discriminate fine gradations of time using an atomic clock (Clemence, 1966), so that time seems to us to be both psychologically and physically unproblematical. But as soon as we stop to think about it, we become puzzled. Can time speed up or slow down? Does it always go forward? Can time stop? What is the relationship of clock time to our subjective experience of time? Was there a time before the existence of time? If so, why is that not just more time? Will time ever cease? If so, what comes after time? Is that not time? Is time infinite, then? We will try to answer some of these questions, although not all of them. But before we get too carried away, there is an even more fundamental question that we need to ask: "Does time exist?" And, perhaps surprisingly, the answer that is commonly given by philosophers and physicists is: "No. It does not."

http://dx.doi.org/10.1037/15957-004
Transcendent Mind: Rethinking the Science of Consciousness, by I. Barušs and J. Mossbridge

Much of the discourse about time in philosophy has stemmed from a paper by John McTaggart (1927/1967) in which he argued that "time is unreal, and . . . all statements which involve its reality are erroneous" (p. 86). His arguments have turned out to be problematical, and subsequent developments in the philosophy of time have resulted in more "interminable arguments" (Barbour, 2000, p. 18; cf. Gale, 1967; Le Poidevin, 2011; Markosian, 2014). This is complex territory, and we will draw on it only as necessary for our discussion in this chapter. As we covered briefly in Chapter 1, absolute time has also pretty much disappeared from physics (Callender, 2010), in spite of being "one of the most fundamental" variables in physics equations (Schneider, 1994, p. 131). So what are we talking about when we talk about time? What does it mean to ask whether time exists? If there is no time, then what is it that we label as time in our experience? And, wait a minute, for there even to be experience, must there not be time? Experience does not occur all at once but as a linear progression of events following some sort of rules, does it not? So why is that not time?

In approaching an understanding of time, we have found that the academic literature is fragmented. Different authors approach time from different perspectives with different assumptions about the nature of reality that guide their discussions. Many theories of time are essentially based on a sample size of $n = 1$, namely, the writer's own experience of time. Many theories of time seek only to explain clock time as it is ordinarily experienced, or only to explain subjective time as it appears in the ordinary waking state. Many theories of time completely disregard anomalous phenomena. To cast a framework for an understanding of time, we will avoid the availability bias by looking not just at first-person accounts but also at collocations of first-person accounts and third-person accounts. We will take into consideration the occurrence of anomalous phenomena, which tend to be noticed more frequently in altered states of consciousness (Baruss, 2012). And we will bring in data from altered states of consciousness.

As we proceed in this chapter from physics, through psychology and neuroscience, and finally to discussions of anomalous phenomena, we will see that, far from being a simple linear string of beads strung from an indefinite past into an indefinite future, time can be misshapen, disconnected, and disappear entirely. As we review the evidence, a framework will begin to emerge suggestive of two times, an *apparent time* to which we ordinarily have access, and a *deep time* that structures the nature of consciousness and physical manifestation, and a possible relationship between the two. We shall explore these ideas as we go along and return to them again in Chapter 8, where we suggest a framework for a model of consciousness.

THE NOTION OF TIME IN PHYSICS

There is no single notion of time in physics, with different character-izations appearing within different subdisciplines (Ruhnau, 1994). Physicists can hold diametrically opposite views, with Julian Barbour (2000), for instance, maintaining that there is no such thing as time. On the other hand, Lee Smolin (2013) has counterargued that time actually does exist as a fundamental reality. Even within quantum theory, there is disagree-ment about how to treat time, for instance, as just measured by a clock on the laboratory wall (Zimmerman, 1966) or time as an interaction with oscillating subsystems that play the role of clocks (Milburn & Poulin, 2006) so that we should not "rely very heavily upon arguments from quantum theory to support any particular philosophical point of view about the nature of time" (Zimmerman, 1966, p. 498). We will extend that caveat to all of physics. Given the importance of the apparent disappearance of time as an actual reality according to many physicists, physics is perhaps the place to start our discussion of time.

For Isaac Newton, time and space formed the container within which physical events took place, in such a way that each event could be assigned a specific time and place of occurrence. Time was uniform and well ordered from the past into the future. In contrast, in his special theory of relativity, Albert Einstein showed that time is necessarily linked to space, so that time slows down for someone who is moving through space relative to a stationary observer. This idea led to the *twin paradox* whereby a twin that left the earth and returned would be physically younger than the twin who stayed behind because for the travelling twin, less actual clock time would have passed (Kennedy, 2003). This conjecture has been validated empirically with atomic clocks (Hafele & Keating, 1972). As well, other experiments with optical atomic clocks moving at different speeds have confirmed the occurrence of *time dilation* as predicted by the special theory of relativity (Reinhardt et al., 2007).

Another consequence of Einstein's theory is that two causally unrelated events can be perceived as occurring one before the other by some observers and as occurring simultaneously by other observers. Being observed simulta-neously, such events are thought to be equally real and thus, remain equally real even when observed as being temporally displaced by other observers. In other words, anything that is in the past or the future is just as real as anything in the present, thereby vitiating time. This has been considered the "most frequent and superficially most plausible argument" for the disappearance of time as an actual reality (Čapek, 1966).

In Einstein's special theory of relativity, there is something that is not relative, and that is the *speed of light* in empty space. The idea is that light always leaves from and arrives at an observer at the same speed, irrespective of the speed of the observer (Kennedy, 2003). At the speed of light, time has stopped completely (Ruhnau, 1994), a fact that is consonant with experiences of timelessness that we will discuss in a bit.

Because the speed of light in empty space is constant, it can be used as a measure of elapsed time. In other words, there is a one-to-one correspondence between time and distance. So, if we wished, we could express any time as a distance. Doing so is known as the *spatialization of time* (Smart, 1967). When we add this spatialized time to our three spatial dimensions, and assume that all physical events must be locally causally determined, then we get a four-dimensional *block universe*. Everything that ever happened and everything that will ever happen can be situated in a single four-dimensional block. It is in this way that time has disappeared as an actual reality (Smolin, 2013).

We will find ourselves returning to the notion of a block universe several times in this book, so let us just say a bit more about it. If determinism were to be true, and the universe were to function the same way as a clock, then whatever has already happened in the past and whatever will happen in the future has already been determined. In that case, all of reality is already constructed and can be reconceptualized as a single block of events. In other words, there is nothing essentially dynamic about reality. Any apparent change from that which is expected is an illusion, as even that change would have been predetermined. That is the notion of a block universe.

Historically there has been a great deal of agonizing over the spatialization of time, with the frequent acknowledgment that space and time are not the same types of dimensions (Čapek, 1966). For instance, for Henri Bergson (1922/1965), spatializing time supposes that any of the times in a block universe are realities that can be lived. According to Bergson, they are not. All we have is the experience of what Bergson called "duration" in which the past is seamlessly enfolded in the present. As soon as we apply spatial attributes to time and make it measurable, we have misrepresented its inherent nature (Bergson, 1913/2001). Similarly, for Smolin (2013), time is an interactive reality in nature, which has an occurrent now, something that is missing from the mathematical descriptions of time. By Smolin's reckoning, not only do we need to restore time to physics, but the existence of real time allows for the laws of nature to evolve and for genuinely novel phenomena to occur. At the crux of this debate is the question of the legitimacy of regarding the lived experience of time as an illusion. For a physicist interested in "objective" events that are "out there" somewhere, all experience, including the experience of time, is incidental, illusory, and uninteresting. For a philosopher or psychologist interested in subjective events, experience is a critical feature of reality, and experience includes temporal features that should not be dismissed in a cavalier manner.

During our ordinary waking state, we feel that not only does time exist, but that it is directed from the past to the future. And, in that context, there has been considerable allusion in physics to the *second law of thermodynamics*, which states that as time passes, closed systems will move toward greater states of *entropy*, which is to say that they will move toward greater states of disorder. It has been proposed that such a situation introduces an *arrow of time* (Schlegel, 1966). However, there are several things to note about this second law of thermodynamics. One is that it was written for closed systems, and it is not at all obvious that the universe as a whole is a closed system, so it is not clear that there need be a universal arrow of time (Smolin, 2013). The second point is that the second law of thermodynamics is essentially a statistical heuristic for describing the activity of a large collection of molecules (Schlegel, 1966; Smolin, 2013). Physical theories are reductionist in nature so that phenomena at larger scales are to be explained by phenomena at lower scales. Thus, the collective activity of molecules is ultimately to be understood in terms of theories of molecules and their constituent parts. And those theories are quantum theories. Thus, it is not clear how helpful the second law of thermodynamics is for understanding anything about time.

In quantum theories, playing events backward in time does not usually violate any laws, although there are conceptualizations of quantum theories in which an arrow of time emerges (Milburn & Poulin, 2006; Poulin, 2005) and some situations in which time reversal fails (Zee, 2003, 2007; see also Aharonov, Bergmann, & Lebowitz, 1964). But there are also specific situations, specifically *delayed-choice experiments*, in which backward causation appears to occur (e.g., Wheeler & Feynman, 1949). In these counterintuitive cases, what is finally observed in an experiment depends on a choice made by the experimenter after the events to be observed have already occurred. This can be understood by considering delayed-choice versions of a famous type of experiment called a two-slit experiment. First we will describe a two-slit experiment, then we will explain the delayed-choice version.

Consider an experimental setup for a classic two-slit experiment. In this experiment, a beam of photons is fired toward a barrier with two slits in it behind which is a recording device such as a camera that can register the impact of the photons. When both slits are open, then an *interference pattern* of light and dark bands is displayed on the recording device. This interference pattern looks just like what one would expect if photons went through both slits of the barrier. However, the interference pattern occurs even when only one photon at a time is sent toward the two slits! This can be interpreted by making the assumption that the photon passed through both slits at once and then interfered with itself as a wave would have done.

Now suppose that we insert special photon detectors behind each of the two slits in such a way as to be able to tell through which of the two slits a photon emerged. When we turn on the special photon detectors, then we find that, indeed, the photon only came through one or the other of the slits; there is no interference pattern. Variations on this experiment have shown that whenever we can tell exactly from which of the two slits a photon emerged, the interference pattern is destroyed. When we cannot tell, then the interference pattern is restored (Feynman, 1985/2006; Rae, 2004).

Suppose now that we wait until after the photon has passed through the two slits before making a decision whether to turn on the special photon detectors. This is the delayed-choice version of the experiment. What we find is that when the detectors are not turned on, then an interference pattern is registered, and when they are turned on, then the interference pattern is lost and we can determine through which of the two slits the photon emerged (Clark, 1992; Kafatos & Nadeau, 1990; Wheeler, 1983).

There are two common explanations for such effects. One is that the choice made by the experimenter causally affects the events that occurred earlier, a phenomenon called *retrocausation* or *retrocausality*. The other explanation is that the choice made by the experimenter occurs in a universe that necessarily matches the earlier events, so that time is always moving forward, in at least two different universes in which different choices are made that match different prior events. Until a choice is actually made, such an experimental system is said to be in a state of *superposition* (Ruhnau & Pöppel, 1991).

What if we start without a notion of time and just look at the occurrence of physical events? This is the approach that was taken by Julian Barbour (2000), who said that all we have is a large collection of *Nows*, the physical events as they actually occur. These Nows are just piled in a big heap from which they emerge one by one as determined by some probabilistic rules. The idea that there ever was a past is the result of the occurrence of Nows that contain references to a past, but no such past exists. Neither does the future. Nor, according to this approach, does time exist as an actual reality (Barbour, 2000).

We started by regarding time as a well-behaved container for physical events and saw that sort of time degraded by time dilation, spatialization, time reversal, and outright dismissal to the point where it seems to have disappeared as an actual reality. It is not clear, though, that time itself has disappeared. Rather, a particular notion of time has disappeared. Even in Barbour's scheme, created by stripping away time and space from the occurrence of events and relegating the experience of temporality to the realm of illusion, the sequence of occurrent Nows is just time by another name. Is it not? So it is not clear what is gained by insisting on the disappearance of time.

At this point it may be helpful to introduce the distinction between apparent time and deep time. In fact, each of those can be subjective and objective. So let us say that *subjective apparent time* is time as it is usually experienced in the ordinary waking state; *objective apparent time* is time as it is measured by a clock; *subjective deep time* is whatever it is that structures successions of subjective events to which subjective apparent time does not pertain; and *objective deep time* is whatever it is that structures successions of objective events to which objective apparent time does not pertain. So, in Barbour's account, there is an objective deep time that enables a sequence of Nows to occur, with each Now containing objective apparent time as measured by a clock.

Before we begin discussing the relationship between time and consciousness, we briefly need to point out that regardless of their lack of faith in time, physicists generally model time as "pushing" events along from the past. In other words, prior events causally generate future events. Even though it has been argued from special relativity and delayed-choice experiments that events in the future are just as "real" as events in the present, the idea that events could also be "pulled" or causally generated from the future has not been well developed. For instance, in both Barbour's and Smolin's worldviews, whatever happens in the present is weighted by the past but not by the future (Barbour, 2000; Smolin, 2013). As our discussion proceeds, we will see that this emphasis on the past might not be warranted, given the apparent influence of the future on the present.

This pushing and pulling raises the issue of causality. What do we mean by causation anyway? Does influence have to go from past to future to be called "causative?" If so, retrocausation is impossible by definition. Is causation just one "thing" pushing on another "thing" that is spatially beside it? In what sense does anything cause anything else? Much hinges on the answers to these questions. For our purposes, we will say that event A *causes* event B if the occurrence of event A is necessary for the occurrence of event B. Now, of course, we are left wondering what necessity is, but with this definition at least we can consider retrocausation as a possible actual occurrence.

THE CENTRALITY OF TIME TO CONSCIOUSNESS

Time and consciousness are so related that it can be difficult to disentangle them. Considering one of the critical aspects of time, the experienced duration of events, a thought experiment may help underscore the critical nature of the relationship between time and consciousness. Imagine that you have no awareness of duration. Your possible conscious states include one of the following: (a) all lifetime events occur at once for you—each word in every sentence and every feeling, sound, and visual impression occurs at once; or (b) only one event occurs for you, forever, with no beginning and no end. Having no awareness of duration means having no way to compare the length of your life to the amount of time it takes to brush your teeth. Such an experience, while interesting, is not consistent with ordinary waking consciousness. An essential aspect of subjective conscious experience is that it occurs over time.

Current physical theory seems ambivalent about whether time is fundamental to the physical universe, but there is widespread agreement among physicists that the experience of a privileged "now" and a past and present related to that "now" are illusions introduced by consciousness (e.g., Davies, 2002). But how can such illusions be both illusory and absolutely central to consciousness? Jonathan Schooler (2015) argued that

> if we grant subjective experience an ontological status equivalent to that of objective reality then we must seriously question any characterization of objective reality that challenges the essential qualities of subjective reality. While much of our subjective experience may be an illusion, it is very difficult to see how the privileged vantage of subjective experience, the flow of time, or the unique status of the present could be such. (p. 24)

On the basis of this argument, here we assume that conscious awareness of subjective time has its own validity, without assuming anything about the nature of physical time outside of conscious awareness. With such an assumption, we can investigate apparent subjective time independently without worrying about whether what we are examining is illusory relative to a physicalist framework.

CONSCIOUS AWARENESS OF SUBJECTIVE TIME

It has been argued that being consciously aware of time actually requires two forms of temporal awareness: primary perception of the extension of events in time and a secondary or metacognitive level of awareness that influences our experience of the passage of time (Wittmann & Paulus, 2008). These two forms of temporal awareness are interconnected (e.g., Lamotte, Izaute, & Droit-Volet, 2012). Here we make the choice to ignore the differences between them and address them together as the phenomenon of the conscious awareness of subjective time.

We will discuss three dimensions of time: duration, order, and flow. *Duration* is used to describe how much "time has passed" between two events used as markers. *Order* describes which of two events we subjectively experience as having occurred first. *Flow* is the common waking experience of one event smoothly transitioning into the next. I experienced a child's version of a year passing between my sixth and seventh birthdays, I experienced my sixth birthday occurring first, and during the year in between the birthdays, events flowed along during each day. Studying the conscious awareness of subjective time currently requires recording the perceived durations or orders of events in an individual's past and comparing these subjective durations or orders with clock times. Because the methods used to assess these two aspects of subjective time are different, first we will discuss the phenomenon of subjective duration, then temporal order.

In a classic duration-reproduction task, the experimenter presents a participant with a 1-second interval, bounded by two tones. The participant is asked to reproduce the same duration that was just presented to her (Zackay, 1990). In this task, the level of attentional focus, the novelty of a stimulus, and various methodological parameters, including whether the participant is warned of the task ahead of time, can create consistently longer or shorter reproductions relative to the experimenter's clock reading (Allman, Teki, Griffiths, & Meck, 2014; Block, 1990; W. J. Friedman, 1990; Zackay, 1990).

The mismatches between a participant's subjective experience of duration and clock duration can give us a sense of how to understand the subjective experience of time in waking consciousness (Allman et al., 2014; H. Eisler, 2003; Wittmann, 2009). The most consistent of these temporal mismatches include the following effects, all obtained by asking participants to recall the durations of past events (for reviews, see Eagleman, 2008; A. D. Eisler, 2003; Wittmann, 2009):

- Intervals with more subdivisions in them generally produce longer duration estimates.
- Unpredictable events or novel activities, including dangerous situations, seem to take longer than events that are well understood, predictable, or routine.
- The passage of time on the scale of hours, months, and years speeds up as people age.

These effects support an observation made by William James, who suggested that it is the frequency and complexity of changes that mark our subjective experience of duration, at least when durations are recalled after the fact. "Many objects, events, changes, many subdivisions, immediately widen the view as we look back. Emptiness, monotony, familiarity, make it shrivel up" (James, 1890/1981, p. 587). The greater, more novel, and more complex our memory for what happened, the longer it seems to have taken.

Despite these clear mismatches between subjective and clock time, there does not appear to be a single "mind-clock" that is influenced by these factors. Instead, time in one sensory system can be dilated, while another remains unchanged or contracted. These and similar observations have led to the suggestion that the experience of duration attributable to each sensory system expands and contracts with the amount of information processed within that sensory system (Eagleman, 2008). According to this idea, our different sensory clocks must reach some kind of agreement so that a multi-sensory event seems to last for one period of time, not multiple durations as reported by multiple sensory systems. This problem is a temporal form of the more traditional object-binding problem, which Revonsuo (1999) presented as follows: "How are internal subjective percepts, as phenomenally unified entities, constructed by the brain as neural entities, considering that the neural mechanisms necessary for creating different phenomenal contents are distributed all around the cortex?" (p. 174). How this occurs for so-called "static" objects is unclear, and how it occurs for "real" objects, which we universally perceive as dynamic, is even less so.

The second aspect of subjective temporality includes the order of events and the related phenomenon of synchrony. To understand subjective temporal order, researchers perform *temporal order experiments* in which the order of sensory events in time must be determined. For instance, a participant will hear two sounds in quick succession, and her task will be to determine whether the onset of the high tone came before or after the onset of the low tone. Such experiments tell us how close in time the two tones must be before they cannot be ordered, which turns out to depend on one's expertise with the task and the stimuli themselves (Mossbridge, Fitzgerald, O'Connor, & Wright, 2006; Mossbridge, Scissors, & Wright, 2008).

A task related to temporal order tasks is to compare two ordered sounds to synchronous ones and attempt to differentiate the two presentations (Mossbridge et al., 2006, 2008). Such *synchrony experiments* tell us less about how temporal order is processed and more about the temporal acuity of a given sensory system. For example, in the visual system, two images in different locations that are flashed in quick succession will seem simultaneous at a delay that can produce an obvious and clear realization of asynchrony when the stimuli are instead offered to the auditory system as a high-pitched tone followed by a low-pitched one (cf. Mitrani, Shekerdjiiski, & Yakimoff, 1986; Mossbridge et al., 2006). Thus, visual temporal acuity, or the sense of now in the visual system, is generally more extended in time than the auditory now. Further, it turns out that even within the auditory system, temporal acuity as assessed by this synchrony comparison method depends on the features of the sounds used to assess it (Mossbridge et al., 2006, 2008). In other words, the duration of now depends on what is contained in the now. As one psychologist put it, "Subjective time is an entity that, like the path of the atom's elementary particles, is not separable from its measurement" (Zackay, 1990, p. 60). Another psychologist expressed that subjective time is even more tenuous: "The temporal aura that envelops us is really a series of fragile constructions, assembled from the haphazard materials that we are able to find in our surroundings and in our consciousness" (W. J. Friedman, 1990, p. 84).

Beyond the puzzles of duration and order, even less is known about how the common experience of the *flow* of time is created. Many people, in their waking moments, experience a past that has just occurred, a future that has not yet happened, and a present consisting of experiences occurring during a now extended over a brief time. This tripartite and ordered description of time, exactly the same description of time that has been removed from physics, has been discussed at length by philosophers and psychologists (e.g., Dennett & Kinsbourne, 1992; Husserl, 1990; J. M. E. McTaggart, 1908/1993; Varela, 1999). One neuroscientist identified neural networks in the prefrontal cortex that he related to each of these three aspects of subjective temporal experience, calling them "preparatory set" (preparing for the future), "working memory" (maintaining impressions of the immediate past), and "inhibitory control" (Fuster, 2001). In addition to the prefrontal cortex, there are other suggestions as to what areas underlie temporal flow processing in the brain; specifically, in a recent anthology on the neuroscience of subjective time, it appears that most of the brain has been implicated in the encoding of subjective apparent time (e.g., Arstila & Lloyd, 2014). Therefore, there seems to be no particular sensory organ for the experience of time's passage. Instead, it seems to some neuroscientists that our conscious experience of temporal flow is created by input from every sense organ along with the temporally integrated functioning of the brain itself (A. D. Eisler, 2003; Wittmann, 2009).

In this section, we have considered several dimensions of subjective time: duration, order, and flow. There may be other dimensions of apparent time, such as density or brightness, but we will not consider those here. We alluded to the metacognitive level that has to do with our implicit knowledge of the nature of subjective time for us. Let us now take this discussion in a slightly different direction, away from the ordinary waking state, and see what we can learn from nonconscious processing and phenomena that occur in altered states of consciousness. What can they tell us about time?

NONCONSCIOUS PROCESSING OF EVENTS IN TIME

To accompany our currently poor understanding of the conscious experience of time, it turns out that we have even less understanding of how nonconscious processes manage events in time. In a popular article, neuroscientist David Eagleman (2011) highlighted several examples of how our well-trained sensory and motor systems know how to perform complex skills like changing lanes in traffic. As he pointed out, attempting to consciously think about these activities nearly always leads to less grace than just relying on our nonconscious sensory-motor timing processes. Consciousness itself can be considered to be the opposite of such automatic functioning (Pribram,

1976). But what is it about these nonconscious sensorimotor timing processes that makes them so good at handling these timing tasks that were initially difficult when first learned? The current consensus is that after much conscious practice, we have learned these tasks so well that they are stored as nonconscious patterns (for a review, see Ashby, Turner, & Horvitz, 2010). However, those patterns are apparently still flexible enough to be altered on the fly—like when you realize you just caught yourself to avoid falling down a stairway. How we anticipate and respond to events such as an unexpected fall is the topic of the remainder of this section.

Some investigators of sensorimotor function in sports believe that what sets elite basketball players apart from others is an outstanding ability to anticipate upcoming events (Aglioti, Cesari, Romani, & Urgesi, 2008). To investigate the mechanisms underlying such anticipation, one investigator created a multisensor device that charts motor movements and muscle twitches over time as participants respond to changes that demand quick and agile responses (Nadin, 2013). Most of these researchers assume that any special skill in anticipating upcoming changes draws from nonconscious learning of visual, tactile, or auditory cues that allow us to predict the upcoming event of interest. Although this is almost certainly the case in many circumstances, it is also possible that nonconscious processing has some way of anticipating unpredictable future events without any cues, nonconscious or otherwise. It turns out that this latter speculation sits on solid scientific ground, at least when the upcoming events are emotional in nature.

To test the hypothesis that nonconscious processing can detect unpredictable emotional events without any cues, Dean Radin (1997b) took physiological measures of participants who viewed a series of images. His protocol had a few features that have become standard for all subsequent attempts at replication: (a) generally nonconscious processing is measured via physiological changes like skin conductance rather than button presses, (b) the events to which participants are exposed consist of emotional events interspersed among calm events in a sequence (e.g., a picture of flowers followed by a picture of a plane crash), and (c) the order of these events is randomized and other precautions are taken so that there are no clear cues as to whether the next event will be an emotional or a calm one. Using this protocol, Radin (1997b) discovered that our physiological systems show different behavior before calm as compared to emotional events about 6 seconds ahead of time, suggesting that they can predict seemingly unpredictable events without sensory cues.

This pattern of results has been replicated successfully more than 20 times since Radin's original work (Mossbridge, Tressoldi, & Utts, 2012). The results of a conservative meta-analysis examining Radin's experiment and all known similar experiments indicate that such *presentiment* or *predictive anticipatory activity* seems to represent an effect that is robustly statistically significant (Mossbridge et al., 2012). Unless some methodological flaw is found in these experiments or the analyses, it appears that for some, and perhaps many people, nonconscious processing seems to "know" about events that will happen soon, even without subtle cues.

The results of the statistical meta-analysis of presentiment were considered provocative by some (e.g., Schwarzkopf, 2014; see response by Mossbridge, 2015), but they did not have to be seen that way. There has historically been resistance to the idea that the nonconscious mind can do things that the conscious mind cannot do. For instance, the existence of subliminal perception, which is now discussed openly in most psychology texts, used to be ridiculed as preposterous (Hassin, 2013; Kihlstrom, Barnhardt, & Tataryn, 1992). The usefulness of nonconscious information processing in dreams only began to be accepted among neuroscientists in the 1990s with powerful evidence showing that dreaming influences perceptual learning (Karni, Tanne, Rubenstein, Askenasy, & Sagi, 1994). Similarly, there has only recently been greater acknowledgment that in certain circumstances implicit cognitive processes (i.e., nonconscious processing of information) can be used to recall memories, make decisions, and solve certain problems better than conscious awareness (Bowden, Jung-Beeman, Fleck, & Kounios, 2005; Dijksterhuis, Bos, Nordgren, & van Baaren, 2006; Voss, Baym, & Paller, 2008; Voss, Lucas, & Paller, 2012). Is it possible that anything going on in the nonconscious mind has been considered suspect because by definition we do not have direct experience of our nonconscious processing? At the very least, the historical resistance to the demonstrated utility of nonconscious processing suggests that we have poor conscious intuitions about the capacities of the nonconscious mind.

An additional reason that the demonstration of presentiment has been considered provocative is that most experimental psychologists and physiologists are not familiar with the data suggesting that nonconscious processing of information about seemingly unpredictable events has been demonstrated not only seconds before an event but also minutes, hours and sometimes days in advance.

Conscious precognition, or the process of consciously identifying future events that seem unpredictable, can be thought of as a bit of a mix between conscious and nonconscious processing of events in time. To create an accurate conscious report of the information obtained by nonconscious processes, by definition, the conscious mind must work together with the nonconscious mind (Broughton, 2010). The added element in precognition is that the information obtained seems to be unpredictable by any conscious means. At this point, we remain agnostic about how this could happen, although we say a little bit about potential mechanisms in Chapter 8. Here, we briefly review the large body of evidence supporting some kind of generally nonconscious access to information about future events, including results from investigations of precognitive dreaming, implicit precognition, and precognitive remote viewing.

PRECOGNITIVE DREAMING

Anecdotal reports of seemingly precognitive dreams include some famous cases, with which the reader may already be familiar. For instance, on the three nights preceding his assassination, Abraham Lincoln's bodyguard reported that the President told him he had been dreaming of the event (Lewis, 1994), and Samuel Clemens ("Mark Twain") claimed to have dreamed of the death of his brother as a result of a steamboat accident (Zohar, 1982). It appears that such experiences are not uncommon, having been reported by about 22% of student participants in a recent survey (Parra, 2013) and between 17% and 38% based on older surveys (for a review, see Lange, Schredl, & Houran, 2000). Further, analyses of the delays between precognitive dreams and the events they seem to predict indicate that around 40% of the predicted events occur on the day following the dream (Sondow, 1988). This temporal drop-off could be due to loss of memory of the dream (Sondow, 1988) or some general mechanism underlying precognition (Orme, 1974). Supporting the latter explanation, a meta-analysis of conscious precognition experiments, in which awake participants consciously attempted to guess the contents of an unknown future stimulus, indicated a clear drop-off of the effect as the time between the participant's guess and the subsequent feedback increased from less than 1 second to minutes, days, months, and years (Honorton & Ferrari, 1989).

As intriguing as spontaneous precognitive dreams may be, problems with using them as evidence for precognition include the following: (a) there can be subtle and complex ways in which any event could be predicted with nonconscious cues available through sensory means; (b) statistical analysis is difficult if not impossible as the number of events in the dream can be quite large, and some of these events could potentially be matched to an upcoming event even if there were no link between the dream and the event; and (c) there is little control for the possibility of fraud. Because of these problems with spontaneous cases, controlled investigations of precognitive dreaming seem to promise greater insight into the phenomenon.

To our knowledge, only a few controlled precognitive dreaming studies have been published in peer-reviewed journals. Three of them revealed statistically significant results supporting the idea that dreams can reveal the content of selected future targets (Krippner, Honorton, & Ullman, 1972; Krippner, Ullman, & Honorton, 1971; Watt, 2014), and three of them did not support this hypothesis (Luke, Zychowicz, Richterova, Tjurina, & Polonnikova, 2012; Sherwood, Roe, Simmons, & Biles, 2002; Watt & Vuillaume, 2015). One study is not discussed here because the participants who were doing the dreaming received a target in an envelope before the dreaming period began (De Pablos, 2011), allowing the possibility that some participants may have opened the envelope to view the target before the dreaming period. The other studies followed practices designed to guard against the three problems just described. First, instead of using spontaneous events that could potentially be predicted in complex ways, they used random methods to select target events that were intended to be experienced by the dreamers. For instance, in Caroline Watt's (2014) successful study, targets were videos that were selected by experimenters who did not know what the dreamers in the study had dreamed. The dreamers were given a link to the target video only after they reported on a week of dreams in which they had attempted to focus on the future target video. Second, statistical analyses performed by judges who were blinded as to the selected target rated the participants' dream descriptions in terms of their similarity to a pool of events, including targets and dummy targets. This made statistical analysis easier, as judges' ratings could be compared against chance associations between dreams and targets. Finally, these researchers guarded against fraud by ensuring that experimenters who knew the content of the targets did not communicate with participants. The unsuccessful study by one of the same authors (Watt & Vuillaume, 2015) used fewer than half the participants, who each provided fewer trials than in the previous, successful study by the same first author (Watt, 2014), suggesting that this unsuccessful study did not have enough statistical power to show the precognitive dreaming effect.

Another possible explanation for why two of the studies did not find significant effects has to do with their method of scoring precognition. In these studies, participants themselves were the judges, and as such, they viewed four images or videos after recording their dreams (Luke et al., 2012; Sherwood et al., 2002). Without knowing which video or photo was the target, participants ranked these stimuli according to which one was most like their dreams. The problem here is that the participants saw all four stimuli, but only one was considered to be a target stimulus. So it might not be surprising that a test for dream precognition would fail, because all four stimuli could potentially be targets of precognition! Meanwhile, in the three peer-reviewed controlled studies that found significantly more accurate dream precognition for targets versus dummy targets, participants were only exposed to the target stimuli (Krippner et al., 1971, 1972; Watt, 2014). In sum, the moral of this story may be that anything that is experienced by a participant may be the target of a precognitive dream, not just what is selected by the experimenters to be the so-called target experience.

IMPLICIT PRECOGNITION

In implicit precognition tasks, participants are asked to perform behaviors seemingly unrelated to precognition, while precognitive effects are examined by analyzing the patterns in their behavior. For instance, in one study, experimenters determined whether performance on a shape-recognition task could be influenced by practice with recognizing a particular shape (Franklin, Baumgart, & Schooler, 2014). Of course, practice on almost any task helps future performance, but they found that this effect could be reversed in time. That is, they gave participants practice *after* the task had been performed, and they found that participants were better at performing the task using the shape for which they received practice. This result echoed an earlier and much discussed finding from psychologist Daryl Bem's (2011) laboratory, in which it was shown that practice on a list of words following a memory task seemed to produce improved memory performance for the words that would subsequently be practiced.

More than 90 similar implicit precognition experiments were conducted between 2000 and 2013. Some produced results matching Bem's original results, and some did not. A recent meta-analysis that examined these studies showed that, taken together, the results seem to be robustly statistically significant and in support of implicit precognition (Bem, Tressoldi, Rabeyron, & Duggan, 2016). One result of this meta-analysis seems especially pertinent to our understanding of potential mechanisms underlying implicit precognition. Specifically, tasks that demanded faster responses (in the millisecond range) and provided immediate feedback were more likely to produce significant results than those that demanded slower responses. In fact, one of the strongest results in the original study, that practice with words following a memory test improves performance on that test, was among the slower response tasks that was generally not replicated (Bem et al., 2016). One reason for the disparity between fast- and slow-response tasks given by the authors of the meta-analysis is that cognitive systems operating quickly suffer less from conscious judgment and alteration of the information that was originally derived from nonconscious sources (Bem et al., 2016). Another explanation is that the tasks requiring faster responses also used more emotionally charged stimuli, which are known to be more engaging to participants (Baruš̌ & Rabier, 2014). A third possibility is that implicit precognition may follow a similar time course as that found for direct or conscious precognition (Honorton & Ferrari, 1989). If so, this would suggest that both conscious and implicit precognition rely on nonconscious processes that seem to access information about future events, but that for some reason these nonconscious processes have more accurate information about events in the very near future.

PRECOGNITIVE REMOTE VIEWING

We already discussed the evidence for remote viewing in Chapter 2, but there was one thing we left out. Remote viewing has often been done without regard to the time of the event. In fact, many of the thousands of government-sponsored remote-viewing experiments performed between 1972 and 1995 can be explained by precognition, as in many cases the targets were not picked until after the remote viewing was completed (Utts, 1996). In her analysis of these studies, statistician Jessica Utts (1996) stated:

> Precognition, in which the answer is known to no one until a future time, appears to work quite well. Recent experiments suggest that if there is a psychic sense then it works much like our other five senses, by detecting change. Given that physicists are currently grappling with an understanding of time, it may be that a psychic sense exists that scans the future for major change, much as our eyes scan the environment for visual change or our ears allow us to respond to sudden changes in sound. (p. 3)

This idea that precognition is especially tied to dynamic events is based on observations made by Ed May, who noticed that precognitive locations with a great amount of energetic change, such as nuclear reactors and wind-power generation sites, were more accurately recognized in remote-viewing sessions than those locations not accompanied by such obvious energetic change (May & Lantz, 2010). May replicated this effect by showing that when an assistant opened a canister of liquid nitrogen and poured it into a bucket, nearby targets were significantly more likely to be correctly viewed than when the same assistant did not open the canister. Because pouring liquid nitrogen into a bucket represents a large thermodynamic change, he concluded that there is something about the processes underlying precognition that are best at encoding or accessing events that are associated with thermodynamic change (May, 2013). A potentially related relationship between *informational* change and precognitive remote-viewing accuracy is supported by previous comparisons of success rates between different targets that either have greater or lesser gradients of informational change. For instance, a high-contrast picture with lots of variation in shape and luminance would be a target with a high degree of informational change across the image (May & Spottiswoode, 2014). Thus, both thermodynamic and informational change within the target are candidate parameters of the nonconscious processes underlying precognition.

POTENTIAL MECHANISMS OF NONCONSCIOUS PROCESSING OF EVENTS IN TIME

Overall, the mechanisms that explain nonconscious access to information about future events are, to say the least, unclear. Not only are they unclear, it is not known how many separate mechanisms need to be found. For instance, one might argue that presentiment likely relies on the same basic mechanisms as precognitive remote viewing, as they both access future events. On the other hand, the time frames are so different that it is reasonable to assume that their mechanisms are different (e.g., seconds for presentiment; minutes to days or months for precognitive remote viewing).

What we do know is that when it is taken seriously, most laboratory evidence supporting access to information about unpredictable future events could be explained using an *advanced perception* argument or a *psychokinetic* argument. That is, it could be that people are doing exactly what they experience doing in a precognitive remote-viewing task: retrieving information about the target they will see in the future. This is the advanced perception argument. Or it could be that people are unaware of what is truly going on, which is that they are psychokinetically causing a particular target that matches their physiology to appear; this is the psychokinetic argument. It turns out that no one has found a controlled laboratory experiment that can differentiate these two explanations, although they could reasonably be differentiated for rare spontaneous cases of precognition. For instance, we assume that those who dreamed of the destruction of the terrorist attacks on the United States on September 11, 2001, before that day's disaster did not, in fact, make the planes fly into the Twin Towers or the Pentagon. Regardless, at least in terms of laboratory results, for now we are stuck not knowing for sure if we should look for a remarkable perception-like skill or a remarkable motor-like skill.

In cases for which there is no clear experimental way to differentiate between two alternatives, it is also possible that the two alternatives are not actually different but only appear to be so.

> It is very hard to resist the view that the subliminal self exists outside temporal conditions as we know them, or at any rate exists in a different kind of time. Time, as we know it, may be a special condition applying only to the physical world or to conscious appreciation of it. (Tyrrell, 1947, p. 96)

If time progresses differently for nonconscious processes compared with conscious ones, then the usual time-based differentiation between sensory events (first they appear in the world and then we perceive them) and motor events (first we want our bodies to move and then we perceive that they move) could be moot. It seems that for the physicists and others among us who are convinced that our waking conscious experience of apparent time is an illusion, an alternative to Tyrrell's idea may be that nonconscious processes are actually *better* able to represent physical reality than conscious processes (Mossbridge, 2015).

Tyrrell's idea that nonconscious processing has a different relationship to time than explicit consciousness was echoed more recently by Jim Carpenter (2012). He spoke about the relation between the borders of our sensorimotor systems and the so-called external world. To describe his model, he introduced the analogy of a gecko's footpads, which help the animal adhere to walls and ceilings using very weak electrostatic forces called van der Waals' forces. These are some of the same forces that hold the molecules of the gecko together, as well as the molecules of the wall. In other words,

> At this very fine level of contact, gecko and ceiling are energetically merged. . . . there is an analogous blur at the edge of our mental being. At the leading edge of perception and intention, organism and surround lack distinguishable identity. In this transactional zone, they are one another. (Carpenter, 2012, p. 43)

As appealing as this analogy may be, there remains much room for explanation and clarification. If nonconscious processes are outside of the normal flow of time, why does the delay between prediction and feedback matter when we assess nonconscious presentiment and precognition? Further, what is the relationship between nonconscious processes and the physical world? Exactly how do nonconscious processes pass their information about future events to the conscious mind? How does the intention to predict a future event influence the accuracy of the information received about that event?

So, at this point in our discussion we have examined the way in which time has come apart in physics, we have seen that there is no unified temporality in the brain driving the structuring of our perceptions, and we have considered evidence that the future can influence the past both in physics and psychology. Apparent time is far from being the rigid structure that we imagine it to be. Moving forward, we want to see what happens to our experience of apparent subjective time during some anomalous phenomena in altered states of consciousness. We have already taken apart a naïve notion of apparent time in what we have said thus far, so that looking carefully at these additional exceptional cases could actually give us some clues about what underlies apparent time. And, indeed, the evidence gives rise to some suggestive ideas about a possible *deep time* and its relationship to apparent time. Although a bridge between the understanding of the physics and psychology of time and anomalous temporal experiences has not yet been clearly developed, we hope the remainder of this chapter inspires scientists to examine how such a bridge could be constructed.

LIFE REVIEWS

Sometimes when people are close to death and subsequently report having had a near-death experience (NDE), or they think they are close to death, they experience a *life review*. A life review consists of a review of the events that have occurred for a person in her life, usually accompanied by critical self-evaluation (Ring & Valarino, 1998). Life reviews have been reported more commonly in NDEs where death was unexpected, such as drownings, car accidents, and falls (Noyes & Kletti, 1977), than those where it was expected, such as terminal illnesses (Greyson, 1985, 2014).

Before examining the variety of temporal experiences that have occurred during life reviews, we note that actual experiences of life reviews vary widely. Some experiencers have seen only highlights from each of the years of their lives. Others have claimed that they had observed everything, including whatever thoughts and feelings had occurred. Some experiencers have said that they had relived their lives as though they had been experiencing everything again for the second time. Other experiencers have said that they had witnessed the events of their lives as though they had been watching someone else. In some cases there has been dual consciousness, as both of those perspectives occurred simultaneously. Occasionally experiencers have said that they had had the perspective of those whom they had affected by their actions, including, in some cases, also those who were secondarily affected by the ramifications of those actions (Beck & Colli, 2003; Draaisma, 2001/2004; Ring & Valarino, 1998). During a life review, time can run backward, forward, or seemingly stand still in a kind of "spatialized" time (Ring & Valarino, 1998, p. 150).

A commonly used metaphor for a life review is that of a film on fast forward. Before the invention of film, the metaphor of a succession of photographic images was used. And before the invention of photography, one writer said in 1821 of his relative's near drowning in a river that "she saw in a moment her whole life, in its minutest incidents, arrayed before her simultaneously as in a mirror" (De Quincey, 1866, p. 111). Again, there is reference to a visual metaphor (Draaisma, 2001/2004).

Film, as a metaphor for life reviews, allows us to understand some of their characteristics. Like film, a life review can run forward or backward; it can be speeded up; it can stop; and some frames can be deleted. Occasionally there is *scenic dilation* whereby the details of a specific event can be held in place while they are examined at leisure. As one experiencer said, "it was as if we were able to wander about, back and forth, in a static landscape, the features of which were not trees and hills, but actions, words, and emotions" (Ring & Valarino, 1998, p. 153). Related to this is the assertion that events during the life review can be experienced in sensory detail that is not possible during physical life. For example, one experiencer said that he had been aware of the air temperature at the time of one of the events in his life review and that he "could have counted the number of mosquitoes present" (Ring & Valarino, 1998, p. 174).

Before examining these experiences further, we need to question the accuracy of the claims of experiencers. Are these veridical memories of events that occurred, or are they confabulated false memories? Can the metacognitive features of these experiences be trusted? Some experiencers have claimed to have remembered their conception or birth (Stevenson & Cook, 1995), memories that may or may not be accurate. But claims of having reexperienced everything from one's life could be formally tested by having experiencers write down lists of the events that they claim to have remembered, something that does not appear to have been done. Of course, such a strategy would introduce a reporting problem in that an experiencer may have perceived far more during a life review than she can subsequently recall and report. Furthermore, few of the recalled events could realistically be checked against verifiable data. Some NDE researchers have tended to regard the stated events of a life review to have been actual events in a person's life, but that is something that needs to be verified. In the meantime, we should not let this stop our inquiry, but we do need to proceed cautiously. We can at least say that some experiencers of NDEs report having life reviews.

Perhaps not surprisingly, an experience of a life review can not only reach backward in time but forward as well. In one case, an experiencer reported imagining seeing his mother at the door of her house being given a notice by a messenger that the experiencer had died (Draaisma, 2001/2004). About one third of experiencers have reported "visions of personal future events," some of which have been subsequently verified to have actually occurred (Ring & Valarino, 1998, p. 151). For example, a 38-year-old woman had seen "an enormous TV screen" in front of her that had displayed her life events from age 13 months to 38 years "all at the same instant" (Ring & Valarino, 1998, p. 150). And once she had decided to return to her body "there was a second TV screen, which was just as big as the first. It showed [her] glimpses of what was to come." And, according to Kenneth Ring, who was familiar with her situation, those events "did indeed take place, just as she was shown" (Ring & Valarino, 1998, p. 151). From examples such as these, we can see that a type of precognition occurs during some NDEs, although there also needs to be more careful verification to determine whether verifiable events are accurately predicted.

If we are to accept the main features of life reviews as reported experiences, then there are several observations that we would like to make. First, life reviews appear to comprise a large number of cognitive events within a short time span. "My whole life was there, every instant of it" (Ring & Valarino, 1998, p. 149); this adds up to a lot of cognitive events. And these events occur quickly (Stevenson & Cook, 1995). Francis Beaufort (1858), who nearly drowned in 1795, said that the rapidity of his thoughts was "not only indescribable but probably inconceivable, by any one who has not himself been in a similar situation" (p. 8). A second observation about life reviews is the clarity, detail, and vividness with which these events are ostensibly recalled. In some cases, rather than a person's capacity being diminished when brain functioning has been compromised, it seems to have been enhanced (Stevenson & Cook, 1995). We shall comment further on this second observation in Chapter 5. Here we just want to look at its implications for an understanding of time.

Such observations prompt the question of whether experiencers' awareness has entered a domain in which the usual experience of subjective apparent time has ceased. In fact, that is what some of them have said. For instance, "I learned that time as we think of it doesn't exist" (Ring & Valarino, 1998, p. 176). Or as another experiencer said,

> Time did not make any sense. Time did not seem to apply. It seemed irrelevant. It was unattached to anything, the way I was. Time is only relevant when it is relative to the normal orderly sequential aspects of life. So I was there for a moment or for eternity. I cannot say but it felt like a very long time to me. (Grace Bubulka, as cited in K. Williams, 2014)

During an NDE, there appears to be a greater variety of temporal expression (cf. Noreika, Falter, & Wagner, 2014). Sometimes time seems to resolve itself into timelessness:

> We go beyond nanoseconds into a space-time measurement we cannot know here on Earth. It is the eternal now where past, present, and future are all merged into one. Eternity is the present, the now that never ends. (Gerard Landry, as cited in K. Williams, 2014)

An NDE appears to take place within some sort of subjective deep time. It is almost as though a person has "popped out of" subjective apparent time for a while.

The quality of life reviews raises the question of whether the lives lived during life reviews are as "real" as lives lived physically, given that events in life reviews can seem as real or more real than events in the ordinary waking state. We can consider that there are a number of dimensions along which altered states of consciousness can vary. One of those is *discrimination*, the ability to identify the altered state of consciousness in which one finds oneself. For example, lucid dreams are dreams in which a person knows that she is dreaming (Barušs, 2003a). A person having a life review usually knows that these are events that are occurring while she is close to death. Another of the dimensions is the *sense of reality*, the degree to which whatever is happening feels as though it were real. *Feelings of reality* are an aspect of subjective experience of which one is usually not explicitly aware but which condition the nature of what is experienced. Most people have set feelings of reality during the ordinary waking state. In depersonalization/derealization disorder, feelings of reality are diminished (American Psychiatric Association, 2013). In some lucid dreams and some NDEs, feelings of reality are enhanced (Barušs, 2003a, 2007b; Sangster, 2004). In particular, sometimes life reviews have been reported as multisensory experiences that have been qualitatively equivalent to living physically.

How is the life review to be explained? We generally have assumed that these life reviews are imaginary experiences of some sort. In Chapter 5, we discuss potential physiological explanations for life reviews and other phenomena experienced in NDEs. But the key observation here is that whatever their ontological status, life reviews tend to take on the properties of lived experiences themselves, to the point where they are indistinguishable from lived experiences. They are sometimes experienced as being "real" for those for whom they occur. Or they are recalled as having been real so that their apparent reality is created during recall. Nonetheless, the apparent reality of life reviews could be an important clue to help us to understand how reality works.

ALTERED TEMPORALITY

There is a psychedelic brew, sometimes called *ayahuasca*, drunk by people living in the Amazon basin. The psychologist Benny Shanon ingested the brew over 130 times and interviewed 178 people for information gathered from an additional 2,500 ayahuasca sessions (Shanon, 2002). In particular, he analyzed the experience of time under the influence of ayahuasca and found that distinctions between memories, perceptions, and thoughts about the future become blurred and that every element of temporality can be altered. In particular, in some cases the temporal distance between the past and present, or the future and present, can appear to be altered so that events that occurred during historical time periods seem to be temporally close to oneself (Shanon, 2002). In addition, an ayahuasca drinker can have the experience of remaining in her own temporal frame but looking in on events as they proceed during another time period. These experiences do not have the characteristic of being remembered but of being observed. Shanon speculated that such experiences represent the confluence of two points in a "non-temporal realm of eternity" (Shanon, 2002, p. 233; see also Shanon, 2001).

One does not need to be intoxicated to experience the sorts of alterations of temporality just described. The historian Arnold Toynbee said that he "slipped into a time pocket" while standing on Pharsalus, in Greece, in January of 1912 (Brennan, 2013, p. 321). For him, bright sunshine gave way to mist, which parted to reveal the visceral slaughter of Macedonians during a Roman attack in 197 BCE. As he averted his gaze from the slaughter, he found himself back in the "peaceful, sunlit present" (Brennan, 2013, p. 321).

Those who have had NDEs sometimes subsequently report episodes of events that are experienced as though there had been a break in the ordinary temporal stream of subjective primary time. According to Phyllis Atwater (2011), such *future memory* can occur in the ordinary waking state. There can be a sensorially experienced series of events that can include physical sensations such as the sweeping of energy, the freezing of time-and-space relationships, expansion of space along with oneself, followed by an overlay of future events on the present. Afterward, present space and time relationships are resumed and regular living is restarted with the person being "startled, chilled, or puzzled" by the event (Atwater, 2011, p. 80). The future memory episode later actually manifests in the person's life. Living such an experience "is so thorough, there is no way to distinguish it from everyday reality while the phenomenon is in progress" (Atwater, 2013, p. 24).

Atwater (2013) described the first of her own future memory episodes. She said that she was sitting at her desk at work, with her pencil in her hand, when everything "froze in place," including her body. There was a surge of heat through her "paralyzed frame from feet to head." Her desk disappeared from view as "a field of brilliant sparkles descended from the ceiling and spread out to encompass the entire office." As this occurred, she found herself back in the nondual state of consciousness that she called "The Void," in which she had found herself during the second of her three NDEs. She was drawn into a swirling mass of energy that sucked her into itself. When it stopped spinning, she found herself preliving almost the entire following year of her life in which she left Idaho and travelled across the United States to end up in Virginia, near Washington, DC, a trip that she had had no intention of taking (Atwater, 2013, p. 33). "This scenario I both watched and lived simultaneously and in great detail, as if each physical motion was being performed in actuality, each thought, feeling, taste, touch, and smell thoroughly experienced" (Atwater, 2013, p. 34). When the future memory was over, The Void disappeared, and Atwater was left still sitting at her desk holding her pencil. She estimated that about 10 minutes of clock time had elapsed. No one else in her office had noticed anything (Atwater, 2013).

Atwater (2013) said that she was upset, that it was uncomfortable to sit and think, and that her eyes filled with tears. "Then the whole scenario replayed itself once more, as if to make certain I would remember each detail"

(p. 35). Except that this time the future memory extended into a future in which she said that she met someone during a walk in the countryside in the southern part of Virginia whom she ended up marrying. She immediately started making arrangements for the trip, which proceeded both as scheduled and not as scheduled, in that sometimes events would follow the future memory scenario and other times they would not. According to her, she did end up encountering and marrying a man matching the description of the one in her future memory scenario while on a walk in the countryside in the southern part of Virginia.

Cynthia Larson (2012) said that she felt compelled to read two stories from picture books for her daughter while sitting in a waiting room, but she had time for only one of them. She decided to go ahead with both of them anyway and looked up at the clock in the waiting room, which said 4:08 p.m. She read the first story at a leisurely pace and looked again at the clock to see that it was still 4:08 p.m. When she subsequently timed reading the story, it took her 11 minutes to do so. In other words, it appeared to Larson that time stopped when she began reading the first story and started again after she had finished reading it. After she read the second story, the clock in the waiting room said 4:30 p.m., which was consistent with the time on the clock in her car. Of course, this is Larson's account of what occurred. It is possible that the clock on the wall had been stopping and starting intermittently, that she had read the clock incorrectly, that the clock in her car had also not been functioning or had been misread, or that her story was embellished. If none of these more mundane events occurred, it would appear that apparent objective time stood still for about 11 minutes while Larson read a story.

In each case, in the events that we have discussed, there has been an alteration of apparent temporality. In particular, in many of these cases, including some of the cases of life reviews, people have reported the appearance of events occurring while the temporal stream has slowed or stopped. In that context, it is interesting to consider the following case in which the apparent temporal stream has continued as usual, but it seems as though time should have slowed or stopped.

Pearl Curran was a woman living in Missouri who ostensibly channelled an entity calling itself "Patience Worth" for almost 25 years, resulting in 4,375 pages of literary material deposited with the Missouri Historical Society in St. Louis. The literary material has received "very favorable, and sometimes lavishly complimentary, reviews" (Braude, 2003, p. 139) and has been considered to be well beyond Pearl Curran's ability, although this does not rule out the possibility that the material was produced by some non-conscious aspect of Pearl's psyche (Braude, 2003). There is good evidence that this material emerged in completed form without subsequent editing (Prince, 1927).

What is interesting for our purposes is that Pearl Curran could compose material on demand as quickly as it could be written down. For instance, on February 17, 1926, Walter Prince asked her to compose a poem whose lines began with each of the letters of the alphabet, except the letter "X," in order, which she did "at a speed regulated only by the ability of the scribe to take it down in shorthand" (Prince, 1927, p. 285). The following day she was asked to produce a dialogue "between a lout and a wench, at a Fair" (Prince, 1927, p. 291) in her characteristic archaic vernacular interspersed with the lines of a poem about "The Folly of Atheism." The request was followed by a span of about 8 seconds before the interlaced composition was produced "about as rapidly as it could be taken down" (Prince, 1927, p. 291).

According to Pearl Curran, while channelling, she would see each word, along with images related to the meaning of that word, which she would then enunciate. She was also aware of somatic sensations in her body and the reactions of people around her, and she could think about other things, such as what she would eat later. She appears to have been in a dissociated state, and whatever the source of the material, it does not appear to have been due to the usual effortful processing required for literary production (Braude, 2003).

The quality of the writing and the speed with which she produced it opens the door to the speculation that some kind of additional time elapsed between the time at which a request was made of her and the time at which she began to produce her writing, but that the additional time was not apparent to Pearl Curran or to her onlookers. An alternative speculation is that whatever intelligence, inside or outside Pearl Curran, created these literary productions, precognitively anticipated the requests. A second alternative speculation is that whatever accelerated cognition occurs during life reviews also occurred during the production of this literary material. In other words, Pearl's usual sense of time proceeded unimpeded, but something appears to have been gathered together and inserted into a time frame that was insufficient for what had been inserted.

THE EXPERIENCE OF TIMELESSNESS

Is time friable? Can it come apart completely? One way to think about the previous scenarios is to suppose that there has been an incursion into explicit awareness by processes that are active within a nonconscious domain of the psyche. And time does not work the same way in that nonconscious domain. Or maybe the passing of subjective apparent time does not exist at all in some states of consciousness. Let us end this chapter by looking more carefully at experiences of timelessness.

Psychedelic drugs often transport the user into magnified awareness of the present, resulting in a feeling of timelessness (Grinspoon & Bakalar, 1979). Christopher Mayhew (1965), who had taken 400 mg of mescaline under the supervision of Humphry Osmond, experienced timelessness in the drawing room of his home. He felt that an "essential part" of himself existed in a "timeless order of reality outside the world as we know it" (Mayhew, 1965, p. 294) whose "countless years of complete bliss" were "interrupted by short spells in the drawing-room" (Mayhew, 1965, p. 296). For him, existing "outside time" was not to be taken "metaphorically, but literally" (Mayhew, 1965, p. 294). Being outside time, for Mayhew, allowed for experiences of hopping around in time, and temporal insertions during which he spent what seemed to him to be years of time in activities that only took up moments of clock time, as evidenced by film taken of his drug experience.

Shanon (2002) also found that when the effects of ayahuasca were "strong," drinkers felt that they were "outside time" (p. 234). For instance, this could occur while dancing, so that the dance seemed to go on outside of time. For Shanon, such experiences of atemporality are associated with an increase in "visual stimulation and a corresponding increase in the rate by which psychological time is experienced to flow" (Shanon, 2002, p. 235) to the point where one leaves the realm of time altogether. Although not parallel, this is reminiscent of the fact that time slows down more and more as one approaches the speed of light and would stop altogether could the speed of light be reached. From the vantage point of this experience of eternity, like the block model of spacetime, everything that has ever happened, everything that is happening, and everything that will ever happen are all equally available. This can also be associated with the feeling that one has become "all-knowing" (Shanon, 2002, p. 236). Thus, this appears to resolve Bergson's dissatisfaction with the spatialization of time, in that events in the past and future are experienced as lived events just as are those in the present.

Timelessness is often also regarded as one of the defining features of *mystical experiences* (e.g., Stace, 1960). Mystical experiences are experiences that occur during particular types of transcendent states of consciousness and that have considerable overlap with psychedelic and near-death experiences (Baruss, 1996, 2003a; E. F. Kelly & Grosso, 2010b; Wulff, 2014). Rather than trying to survey ideas about time in mystical experiences, let us just consider what the American mystic Franklin Merrell-Wolff had to say about the nature of time, given that his was a particularly clear exposition of the transcendent events that occurred for him.

For Merrell-Wolff, ordinary experience is structured by dualities, including those of subject versus object and time versus timelessness, whereas events that occur during transcendent states of consciousness transcend all dualities. In fact, Merrell-Wolff restricted the use of the term *experience* to mental events that have the subject–object structure of intentionality and invented the neologism *imperience* for whatever goes on in the nondual realm. For Merrell-Wolff, there is a discontinuity between the ordinary and transcendent realms with the *escalating self* capable of moving easily back and forth from one to the other in response to small changes in consciousness (Baruš, 1996; Merrell-Wolff, 1966).

Consciousness, as imperienced by Merrell-Wolff during a transcendent state, is primary and gives rise to time, rather than being bound by it. How does it do so? For this, Merrell-Wolff (1995) used "the notion of a 'life-current' constantly moving but, at the same time, so turning upon itself that there is no progress from past to future"; he acknowledged that this does not make any sense but said that "that did not change the fact that I knew what I knew" (p. 132). This is similar to Alan Watts's (1965) conception of time under the influence of psychedelics when he said,

> The present is self-sufficient, but it is not a static present. It is a dancing present—the unfolding of a pattern which has no specific destination in the future but is simply its own point. It leaves and arrives simultaneously, and the seed is as much the goal as the flower. (p. 33)

Taken together with the previous examples of anomalous experiences of time, the actual nature of time as it is experienced is starting to look like the redacted time of physics.

RETHINKING TIME

What do we have available to us to help us understand time in the context of a discussion of consciousness? We know that we have a richly textured present. As far as we know, the past and the future might not exist as anything other than schemata for structuring our experience. So, there is an indefinite past and an indefinite future, neither of which may actually exist. But the richly textured present keeps recurring, bringing into existence the perception of temporal progression and the existence of an apparently objective sequence of events that is interpreted as being separate from the subjective vantage point associated with it. In this way, there can be a continuously regenerating present without a past or future. This is similar to Julian Barbour's conception of time and one way to think about the view of Franklin Merrell-Wolff. But this idea is still not satisfying, as it does not explain the rules that bring us from one point to another in the chain of events. At the same time, pun intended, it may be as far as we can go.

There are two concluding observations that we would like to make about time, before closing this chapter. The first is that apparent time, whether objective or subjective, is a construction that only applies to limited situations. In particular, subjective apparent time is explicitly experienced during the ordinary waking state, in part by binding information across multiple sensory inputs. The deep time of some nonconscious processes does not appear to be the same as subjective apparent time. And it appears that some of these nonconscious processes seem to become conscious in altered states of consciousness. Further, some of these nonconscious processes appear to be able to access events that are spatially and temporally not within apparent time, implying that the deep structures underlying our waking consciousness are fundamentally spatially and temporally nonlocal in nature. This is a key reframing of our understanding of consciousness in that consciousness now has been extended into temporal domains beyond apparent time.

Our second concluding observation is that the time experienced during timelessness and the time that characterizes some nonconscious processes are both aspects of deep time, a sort of time that structures subjective apparent time. Deep time may run concurrently with apparent time, but the relationship between the two needs to be established and understood. We will keep these ideas about time in mind as we proceed to look at other phenomena suggestive of the transcendent nature of mind.

4

INTERACTIONS WITH
DISCARNATE BEINGS

Think ye the earth aholdeth none save those atrack 'pon clay?
—Patience Worth (ostensibly, channelled
by Pearl Curran, as cited in Prince, 1927, p. 295)

Penny Sartori was a staff nurse on a night shift in the Intensive Therapy Unit at Morriston Hospital in Wales when she had an experience with a patient that made her question the manner in which we treat the dying. The man, who knew that he was going to die, was in agony when she adjusted his bed to bathe him. Sartori called a physician, who could do nothing other than to increase the patient's dose of painkillers. Because he was connected to a ventilator via a tracheostomy, the man could not speak, but he mouthed the words "Let me die, leave me alone, just let me die in peace." Sartori said that she would never forget the look in the man's eyes (Sartori, 2008, p. 2; see also Gawande, 2014). Would we try to hold on so hard to the dysfunctional bodies of the dying if we were aware of evidence that consciousness continues after death? And if consciousness continues after death, then how are we to understand consciousness?

http://dx.doi.org/10.1037/15957-005
Transcendent Mind: Rethinking the Science of Consciousness, by I. Baruss and J. Mossbridge

The question of whether we survive death has profound practical consequences for the manner in which we live. We have a basic survival instinct. But if consciousness, sentience, and personality are mere by-products of a brain encased in a physical body, then we cling even harder to whatever vestiges of life remain in corporeal form because we believe that once life leaves the body, then so do the qualities that we identify with being human. That is the normative, materialistic attitude entrenched in the structures of Western civilization. And to try to think otherwise can seem impossible, as illustrated by philosopher Michael Grosso's (1994) self-reflection:

> When I look closely within myself, I feel pulled toward belief in probable extinction. This is due to what has been called the spell of the paradigm, the feeling that I do not inhabit the kind of universe where the leap into a new mode of existence after biological death is possible— or at any rate, probable. This has something to do with my educational experience. The model of reality that was in the air at Columbia University where I studied philosophy and classics in the 1960s was simply not congenial to belief in postmortem survival. (pp. 18, 20)

So at the same time that it is necessary for practical and scientific reasons to scrutinize the notion that consciousness can survive the death of the body, we need to take into account that many of us have been conditioned to assume that such survival is not possible. Therefore, we will move ahead to logically examine the empirical evidence as dispassionately as possible.

The proposition that consciousness survives the death of the body, at least for a while, is formally known as the *survival hypothesis* (Irwin, 1994, p. 183). Scientific investigation of survival, in spite of suppression, has been ongoing since at least the founding of the Society for Psychical Research in 1882 (Grosso, 1994; Irwin, 1994). There have been a number of thorough evaluations of that material (Assante, 2012; Braude, 2003; Carter, 2012b; Fontana, 2005; see also Shushan, 2009). However, rather than reviewing the history of survival research here, we will take a somewhat different approach. If human beings do survive the death of the body, then those who have died must still be around somewhere in some form or other. If so, is there any way in which we, the living, can interact with the dead? In fact, have we already done so? Is it possible that we do so on a regular basis? Are there ways in which the dead can interact with us? And, to complicate matters, if deceased human beings are out there, then who else might there be? And are they all friendly?

Perhaps it is best to ease into this subject matter. So let us start by reviewing cases of people who feel that they have had spontaneous contact of one form or another with the deceased, then consider cases in which there has been deliberately induced contact with the deceased as a way of treating grief. *Mediums* are people who can ostensibly do this on a regular basis, so we will look at mediumship as a way of interacting with the deceased on demand. We will talk about yet more intimate forms of contact whereby invisible beings apparently take over a person's body or parts thereof, including cases of unwanted intrusions. Finally, we will draw some conclusions about the implications of ostensible interactions with the deceased for our understanding of consciousness.

SPONTANEOUS CONTACT WITH THE DEAD

Considering that these sorts of things are not supposed to happen, it might be surprising to learn that many people have reported having had contact with the dead. In a 1973 National Opinions Research Council poll in the United States by the University of Chicago, 27% of respondents claimed to have had contact with the dead. In a National Opinions Research Council poll in 1984, that number had gone up to 42%. The numbers for widows who felt that they had had contact with the dead were even higher: 51% in 1973 and 67% in 1984 (Greeley, 1987). In other studies, 74% of 39 widows had "sensed the presence of the dead spouse" (Lindström, 1995, p. 14), 60% of 87 bereaved participants reported the perception of a presence (Datson & Marwit, 1997), 49% of 47 next-of-kin of the deceased had had a "hallucination or significant dream" associated with the deceased within the first month of bereavement (Barbato, Blunden, Reid, Irwin, & Rodriguez, 1999, p. 32), 31% of a 1974–1975 representative sample of 902 people from Iceland claimed to have "been aware of the presence of a deceased person" (Haraldsson, 2012, p. 1), and 48% of 33 pet owners had a sense of their deceased pet's presence (Carmack & Packman, 2011). These numbers are probably low given that people would likely be reluctant to report experiences that could cast doubt on their mental health (A. S. Berger, 1995; Hall, 2014; see also Baruš, 2014b; Greeley, 1987).

Exactly what kind of experiences are people having? In an Icelandic sample of 449 people who had "been aware of the presence of a deceased person" (Haraldsson, 2012, p. 1), 67% of the experiences had been visual, 28% had been auditory, 13% had been tactile, and 5% had been olfactory. About one fifth of the accounts involved more than one sensory modality. In addition, 11% of the accounts involved only the "sensing of an invisible presence" (Haraldsson, 2012, p. 37). The perceptions can be fragmentary, such as just the smell of cumin coffee that the deceased used to drink (Haraldsson, 2012), or so complete that a deceased person appears to be physically present (Haraldsson, 2012) or capable of physical interaction, such as writing a note (Kübler-Ross, 1977, 1997), and pretty much anything in between. One way to think of purely perceiving someone without any sensory accompaniment is to think of this information as arriving in whatever anomalous way it arrives in cases of remote viewing or precognition. As far as being able to identify a sensed presence as being someone in particular, it is possible that there are qualities of the sensed presence that correspond to those with which we identified the person during life. In other words, sometimes a person just gets a feeling that a certain deceased person is around (Assante, 2012, p. 288).

Sometimes significant dreams associated with the deceased are included in such frequency counts and surveys (Barbato et al., 1999). These are typically dreams in which the deceased person appears in such a way as to leave an impression that one has actually interacted with her (Assante, 2012; Guggenheim & Guggenheim, 1996). For instance, Carl Jung (1961/1989) had two dreams of his father after his father's death that made Jung "think about life after death" (p. 97).

There are also other types of experiences in which the deceased do not themselves appear, but that the living interpret as being associated with them. These experiences can include lights apparently turning on and off by themselves, pictures of the deceased seeming to glow or vibrate, broken electronic equipment suddenly starting to work, cars seeming to start themselves, and so on (Assante, 2012; Barbato et al., 1999). Such statistically rare or possibly anomalous phenomena are sometimes labelled as *poltergeist* activity, with the word *poltergeist* literally meaning something like "troubling spirit" (Irwin, 1994, p. 190). But why should such events be attributed to the dead? Let us consider an example.

When giving examples of experiences in this book, we have been careful to choose anecdotal accounts and case studies that appear to have genuinely occurred. It is possible that some of these, as well as some of the field studies and laboratory studies that we cite, are fraudulent. In any scientific field, any report could consist of well-constructed fraudulent data that we and others have been unable to recognize as fraudulent. There is no way around this problem except to take great care in choosing the material that we do share in this book and to let the reader know the source of the material so that she can decide for herself what to make of it.

In June of 2014, Michael Shermer, the publisher of *Skeptic* magazine, was getting married in California to Jennifer Graf from Germany. Three months prior to the wedding, Shermer had tried to fix Graf's deceased grandfather Walter's 1978 Philips 070 transistor radio. The radio had not worked for decades. Shermer had tried to restore it by putting in new batteries, checking for loose connections, and giving it a good whack. He and Graf had not been able to get it going and had ended up placing it at "the back of a desk drawer in [their] bedroom" (Shermer, 2014, p. 97).

On the day of the wedding ceremony, which was being held at their home, Graf missed her grandfather and wished that he were there. At one point, Shermer and Graf went to the back of the house, where they could hear music coming from the bedroom. It turned out that it was emanating from Walter's radio, which had apparently begun playing within minutes before the beginning of the ceremony. "My grandfather is here with us," Graf said, "I'm not alone" (Shermer, 2014, p. 97). In spite of her skepticism, Graf had the feeling that her grandfather was present and that the music was his "gift of approval" (Shermer, 2014, p. 97). The radio stopped working the following day and remained silent. Shermer acknowledged that infrequent events sometimes do occur but that that does not strip them of their evocative nature or emotional significance. In addition: "I have to admit, it rocked me back on my heels and shook my skepticism to its core as well" (Shermer, 2014, p. 97).

Erlendur Haraldsson listed six noteworthy features of afterlife encounters on the basis of his detailed examination of 449 accounts of such experiences among the Icelandic population. The first is that 28% of the deceased who appeared in these accounts had died a violent death when only 8% of the Icelandic population had died violently. That figure of 28% is consistent with those found in other studies for other populations. In many cases, those apparently perceiving the deceased were unaware that the person had died. Because an unanticipated death leaves the dying with no chance to finish unfinished business, the violent nature of someone's death suggests that the motivation to have some form of contact with the deceased, at least in some cases, could lie with the deceased rather than the living. Second, 14% of encounters occurred within 24 hours of death, often in cases where the person having an experience of the deceased did not know that the person had died, again suggesting that the motivation for contact lies with the deceased. Third, sometimes more than one person simultaneously has similar experiences associated with the deceased, suggesting that some of these apparent encounters could have veridical features. For instance, in the case of the smell of cumin coffee mentioned previously, the experiencer's mother admitted that she also smelled something but did not want to say more about that. Fourth, participants sometimes described a person whom they did not know, who was only identified afterward from the description given by the person having the encounter. Fifth, some participants discovered information that had been previously unknown but later proved to be correct, again suggesting veridicality in these cases. Sixth, in some encounters there appeared to have been a deliberate intervention in a person's life, such as warnings of danger or apparent healing of illnesses (Haraldsson, 2012). Other researchers have found similar features of afterlife encounters (e.g., Barbato et al., 1999; A. S. Berger, 1995).

DELIBERATE CONTACT WITH THE DEAD

In contemporary grief therapy it has been acknowledged that *continuing bonds* with the deceased could be beneficial for the bereaved (Hall, 2014; Neimeyer, 2014). The idea usually is that it is acceptable to allow mental representations of the deceased to continue to evolve in the absence of actual physical proximity (Field & Wogrin, 2011; Neimeyer, 2001). Not surprisingly, spontaneous contact with the dead can emerge as an aspect of continuing bonds, although the incidences of such occurrences are thought to be under-reported because of clients' fears of being ridiculed or considered to be mentally ill or "stupid" (Hall, 2014, p. 10). Indeed, some psychotherapists do consider "illusions or hallucinations of the deceased" to be lapses in reasoning (Field & Wogrin, 2011, p. 39).

Barbato, Blunden, Reid, Irwin, and Rodriguez (1999) considered apparent contact with the deceased, along with any accompanying anomalous phenomena, to be so common during grief that they should be regarded as a normal part of the grieving process. In their self-report survey of the next of kin of 47 patients who had died in a palliative care unit in Australia, they found that 18 respondents had "had direct experience of something unusual within the first month of their loved one's death" (Barbato et al., 1999, p. 32). Most frequently, at 50%, was a "sense of a presence," while 33% experienced "auditory hallucination," 33% experienced "olfactory hallucination," 16% experienced an "unusual occurrence," and so on (Barbato et al., 1999, p. 32). In one case, ostensibly a picture of the deceased hanging on the wall vibrated so quickly as to emit a hum. Barbato et al. noted that initial contact experiences can be disturbing, but that as the number of such experiences increases, "experients become more reassured and comforted" (p. 35). They maintained that unusual phenomena associated with death for those who are dying, as well as those who are bereaved, can be therapeutic and counseled palliative care workers who witness or hear of such an experience to "listen attentively and to validate the experience as normal" (Barbato et al., 1999, p. 35).

Other investigators have also urged acceptance of apparent contact experiences. "Perceiving the presence of a deceased loved one is a frequent enough occurrence to be considered a relatively normal correlate of bereavement" (Datson & Marwit, 1997, p. 132). Others have said that "these paranormal experiences must not be discarded as 'hallucinations'" (A. S. Berger, 1995, p. 3). In fact, where apparent interactions with the deceased are accepted as real by the bereaved, they can become part of the "primary source of emotional comfort" for them (T. A. Richards & Folkman, 1997, p. 546). This also applies in cases of mediumship (Darghawth, 2013), which we discuss next. The idea is that if a person were to accept experiences of apparent contact as actual experiences of contact, they could be reassured of the survival of the deceased, which then could have a therapeutic effect, supportive of the continuing bonds model.

If the bereaved are comforted by experiences of apparent contact with the deceased, can such experiences be induced in those who are not having them otherwise? A point to note is that all of the previously mentioned information about contact experiences comes from various surveys and from psychotherapists' observations from clinical practice. Although the results of this work can usefully inform the continuing bonds model, from the point of view of attempting to understand consciousness, it would be desirable to have greater control over such experiences so as to be in a better position to examine them to determine whether they could possibly qualify as verifiable contact with conscious, but deceased, beings.

There have been several techniques that have been used to induce apparent communication with the deceased. One of those involves the use of mirror gazing, whereby people look into a mirror in a darkened environment with the intention of perceiving an apparition of someone with whom they wish to communicate who is deceased (Merz, 2010; Moody, 1993; Terhune & Smith, 2006). However, the technique that we consider here is one that was developed by Allan Botkin (2014).

Botkin (2014) was using a procedure known as *eye movement desensitization and reprocessing* (EMDR) at a Veterans Affairs hospital in the Chicago area for treating posttraumatic stress disorder. This procedure involves having a patient attend to a disturbing thought while following a target (e.g., a psychotherapist's fingers, a wand) with her eyes as the psychotherapist moves the target laterally back and forth at eye level in front of the patient's face. In the context of posttraumatic stress, this procedure appears to allow distressing content to more easily enter a patient's awareness than it otherwise would and, once having become explicit, to shift the status of that content from that of a relived experience to a more abstract memory. Botkin has claimed that EMDR therapy was strikingly successful for treating the symptoms of posttraumatic stress disorder and that it was particularly successful for treating grief, including traumatic grief.

At one point, Botkin (2014) was working with Sam, a Vietnam War veteran, who had been traumatized by the death of a 10-year-old Vietnamese girl during a firefight. Botkin administered EMDR several times to help Sam resolve his grief. After administering a final set of eye movements, Botkin asked Sam to close his eyes. The tears that Sam had been crying stopped, and he smiled, giggled, and became euphoric. Afterward, Sam said that when he had closed his eyes, he had seen the Vietnamese girl "as a beautiful woman with long black hair in a white gown surrounded by a radiant light" (Botkin, 2014, p. 13). The woman in the image had seemed happy and thanked Sam for having taken care of her before she had died. They had told each other that they loved each other, and the woman in the image had embraced the war veteran before fading away. Sam was convinced that he had actually communicated with the Vietnamese woman.

Botkin (2014) did not know what to think. However, over the following weeks, several other patients had the same sorts of experiences, so he decided to try to induce them deliberately. He did so at the end of EMDR sessions by asking "patients what they would say to the deceased if they could talk to him or her," reminding them of going into a "receptive mode" of mind that he had discussed with them at the beginning of the session, telling them to allow whatever happens to happen, and then having patients make the eye movements and close their eyes after having made them (Botkin, 2014, p. 224). That worked. In fact, Botkin claimed that he "was able to induce the experience with 98 percent reliability by following the sequence precisely" (p. 19).

One of the authors of this book, Julia Mossbridge, went to Allan Botkin in 2003 to experience this procedure for herself. She blamed herself for the death of a college friend, Josh (whose name has been changed to protect his family), who had died in an automobile accident on his way to a dance at Julia's college. Mossbridge had some residual guilt about the death of her friend because she had invited him to the dance. When she sat down with Botkin, she was skeptical of the white stick with a blue marker cap stuck to the end of it that Botkin used for guiding the eye movements. Nonetheless, as she watched the stick and listened to Botkin encouraging her to get in touch with her grief, she was filled with images of her last fateful interaction with Josh. A few more waves of the wand and she began to cry, "seeing images of his death" until sadness gave way to happy memories. And then, when she closed her eyes again:

> Simply, without pretense, I saw Josh walk out from behind a door. My friend jumped around with his youthful enthusiasm, beaming at me. I felt great joy at the connection but I couldn't tell whether I was making the whole thing up. He told me I wasn't to blame and I believed him. Then I saw Josh playing with his sister's dog. I didn't know she had one. We said good-bye and I opened my eyes, laughing. (Mossbridge, 2003)

Mossbridge was surprised to subsequently discover that Josh's sister had, in fact, had a dog that also had died in a car accident, just like Josh. It had been a golden retriever, the same breed as the one that Mossbridge had seen playing with Josh. If Mossbridge's experience was correctly remembered and was not an unintentionally biased account of what occurred (see Chapter 7, this volume), this may be an example of an induced interaction with a deceased person in which verifiable information, not known at the time to the percipient, was revealed. Regardless of whether her memory was accurate, her experience suggests the possibility of induced interactions with the deceased as a method of relieving grief and guilt and deserves further research.

MEDIUMSHIP

We started this chapter by considering fleeting, spontaneous, apparent contact with the dead, and then we examined deliberately induced, somewhat steadier, apparent contact. Let us now consider mediumship as a yet more stable way of ostensibly interacting with the deceased. A medium is a person who appears to be able to talk to the dead or, more generally, appears to communicate with invisible intelligences or receive "energy" from other dimensions of reality (Baruša, 2003a, 2014a). Mediums are sometimes sought out by the bereaved as a way of trying to confirm the continuing existence of the deceased, so that mediumship also has relevance for the treatment of grief (Beischel, Mosher, & Boccuzzi, 2014–2015). Let us start with an example.

One of the authors of this book, Imants Baruš, had a tape-recorded session with a medium in his home office. Baruš mentioned to the medium that a recently deceased friend with whom he had played ice hockey had been on his mind. The medium asked if his friend had been a beer drinker and then, whether he had drunk "Canadian," which is a type of beer. He was likely a beer drinker, but Baruš did not know what his beer preferences had been. The medium said that he had had short dark hair and had been lean. She said that he had been a good listener and had tried to be very present when he listened. All of that had been correct. The medium was not sure whether Baruš or his friend had been a defenseman. It was the deceased who had been a defenseman. She asked if he had been a Boston Bruins fan, because she said that she was seeing the previous night's Stanley Cup playoff game between the Boston Bruins and the Montreal Canadiens. To Baruš, that seemed unlikely. It seemed more likely that Baruš's friend had been a Montreal Canadiens fan given that he had lived in Montreal at one time. In fact, the earlier "Canadian" may have been an allusion to the Canadiens team and not the beer. Then she asked "Is there a 'Lafal' or 'Laval' or a place that sounds like that?" (Baruš, 2013a, p. 95). Baruš commented that there was a university as well as a district in Montreal called "Laval" but that neither of those was relevant to his friend, so, at the time, this seemed like a miss. However, subsequent investigation revealed that Baruš's friend had lived at the corner of Laval Street and Carré Saint-Louis in Montreal (Baruš, 2013a).

In this example, the medium was ostensibly communicating correct information that she could not reasonably have known through ordinary sensory processes. Does that really happen? Can mediums obtain correct information through anomalous means? That is an empirical question for which it is easy to design appropriate experiments. An investigator finds a medium who has a reputation for getting correct information and then pretests the medium. The investigator brings her own *sitter*, as the person for whom the information is provided is called. To eliminate the possibility of *sensory leakage*, whereby information is gathered by normal sensory means, the investigator isolates the sitter. The experimenter then gets a second experimenter, who does not know the identity of the sitter, to interact with the medium. This second *blinded* experimenter gets the medium to provide information about the sitter's *discarnates*, as the deceased relatives and friends of the sitter are sometimes called. This can include having the medium provide specific information about the physical appearance of the discarnate, the discarnate's personality, her hobbies and interests, or her cause of death. Then the sitter scores the transcript of what the medium said against the facts as she knows them. And she does that also for the transcript of a session that was intended for another sitter, without knowing which transcript was hers and which was for the other person, thereby providing a control condition (Beischel, 2007, 2013).

Using such a protocol, Beischel, Boccuzzi, Biuso, and Rock (2015) found that 38 of 58 sitters, or about 66%, chose the transcript intended for them rather than the control transcript. That result is statistically significant. In a separate study, a statistically significant 13 of 16 transcripts (81%) chosen by sitters were the transcripts intended for those sitters (Beischel & Schwartz, 2007). Other investigators, using various protocols, have found similar results (e.g., E. W. Kelly & Arcangel, 2011; Robertson & Roy, 2004; Rock, Beischel, Boccuzzi, & Biuso, 2014; G. E. R. Schwartz, Russek, Nelson, & Barentsen, 2001). There have been several studies in which no effect was found (Jensen & Cardeña, 2009; O'Keeffe & Wiseman, 2005), but there are several aspects of those studies that minimized the likelihood of finding an effect, such as the lack of pretesting prospective mediums to see whether they could perform effectively in the research setting (Beischel, 2007).

So, good mediums can produce correct information, at least some of the time. That is consistent with some of the cases of spontaneous and induced after-death communication that we have already considered. But is that information coming from dead people? Could mediums, and others experiencing apparent after-death communication, just be good at picking up information from the living or from physical sources wherever the necessary information might be found? The former explanation has been called the *survival hypothesis*, whereas the latter explanation has been called the *super-psi hypothesis* (Braude, 2003; see also P. F. Cunningham, 2012). So the question becomes, does the survival hypothesis fit the data better than the super-psi hypothesis? This is where the story becomes more complicated.

SUPER-PSI VERSUS SURVIVAL

To think about this, let us flip our perspectives. Suppose that we are dead. But we realize that we still exist and that we are still pretty much the same as we used to be except that we no longer have a physical body. And we get a chance to talk through a medium to those who used to know us. What could we try to do to convince them that we are still around and that what we are saying is not just an artifact of the medium's ability to extract information from sources in the physical world using clairvoyance or telepathy? Well, there could be several things we could try. Suppose that we used to be a famous poet. If we recited one of our own poems, then observers could just say that the medium was using super-psi. But what if we produce a new poem, in the same style as our original poetry, that no one has ever seen? There has been such a case, sort of, in the context of the *Scole experiment*.

Two couples used to meet twice a week in one of their homes in Scole, England, for the purpose of contacting discarnates. Two of the people in the group were mediums, who would go into an altered state of consciousness for 2 to 2.5 hours at a time, ostensibly allowing 10 different spirits to speak through them. In addition to apparent conversations with the spirits, various anomalous physical phenomena occurred. A number of investigators attended 37 of the sessions from October 1995 to March 1998. During some of the sessions, rolls of 35-millimeter photographic film were present in the room, usually left unopened in their cases. Upon development afterward, the film was often found to contain writing in various languages, drawings, and Chinese ideograms. In particular, a handwritten German poem appeared on a film used on July 26, 1996. The poem had been written in the style from around 1840 and was of good quality. Indeed, it resembled the poetry of Friedrich Rückert, although no such poem written by him has ever been found (Keen, Ellison, & Fontana, 1999). There are issues regarding appropriate controls for this film, although the phenomena reported by the investigators overall appear likely to have been genuine (Keen, 2001). Did Rückert create a poem after his death to show that he is still around?

What else could we do to show that we still feel alive? How about playing chess? In 1985, Wolfgang Eisenbeiss, himself an amateur chess player, persuaded Victor Korchnoi, ranked third in the world at the time, to play chess with a deceased grandmaster. Eisenbeiss gave the medium Robbert Rollans, who himself did not play chess, a list of deceased grandmasters and asked him to find one who would play. On June 15, 1985, the deceased Hungarian grandmaster, Géza Maróczy, ranked third in the world around 1900, ostensibly said, through Rollans the medium, that he would play, and Maróczy ostensibly opened the game by playing a move by white. The move was relayed to Eisenbeiss, who gave it to Korchnoi, who then played his move, told Eisenbeiss what it was, who then gave it to Rollans. This process was repeated for 7 years and 8 months until the ostensible Maróczy resigned at the 48th move (Carter, 2012b; Eisenbeiss & Hassler, 2006; Neppe, 2007).

Analysis of the chess match revealed that the ostensible Maróczy played at a master level or, arguably, at a grandmaster level (Targ, 2012). The ostensible

Maróczy played a variation of the French Defence that would rarely have been played after advances in opening theory in the 1950s led to a recognition of the weaknesses created for white. This is significant because by the 1980s chess players had the advantage of training in opening theory that chess players of the early 1900s did not. However, the ostensible Maróczy finished strong, a trait for which the living Maróczy was known. In fact, at one point Korchnoi thought that he was going to lose the match. In other words, the style of play was consistent with the way in which Maróczy would have played the game while alive. Computer programs of the 1980s could not have played the moves made by the ostensible Maróczy, nor is it likely that living grandmasters surreptitiously provided Rollans with the Maróczy moves (Carter, 2012b; Neppe, 2007).

In addition to playing chess, the ostensible Maróczy was asked 81 questions that could be authenticated about the life of Géza Maróczy. Of those, 79 were answered correctly. For the questions that were the most difficult to verify, the ostensible Maróczy correctly answered 31 of 31 (Carter, 2012b; Eisenbeiss & Hassler, 2006; Neppe, 2007). So, in this case, we have correct information provided by a medium along with a set of master-level chess moves in the style of a deceased grandmaster. Was Maróczy the source of that information, or is this super-psi on the part of the medium? Or is there some other explanation?

One way to approach such questions is to look at what mediums themselves say about the process of mediumship. Julie Beischel (2014) asked some mediums who could produce correct information under experimental conditions about their experiences. On reading the accounts they produced, it is clear that some mediums attribute what is happening during a reading to discarnate entities. In many cases, mediums simply receive information as though daydreaming or watching a movie. But some mediums claim to see discarnates in the space around themselves and seem to mentally interact with them the way that they would interact with someone who is living (Beischel, 2014).

Let us think about this for a moment. How do we know that the person standing in front of us, when we are in an ordinary waking state of consciousness, has any independently real existence apart from us? The answer may seem obvious, but it is not. All we have is our assumption that there is really someone out there. In actuality, what we have are mental events that go on privately for us that we interpret as the presence of other people. As long as we are confined to the machinations of our own minds, we can always find a way to account for whatever occurs in our minds as a product of our minds (cf. Lipson, 1987).

The same argument applies to mediums who see discarnates in the space around themselves. Logically, we cannot avoid the possibility that these are experiences confined to the mediums' minds rather than encounters with beings somewhere out there apart from the mediums, precisely because they are experiences that occur in the mediums' minds. We are usually happy to point this out in the case of mediums and say that the mediums are hallucinating, yet we are reluctant to apply the same reasoning to our own experiences of others in the ordinary waking state of consciousness and admit that we could be hallucinating (cf. Hoffman, 1998). Of course, one major difference between a medium's experience of discarnates (for those who claim to perceive discarnates) and the ordinary perceptual experience of other people is that it is relatively easy to find two or more people who agree that a given person is there, whereas it is more difficult to find two or more people who see the same discarnate. Regardless of whether mediums' experiences of discarnates reflect some sort of public reality, mediums can make judgments about the similarities and differences between seeing people out there in the ordinary world and seeing people out there in a not-so-ordinary world, and decide to what extent those experiences are more similar than different. In other words, a medium could reasonably become convinced that she is actually interacting with another person, whether that person is alive or dead.

If our bodies were dead, but we wanted to demonstrate that we still experienced ourselves as being alive, we could initiate activities. The previous examples we have discussed represent cases in which a medium or another living intermediary initiated the process of apparent communication. Such a process initiated by the living could be thought of as more likely to be consistent with a super-psi explanation of apparent communication with discarnates. So, if a medium is not looking for information, but the information finds her, then an argument can be made that the dead are in some ways still functioning as live beings because they are trying to do things. The strategy here is to pay attention to *drop-in communicators*—entities that show up for a medium but were not invited and might be unknown to everyone who is present. In some cases, there has been a clear motivation of unfinished business that the dead seem to have wished to complete, such as having one's thigh bone buried with the rest of one's remains (Braude, 2003), although it is not clear why that should matter. Of course, it is still possible that even such apparent communications are somehow initiated by mediums.

Drop-in communication is not as rare as some of the survival literature makes it seem. In fact, based on the descriptions of mediums' experiences gathered by Julie Beischel, the reverse is the case. For some mediums, discarnates show up at all times of the day and night, and during pretty much any activity in which a medium is engaged. Let us think about this from our imaginary point of view of being dead. Our living relatives and friends cannot find the will, or think that we committed suicide when we did not, or whatever. How do we tell them? The problem is that none of them can see us or hear us. Or if they can, then their therapists have assured them that we are just a hallucination caused by their grief, so that we are not being taken seriously. But wait. We find someone who can see us, or notice us in some way—a medium. So we start pestering her. In fact, some mediums have claimed that they are constantly surrounded by discarnates who want their attention and that they have had to learn how to tune them out so that they can live ordinary lives (Beischel, 2014).

We have seen that mediums can receive information mentally, some can communicate with seemingly physical discarnates, and some can feel sensations in their bodies as a way of receiving information. There are others who claim to allow discarnates to take over their bodies and use them. For instance, one medium described how she can feel discarnates pressing outward against her skin upon allowing them to use her body. She has said that she sees what the discarnates see, she takes on the personalities that the discarnates had, and she reportedly behaves as the discarnates would have behaved, sometimes apparently to the shock of those watching her who knew the discarnates when they were alive (Beischel, 2014). So now we have not only correct information that is relayed to sitters but also distinctive mannerisms that are attributed to the discarnates. The following is an example of imitative behavior from author Imants Barušs's experience of bringing a medium to one of the college courses about consciousness that he was teaching:

> She told one student that his grandfather was telling him to follow his heart and not "this," where "this" referred to a gesture by the medium whereby she held up her hands and flapped her fingers against her thumbs. I turned to the medium with a quizzical expression on my face, unable to understand the intended meaning of the gesture. The student, however, said that that was what his grandfather used to do to indicate that he should not listen to what other people said. (Barušs, 2012, p. 813)

Assuming that such behavior mimics actual behavior, then it does not rule out the super-psi hypothesis, but it does stretch it toward even more impressive levels of manifestation.

When we consider both the after-death communication literature and the research concerning mediumship, there are a number of features of apparent communication with discarnates favoring the survival hypothesis over the super-psi hypothesis. Two of these are the presence of behaviors demonstrating expert skill on the part of a medium that would be difficult for a medium to match and the display of behaviors that are characteristic of the behaviors of the deceased. Such features reveal the "volume, speed, and accuracy" (Carter, 2012b, p. 218, emphasis removed) of correct information that would need to be drawn through anomalous means from disparate sources such as books, documents, the memories of the living, and so on, and then synthesized in such a way as to allow a medium to make master-level moves in chess or impersonate someone that she has never met, if the super-psi hypothesis were to be correct. The integration of such diffuse material into demonstrable skills and behaviors has not been seen in laboratory research concerning psi (Carter, 2012b). Another two features are the similarity between characteristics of apparent encounters with the deceased and encounters with the living, and the potential presence of motivations that can more easily be attributed to discarnates than mediums. These features are consonant with the apparently objective existence of the deceased. Taken together, features such as these have sometimes been judged to tip the scales in favor of survival (Braude, 2003; Carter, 2012b).

UNWANTED INTRUSIONS

We saw in the previous section that some mediums have reported being inundated by discarnate entities and have said that they have needed to learn to shut them out. If we take such claims seriously, then the presence of such entities is unlikely to be limited to mediums and the bereaved. If these entities are around, then they are probably around everyone. And if they are around everyone, then we can ask the question of whether there are ways in which they are influencing us. We can ask the further question of whether those who have previously been human are the only entities that are present around us, or whether there are other types of disembodied entities of varying intelligence, character, and morality that we could encounter.

Acknowledging that there could be entities out there with which we can interact significantly complicates matters, including our understanding of the nature of consciousness. Also, acknowledging the possibility of interaction with nonphysical entities forces us to reexamine our ethical guidelines, as they were never designed for having to take into account the activities of invisible beings. And it raises questions about the existence of unwanted intrusions and what to do about them. It would be much easier to pretend that these sorts of problems cannot exist, and we are good at doing so.

> A well-known pitfall of scholarly endeavour is our propensity to dogmatize those theoretical postulates which are currently in vogue. It is accordingly fashionable at least in professional circles to dismiss the notions of possession and exorcism as outmoded medieval superstition of, at best, historical interest. (Henderson, 1982, p. 131)

Well, while not much has changed in academia, in the mid-1970s, the public imagination in North America became inflamed with the notion of possession. *Exorcism*, a ritual aimed at alleviating a person from whatever negative influences are ostensibly affecting her (Amorth, 1999), became widely practiced. In some cases perhaps, blaming a malevolent invisible entity for one's problems and having it cathartically excised by an exorcist was more appealing than the effort otherwise needed to deal with one's substance abuse, anxiety, depression, or whatever. How much actual possession took place during this exorcism boom is unknown, with little actual evidence for it (Cuneo, 2001). Neither the attitude that possession is impossible nor the attitude that it is rampant offers useful insights, so let us try to find a rational way into this material.

Perhaps the place to start is with *sleep paralysis*. When sleep paralysis occurs, muscle atonia mechanisms that usually keep one's body from moving during *rapid eye movement* (REM) sleep are engaged when a person is awake, usually either just before falling asleep or just upon awakening (Aldrich, 1999; Barušs, 2003a; Carskadon & Rechtschaffen, 2000). Sleep paralysis itself is not considered to be pathological, although it occurs in 20% to 60% of those who have the sleep disorder narcolepsy (American Psychiatric Association, 2013). During sleep paralysis, people have reported a sense of dread; feeling the presences of invisible entities; hearing footsteps or gibbering; seeing apparitions; having breathing difficulties; having pain; or sensorially feeling something pressing against themselves, sometimes in erotic or terrifying ways (Cheyne, 2005; Gooch, 1984/2007; Hufford, 1982, 1994, 2005). Some of these experiences have been interpreted as threats or assaults by external agents or entities (Cheyne, 2005). It is important to note that some people who have had these experiences and have often come to regard them as intrusions by objective beings had not previously heard of the existence of such phenomena (Hufford, 1982). "The great surprise of the persistence of spirit *belief* in the modern world becomes readily understandable once we know that spirit *experiences* persist" (Hufford, 2005, p. 41, emphases in original; Hufford, 2014). Of course, interpretations of experiences that seem that they could be due to external agents or entities are not necessarily correct interpretations, but they are nonetheless common enough to warrant exploration.

We noted earlier that mediums say they need to learn how to control unwanted intrusions. However, even then, in some cases, they say the spirits come through in dreams. How about during sleep paralysis? Is it possible that sleep paralysis is a point of ingress? In fact, some experiencers believe that intruding entities deliberately turn on sleep atonia mechanisms as a way of gaining access to them (Hufford, 1994).

Another point to note is that to successfully turn off these apparent intrusions, we probably need to be psychologically healthy. Conversely, "If there are devils, if there are supernormal powers, it is through the cracked and fragmented self that they enter" (William James, as cited in Taylor, 1984, p. 110). Is there any evidence that hallucinated entities in psychiatric disorders are actually intruding entities?

Wilson Van Dusen was a clinical psychologist who devised a way of talking to his patients' hallucinations to do a phenomenological analysis of them. These were patients who had problems with schizophrenia, alcoholism, brain damage, and dementia, yet Van Dusen reported that their hallucinated worlds were strikingly similar. For instance, these patients "felt they had contact with another world or order of beings" (Van Dusen, 1974, p. 56). None of them liked the word *hallucination*. The visions and voices they reported did not have the same quality as "thoughts or fantasies" (Van Dusen, 1974, p. 57). Most of the patients realized that no one else could see or hear what they could perceive, so they did not talk about their hallucinations to others.

Van Dusen (1974) found what he called *lower* and *higher* orders of hallucinations: "Lower-order voices are as though one is dealing with drunken bums at a bar who like to tease and torment just for the fun of it" (p. 57). The lower order hallucinations lie, seek to take over specific body parts, have low intelligence, are disdainful of religion, and have a "persistent will to destroy" (Van Dusen, 1974, p. 58). The higher order hallucinations comprise only about a fifth of all hallucinations but are often symbolic and "richer and more complex than the patient's own mode of thought" (Van Dusen, 1974, p. 60). Whereas the lower order hallucinations are disdainful and malevolent, the higher order hallucinations are supportive and respectful of the patient's freedom. Van Dusen was struck by the evident contrast between the good and evil hallucinations as well as the consonance with Emanuel Swedenborg's descriptions of the behavior of spirits. So, are these hallucinations objectified lower and higher aspects of one's nonconscious? Or are the hallucinations of psychiatric patients, at least in some cases, entity intrusions (Guirdham, 1982; Wickland, 1924)?

The patients interviewed by Van Dusen (1974) were pestered by apparent spirits who occasionally managed to take over a body part such as an eye, ear, or tongue, but Van Dusen said that he thought that sometimes the spirits manage to take over the whole body. If that were to occur, then that would be possession. In fact, there is also a unique *possession syndrome* with its own specific symptoms (Ferracuti & Sacco, 1996; Grosso, 2014; Isaacs, 1987; McNamara, 2011; Trethowan, 1976). But perhaps the most suggestive condition in which possession appears to occur is *dissociative identity disorder* (DID), in which a person takes on different personas, called *alters*, at different times (American Psychiatric Association, 2013). In one study, 21% of 236 people with DID had a "personality identified as a dead relative" and 29% had a personality that was "identified as a demon" (Ross, Norton, & Wozney, 1989, p. 415). Are these actual dead relatives and demons (whatever those might be) using the person's body (Barušs, 2003a)?

Ralph Allison (1980), a psychiatrist who has treated people with DID, said that he has "come to believe in the possibility of spirit possession"

(p. 183) because he encountered alters that he said serve no purpose in a person's psyche and that often call themselves "spirits" (p. 184). He gave the example of a patient named Elise. At one point an apparent male alter named Dennis emerged. Upon questioning, Dennis said that his only reason for being with Elise was because he was sexually aroused by Shannon, who appeared to be one of Elise's alters, created when Elise lost a baby. This did not make sense to Allison. How could one alter be in love with another alter? So Allison "asked Dennis how he expected to have sex with Shannon" (p. 185). The answer, according to Dennis, was that he used the body of whichever lover was having sex with Shannon. When Allison talked to Shannon, Shannon concurred with what Dennis had said, and added that Dennis always pinched her after having had intercourse with her with whichever lover he had possessed. When Allison talked to Elise's inner self helpers (alters in a person's psyche that cooperate with a therapist), they told him that Dennis was a spirit and could not be fused into Elise's personality. From Dennis, Allison learned that he, Dennis, had been a stockbroker who had been shot to death on being robbed sometime in the 1940s. Eventually Allison was able to get rid of Dennis along with two other apparent spirits who had been using Elise's body, and Shannon, who turned out to be the spirit of the lost baby. Allison said that "nothing in the psychological literature could account for what I had seen" (p. 192).

So, where does this leave us? Perhaps the first thing to note is that we have looked at different types of apparent interactions with invisible beings, and there is some degree of consistency among them. Such consistency can be entirely the result of that which is visible, or it could be due to regularities in that which is invisible. An analogy would be that of the germ theory of disease. What we now know to be infectious diseases were previously thought to be the result of bad air or other causes that are readily available to our senses, but they were instead discovered to be the result of pathogens that are invisible to unaided vision. Analogously, the pattern of characteristics associated with apparent presences could be the result of misperceptions, memory lapses, and fraud, or they could be the result of invisible beings. Of course, the analogy could fail. But as a logical point, we only need a single legitimate case of an apparent invisible being that cannot be explained solely as a product of misperceptions, and so on, to assert that sometimes there is at least something out there that shows up as a discarnate being. In other words, for there not to be any discarnate entities outside of people's minds, every single instance in which invisible entities could be posited needs to be explained in terms of known psychological processes. And these cannot just be wildly speculative explanations but must have some evidence for them. Given what we have seen just in this chapter alone, that is a tall order.

Second, contrary to the claims of some grief therapists that interactions with the deceased are always benign, that is not true of interactions with apparent discarnate entities in general. In fact, whatever psychological mechanisms allow for pleasant apparent interactions could equally allow for dysphoric apparent interactions were it not for whatever psychological mechanisms protect a person from apparent unwanted intrusions. We need research specifically aimed at understanding both of those types of mechanisms before people subject themselves en masse to an onslaught of apparent discarnate entities. In fact, however those events are explained, there are already lots of cases in which people have ended up in serious trouble by stumbling into various practices for which they were not prepared (Allison, 1980; Baruss, 1996).

Third, let us return to the two questions with which we opened this chapter. What are the implications of these types of experiences for the way in which we care for people at the end of life? Well, people who are at the end of life also have visions of the deceased, sometimes called *deathbed visions* (Fenwick & Fenwick, 2013; Osis & Haraldsson, 1997). Sometimes the dying interact with the person in the vision as though that person were present in the space around the dying person. This can include carrying on a conversation with the envisioned beings as well as with those physically present in a room without confusion as to who is who (Fenwick & Fenwick, 2013).

After presenting some information about end-of-life experiences to the public, Peter Fenwick was overwhelmed with correspondence from people who gave examples of such experiences that had occurred for them in their own lives. Fenwick said that there were three themes that were repeated in this material: the comfort that the dying and other witnesses had felt as a result of these experiences; "the conviction that what had happened was not a dream, or wishful thinking, or a figment of the imagination, or a drug-induced hallucination" (Fenwick & Fenwick, 2013, p. 12); and a sense of relief that the correspondents felt in being able to freely talk about such experiences (Fenwick & Fenwick, 2013). Thus, it appears that we ought to at least reassure people that such experiences are normal and common, and perhaps even veridical. The end of life could well not be the end of life but a transition into other dimensions of being. If that were to be the case, then we would clearly need more research to understand that process and learn how to prepare people for it and to facilitate it within the context of their death (cf. Pearson, 2014; Assante, 2012).

Fenwick's findings, taken together with the material discussed in this chapter, also address the second question we asked at the beginning of this chapter: What are the implications of these types of experiences for our understanding of consciousness? Not only would consciousness appear to be potentially independent of the brain, as we explore in the next chapter, but if the deceased continue to exist in the ways in which we have described such survival in this chapter, then it would appear that our individual experiences and memories apparently do not cease with bodily death. Further, the possibility opens up that physicality may not ever be necessary for certain types of consciousness.

5

SEPARATION OF MIND FROM BRAIN

It is the mind (not the brain) that watches and at the same time directs.
—Wilder Penfield (1975, p. 49)

In this book, we are considering the hypothesis that the mind is not an epiphenomenon of the brain, but instead is independently real even as it exists in some sort of relationship to the brain. There is considerable evidence that one's mind is often in relationship with one's brain, so what evidence do we have that the mind can be separated from the brain? Well, we have already seen phenomena that could be used to support the hypothesis that the mind can function independently of the brain, such as the evidence for an extended mind and for the survival of consciousness after death.

In this chapter, we tackle this question more directly. In doing so, we consider three gradations of the extent to which we can account for phenomena in terms of brain activity. First, we can look for clues to the existence of an expanded mind when the brain is substantially compromised, as it is during dementia, for instance. Second, we can consider cases in which the brain is apparently not working at all, such as during some near-death experiences

http://dx.doi.org/10.1037/15957-006
Transcendent Mind: Rethinking the Science of Consciousness, by I. Baruš and J. Mossbridge

(NDEs). And, third, we can look further at situations in which there is no brain at all, which is the case with apparent communication by discarnates through mediums. The point of our explorations in this chapter is to see what we can learn about the mind when it is not in its usual relationship with the brain.

MIND IN A COMPROMISED BRAIN

Sometimes it appears that the mind manifests in spite of a brain that should not be able to support the activity of the mind. Here we look at several examples of apparent separation of mind from brain, including terminal lucidity, illness-induced lucidity, as well as accounts of anomalous perception during NDEs.

Terminal lucidity refers to "the unexpected return of mental clarity and memory shortly before death" (Nahm & Greyson, 2009, p. 942). In neuroscience, we generally assume that mental clarity requires a functioning brain. Thus, the reason that mental clarity is unexpected in some of these cases is the presence of obvious functional or structural brain pathology, as determined by diagnostic procedures or subsequent autopsies, that seems sufficient to prohibit mental clarity. Pathologies have included brain abscesses, brain tumors, strokes, various dementias, meningitis, schizophrenia, and possible affective disorders. For instance, there have been cases of patients with Alzheimer's disease who have been mute and unreactive to family members for years, yet have suddenly had lucid conversations with them within a day, week, or month of their deaths. One of those cases involved an 81-year-old woman with dementia who had neither recognized nor spoken to any of her family members for a year. At one point, she suddenly sat up, told her son that she was going to recite a verse for him, which she then did, before lying back down and becoming unresponsive again until she died about a month later (Bering, 2014; Fenwick & Fenwick, 2013; Nahm, 2009; Nahm & Greyson, 2009; Nahm, Greyson, Kelly, & Haraldsson, 2012; Normann, Asplund, Karlsson, Sandman, & Norberg, 2006).

Bruce Greyson (2013) described a case of illness-induced lucidity that appears to illustrate a separation of mind from brain. A nurse had tried to commit suicide by taking an overdose of medication and lying down to die. Rather than dying, however, he just became ill, so he got up to try to walk to the telephone to call for help. However, not only was he having problems with walking, but the drug overdose apparently also caused him to hallucinate the presence of people in his room who were impeding his movement. At that point, he experienced leaving his physical body and hovering about 10 feet above and behind it. Now his mind was thinking clearly. He could "see" his confused body staggering around but could no longer "see" the imaginary people in his room that his brain had been hallucinating (Greyson, 2013, p. 72). One interpretation of his experience is that the drugs made his brain hallucinate seeing his body from above, and another possibility is that the drugs were affecting only his brain, with his mind able to separate from the brain and perceive things clearly.

In Chapter 3, we considered mental clarity in the context of NDEs, namely, the exceptional mental clarity that has been reported to have occurred during some life reviews. More generally, enhanced mentation is characteristic of NDEs. In one collection of accounts of NDEs, 45% of near-death experiencers claimed that their thinking was "clearer than usual," and 29% described it as being "more logical than usual" (E. W. Kelly, Greyson, & Kelly, 2010, p. 386, footnote). Furthermore, studies in which the quality of ostensible memories of life events during NDEs were compared with waking life memories of emotionally powerful experiences have revealed that memories of events during an NDE are recalled with at least as much detail, if not more, than real-life emotional memories. Further, in these same studies, it has been shown that memories during NDEs are reported with significantly more detail and emotionality than memories of imagined emotional events (Palmieri et al., 2014; Thonnard et al., 2013). This is in spite of the fact that the brains of those reporting NDEs were often compromised at the ostensible time of their NDE.

Another example of apparent mind–brain separation can be found by examining visual elements of the NDEs of the blind. In a study by Kenneth Ring and Sharon Cooper (1997) of the NDEs of 21 blind participants, 15 claimed to have had some sort of sight during their experience. Of the remaining six participants who were unsure or did not report visual experiences during their NDEs, five had been blind from birth and may have experienced some sort of sight during their experience without having been able to identify it as such. For instance, one of the participants had said that he did not know what was meant by "seeing" and so did not know how to explain the perceptions that he had been having. Some of those who had been congenitally blind nonetheless described clear and detailed visual images even though they had been aware at the time that they could not see. In the case of one participant, who had been blind from birth, this included ostensibly seeing her body and recognizing it as hers from the distinctive wedding ring on her finger. Ring and Cooper could only partially confirm that some of the visual impressions were veridical, so these could have been fictitious images.

People who lose their sight before the age of 5 do not have visual images at any time and, in particular, do not usually have "visual imagery in their dreams" (Kerr, 2000, p. 488). Some of the congenitally blind participants in the study maintained that their NDEs were different from their dreams because of the occurrence of visual elements during their NDEs. This is a crucial point. Those who are blind from birth have not had an opportunity to develop visual processing in the brain (cf. Hirsch & Spinelli, 1971) and would not be expected to have any impressions that could be regarded as being visual, at least not in the way that sighted people experience visual impressions (Baruš, 2003a). So what is the mechanism for this "seeing?"

Well, when Ring and Cooper (1997) queried their participants more closely, the "sight" started to lose its strictly visual nature and become more synesthetic, so that these experiences seemed instead to be those of knowing directly through some sort of synesthetic sense, which nonetheless could have had pictorial aspects to it. As one participant said:

> I think what it was that was happening here was a bunch of synesthesia, where all these perceptions were being blended into some image in my mind, you know, the visual, the tactile, all the input that I had. I can't literally say I really saw anything, but yet I was aware of what was going on, and perceiving all that in my mind. (Ring & Cooper, 1997, p. 134)

Ring and Cooper introduced the term *transcendental awareness* to denote the "seeing" that occurs during NDEs for those who are sighted as well as those who are blind. In other words, the visual images that occur during NDEs are not "visual" in the sense of seeing with the eyes but appear to entail a form of synesthetic perception that gives a person apparent access to knowledge about what is going on around her. "In this type of awareness, it is not of course that the eyes see anything; it is rather that the mind itself sees, but more in the sense of 'understanding' or 'taking in' than of visual perception as such" (Ring & Cooper, 1997, p. 140). In other words, we have the contention that the mind has the ability to perceive what is going on somewhere without the need for physical senses through which to acquire that information. Thus, this line of investigation could be developed further, allowing us perhaps to tease apart the qualities of mind from those of brain.

Perhaps in these cases of terminal lucidity, illness-induced lucidity, and near-death transcendental awareness, what we are seeing is evidence for a clear mind even though there is a poorly functioning brain. The ordinary pathways for the expression of mind through the brain, whatever they may be, seem to have been not working prior to at least some of these incidents. Perhaps there is a nonordinary pathway, outside of the usual connection between the mind and the brain, by which the mind can influence the body, allowing terminally ill patients who have not spoken in weeks to become lucid or allowing individuals who have been blind from birth to have visual-like experiences. We say more about such possible direct mental influence later in this chapter and in Chapter 6, but for now, let us withhold judgment until we have delved deeper into some additional reports that speak to a potential separation of the mind from the brain.

EXPLAINING NEAR-DEATH EXPERIENCES

Because the mechanisms underlying NDEs could shed light on potential separation of mind from brain, let us briefly consider some common psychological and physiological explanations for NDEs. Psychological explanations usually include the idea that NDEs are efforts at depersonalization or wishful thinking as defenses against the fear of death (Trent-von Haesler & Beauregard, 2013). However, it is important to note that not all NDEs are beatific experiences. Some NDEs are markedly distressing and can include explicit hellish imagery that terrifies the experiencer (Greyson & Bush, 1992). If these latter experiences are defenses against the fear of death, they are poor defenses. Of course, we could also speculate that these are exceptions in which the psychological defenses break down, producing dysphoric experiences.

Physiological explanations include the contentions that NDEs are hallucinations caused by lack of oxygen to the head, increased carbon dioxide in the blood, drugs given around the time of death, and synchronous seizure-like neural firing (Blackmore 1991, 1996; Trent-von Haesler & Beauregard, 2013). Loss of oxygen to the head could cause an experience of seeing a tunnel, one of the perceptions sometimes reported during NDEs, as the retina is selectively deprived of oxygen from the periphery toward the center, which could be interpreted by the visual cortex as a tunnel. Loss of oxygen to the brain could also induce endorphin release, creating dreamlike experiences and peaceful feelings (van Lommel, 2013; Whinnery & Whinnery, 1990). A buildup of carbon dioxide in the blood can cause the occurrence of vivid imaginary experiences that can feel real to the person having them. NDEs could be vivid imaginary experiences like these, which an experiencer assumes to be real.

In support of these ideas, the intensity of NDEs in at least one study was positively correlated with the amount of carbon dioxide in the blood (Klemenc-Ketis, Kersnik, & Grmec, 2010). We note that in another study, levels of oxygen were found to be higher, not lower, in the NDE group, suggesting that an explanation for NDEs based on low oxygen levels alone does not work (Parnia, Waller, Yeates, & Fenwick, 2001). An increase in the synchronous firing of neurons during late-stage cardiac arrests has been put forward as a possible explanation for the dreamlike phenomena that are remembered in reports of NDEs, although the study in which this synchrony was observed was performed with rats, and it is not known whether the rats were experiencing NDEs during the neural synchrony or not (Borjigin et al., 2013).

Temporal lobe seizures have been proposed as a physiological mechanism for the experience of life reviews during NDEs (Blackmore, 1993). However, Pam Reynolds, whose NDE occurred during a surgical procedure in which her brain was monitored using an electroencephalograph, did not have any seizures, yet described having had review-like experiences that were "like watching a movie on fast-forward on your VCR" (Sabom, 1998, p. 45). In a brief commentary article, Dean Mobbs and Caroline Watt (2011) proposed that "the life review and REM components of the near-death experience could be attributed to the action of the locus coeruleus-noradrenaline system" (p. 449). Elsewhere they cited evidence that the midbrain noradrenergic system can produce hallucinations, including the experience of a tunnel (Manford & Andermann, 1998). They added, "If one challenge of science is to demystify the world, then research should begin to test these and other hypotheses" so that the discussion can be moved "into the lawful realm of empirical neurobiology" (Mobbs & Watt, 2011, p. 449). For such hallucinations to fully account for NDEs, they would need to explain the rapidity and clarity of a life review and the sense of reality with which it can be accompanied. They would also need to be empirically verified. There have been other neurophysiological mechanisms proposed as explanations of NDEs, including, presumably, life reviews (e.g., Bonta, 2004; Jansen, 1997), but none of them have been empirically verified (Greyson, 2014). At this point, physiological explanations may seem to have potential to explain some of the features of NDEs, but we are not through examining them yet.

There are some additional pieces of evidence that are not easily dismissed by physiological explanations. For instance, one of the defining characteristics of some NDEs is a profound change in outlook. This shift in outlook also needs to be taken into account. A personal description of such a shift is summarized by experiencer Andy Petro (2011), who at the age of 18 developed cramps while he was swimming in a lake and soon became unable to swim. He sank to the bottom of the lake, when everything in his visual field went black. During this time, he felt he became a giant sphere, in which he watched film-like versions of his life surrounding him. As he watched those movies, he could feel the feelings of every person with whom he had interacted. Then he was absorbed by a light that told him that he should not be afraid, and that he was loved.

> If there was some way to do a psychological profile of me before and after my experience, there would be two different people, two very different personalities. I lost my fear as a result of my experience. I lost my sense of being worthless. I came back with a great sense of self-worth, self-love, and a tremendous amount of faith. Now I love people, I love being alive, and I'm having fun being alive, with all its pluses and minuses. (Petro, as cited in Berman, 1996, p. 125)

Researchers have examined post-NDE transformations using quantifiable techniques assessing life changes at varying times after the initial NDE.

These studies all focused on participants who had experienced a hospital-confirmed cardiac arrest.

The reason that cases of verified cardiac arrests are useful in the study of NDEs is that, within seconds of cardiac arrest, blood flow to the brain stops, and within 20 seconds of the arrest, the brain's cortical activity as measured by an electroencephalograph goes silent (van Lommel, 2013). As a result of not being resuscitated within the first 20 seconds after cardiac arrest, such patients are considered essentially brain dead, and most of them die. Of the patients who survive after resuscitation, around 9% to 23% report NDEs (Klemenc-Ketis, 2013; Parnia et al., 2014; Schwaninger, Eisenberg, Schechtman, & Weiss, 2002; van Lommel, van Wees, Meyers, & Elfferich, 2001).

Two follow-up reports of cardiac arrest patients showed that those who had experienced NDEs also reported greater positive improvements 6 months afterward than those who had not experienced NDEs. Furthermore, those who had not experienced NDEs did not report as many life changes during this time period. Because both of these reports used the same scale to assess life changes, and because all participants had experienced cardiac arrests, we can compare significant improvements seen in both studies for those who had reported NDEs to those who had not reported NDEs. Improvements tied to having an NDE included improved appreciation of nature, tolerance for others, concern with social justice issues, and a sense that there is some inner meaning to life (Klemenc-Ketis, 2013; Schwaninger et al., 2002).

Similar to those two studies, a large study of 344 individuals who were resuscitated from cardiac arrest and screened within a few days afterward, 62 of whom (18%) reported NDEs, revealed significant differences 2 years after the cardiac arrest between the self-reports of life changes for those who had reported NDEs and those who had not reported NDEs. These differences consisted entirely of changes that, as a whole, would likely be considered psychologically adaptive. They include showing one's feelings, gaining acceptance of others, becoming more loving and empathic, understanding others, being involved with one's family, gaining a sense of understanding the purpose of life, finding a sense of the inner meaning of life, developing an interest in spirituality, feeling less fear of death, believing more in life after death, developing a greater interest in the meaning of life, understanding oneself, and deepening one's appreciation of ordinary things. These improvements deepened, according to the participants' self-reports, when the same participants were assessed 8 years after their cardiac arrests. However, by this point most of the individuals who could be reached in the group that had not reported NDEs had "caught up" to those who had reported NDEs and reported similar life changes (van Lommel et al., 2001).

The cardiac arrest patients in all three studies were treated similarly in terms of medical interventions. Furthermore, two of the three studies used "clinical death," defined as a "flat line" on an electrocardiogram, as a criterion for admission into the study (Klemenc-Ketis, 2013; van Lommel et al., 2001). Thus, in that sense, all patients underwent similar experiences. Yet at 6 months and 2 years, the patients who had reported NDEs had significantly more positive life changes than those who had not reported NDEs. This difference is difficult to explain in terms of physiology because there were no clear differences between the groups except for the presence or absence of an NDE report. Of course, it is possible that physiological measures that had not been taken could account for the difference in outcome, and indeed, in the largest study, relevant physiological measures such as blood gas levels had not been reported (van Lommel et al., 2001).

On reflection, there is something backward about physiological explanations for NDEs. The brain's functioning is being compromised, for instance, by loss of oxygen and a buildup of carbon dioxide. If that keeps up for a few minutes, the brain stops functioning altogether. If the mind's functioning is a by-product of the brain's activity, then as the brain deteriorates, the mind should deteriorate as well and cease to function when the brain ceases to function. Under the assumption that the brain is required for mental functioning, we should be hearing reports of delirium—incoherent jumbled experiences—followed by an inability to remember anything that happened afterward (Fenwick & Fenwick, 1995).

Of course, the argument could be made that memories of NDEs are not memories of experiences that occurred just before coming close to death but of experiences that occurred at some point following resuscitation when the brain was functioning more or less properly again. But it is not clear why an NDE would occur with any greater frequency in the context of coming closer to death than it would at any other time when the brain is coming out of a state of diminished functioning. Also, as we shall see in a bit, some of the events described by experiencers can be timed to physical events taking place when a person's brain activity was compromised, seeming to place the occurrence of at least some NDEs specifically at the time that the experiencer was close to death.

However, not only do we have accounts of experiences ostensibly from the time that the brain was compromised, but these experiences have been described as some of the most vivid ones that these people have ever undergone. Indeed, as we have already seen, the greater the levels of carbon dioxide, the more the brain is compromised, and the more vivid the NDEs. In Chapter 3, we discussed how extensive, sensorially saturated experiences have occurred during NDEs. In other words, it looks as though the less the brain is able to function properly, the more vivid the experiences that are occurring, assuming that the experiences are occurring at the same time as the brain is shutting down. On the basis of that assumption, the physiological data showing impairment in brain function during NDEs actually undermine physiological explanations for NDEs. We could propose a theory that in fact the brain functions better when all detectable signals from it are shut down, or when the brain has been deprived of oxygen for a long period of time, but such a theory would be contrary to the empirical observation that for a brain to function well, it should have all the hallmarks of a functioning brain, including the production of detectable signals and access to oxygen. An alternative explanation that better fits the facts would be that the mind, loosened from the brain, comes into its own, functioning without the constraints imposed by the brain (Kastrup, 2014; see also Chapter 8, this volume).

In contrast to the lack of success of physiological explanations for NDEs, some psychological explanations could provide insight into the apparent long-term impact of NDEs on an experiencer's outlook. It seems reasonable to suppose that someone who experiences having a positive interaction with "spiritual beings," who experiences a sense of being unconditionally loved, or who sees her life reenacted through a life review might experience greater life changes after these experiences than someone who has not had them.

One needs to be careful about interpreting data about psychological "changes" after NDEs because there have been no measures taken of a person's psychological profile prior to the NDEs to make proper comparisons. It is possible that those who are already more interested in finding meaning in life, and so on, are also those most likely to report NDEs after cardiac arrest. Induced cardiac arrest, a surgical procedure in which patients' heart rhythms are stopped for a period of time during surgery, would be a good "laboratory study" of the impact that NDEs can have, because patients' hearts are not functioning at a scheduled time for a specific duration. Psychological measures could be given to patients receiving such treatment prior to surgery and again afterward, and changes in those scores could be compared for those who reported NDEs and those who did not. That is a straightforward study to carry out. One group of researchers attempted something similar, although no psychological measures were gathered before surgery and no NDEs were reported (Greyson, Holden, & Mounsey, 2006).

The point is that the NDEs that people are having, along with their sequelae, cannot easily be encompassed within physiological explanations. There is a second difficulty with physiological explanations to which we have already alluded that gets us back to the theme of looking at the possible separation of the mind from the brain: Sometimes people report strikingly accurate descriptions of what occurred during their NDEs. Let us examine some of these reports.

NDEs sometimes start with a person having an experience of rising from her body and seeing the surroundings in which her body is found, with one study reporting that "48% of near-death experiencers reported seeing their physical bodies from a different visual perspective" (Greyson, 2010, p. 41), and another study finding the same phenomenon in 24% of NDEs (van Lommel et al., 2001). Is there any evidence that a person perceives accurately what is going on around her when she is seeing the world from outside herself? The answer is yes, with some qualifications. There are several ways to try to answer the question rigorously, one of which is to look at retrospective accounts by experiencers and compare them with the available documentation about what was happening around them at the time. The idea here is to look for low-probability events that an experiencer reports as having occurred during the out-of-body portion of her experience, then examine hospital records and interview staff to determine whether those events indeed occurred at the time that that patient's brain was not functioning properly. We give two such examples.

Cardiac surgeon Lloyd William Rudy, Jr., together with his assistant cardiac surgeon, Roberto Amado-Cattaneo, had completed heart surgery but could not get the patient off the heart-lung bypass machine. After several unsuccessful tries, they decided to give up. They pronounced the patient dead, and his wife was told that he had died. While a surgical assistant closed off the incisions in such a way as to facilitate the legally mandated autopsy, the two cardiac surgeons left the operating theatre. The support staff came in to clean up. However, no one had bothered to turn off the monitoring equipment, so it continued to run, creating a pile of paper on the floor and creating images on a video recorder from a transesophageal echo-probe of the activity of the heart. The cardiac surgeons came back to the operating theatre and stood in the doorway with their arms folded, talking about whether they could have done anything else for the patient. After about 20 to 25 minutes without a heartbeat, and after the surgical assistant had finished closing the body, the cardiac surgeons looked up and saw electrical activity that turned into a heartbeat. The surgeons called their support staff back into the operating theatre and, without reactivating the bypass machine, were able to resuscitate the patient, although he did not regain consciousness until several days later in an intensive care unit (Rivas & Smit, 2013).

What "astounded" (Rivas & Smit, 2013, p. 182; emphasis in original) Rudy was that the patient accurately described the appearance of the room during the time that his heart was stopped. For instance, according to Rudy, the patient had told him, "I saw you and Dr. Cattaneo standing in the doorway with your arms folded, talking" (as cited in Rivas & Smit, 2013, p. 183).

Also, the patient had apparently correctly seen notes stuck to a monitor; these were telephone messages that had accumulated as the operation had progressed, so that he could not have seen them before having been anaesthetized. The assistant cardiac surgeon confirmed the accuracy of the patient's perceptions, including the notes: "The messages to Dr. Rudy I believe were taped to a monitor that sits close to the end of the operating table, up in the air, close enough for anybody to see what it is there, like the patient for example if he was looking at it" (as cited in Rivas & Smit, 2013, p. 185). In this case, the patient was clearly not looking at the messages with his physical eyes, given that he had been anaesthetized and had then been without a heartbeat, blood pressure, or respiration for about 20 minutes or so before being resuscitated to an unconscious state (Rivas & Smit, 2013).

The second example is from a controlled, prospective study of NDEs in 101 cardiac arrest patients. Nine individuals reported NDEs in that study, but seven of the nine did not report auditory–visual experiences that could provide details of the resuscitation. However, two of the patients did have such experiences, although one of these could not participate in the follow-up interview to verify his statements. However, a follow-up interview with the one remaining patient who could comment on his experience during resuscitation suggested that his experience took place about 3 minutes after the onset of cardiac arrest.

> He accurately described people, sounds, and activities from his resuscitation. . . . His medical records corroborated his accounts and specifically supported his descriptions and the use of an automated external defibrillator (AED). Based on current AED algorithms, this likely corresponded with up to 3 min of conscious awareness during cardiac arrest and CPR. (Parnia et al. 2014, p. 1802)

The following is the survivor's account:

> (Before the cardiac arrest) And I was still talking to [the nurse] and then all of a sudden, I wasn't. I must have [blanked out] . . . but then I can remember vividly an automated voice saying, "shock the patient, shock the patient," and with that, up in [the] corner of the room there was a [woman] beckoning me . . . I can remember thinking to myself, "I can't get up there" . . . I felt that she knew me. I felt that I could trust her, and I felt she was there for a reason and I didn't know what that was. . . . and the next second, I was up there, looking down at me, the nurse, and another man who had a bald head. . . . I couldn't see the face but I could see the back of his body. He was quite a chunky fella. . . . He had blue scrubs on, and he had a blue hat, but I could tell he didn't have any hair, because of where the hat was. The next thing I remember is waking up on [the] bed. And [the nurse] said to me, "Oh you nodded off . . . you are back with us now." Whether she said those words, whether

that automated voice really happened, I don't know. . . . I can remember feeling quite euphoric. . . . I know who [the man with the blue hat was]. . . . I [didn't] know his full name, but . . . he was the man that . . . [I saw] the next day . . . I saw this man [come to visit me] and I knew who I had seen the day before.

Post-script—Medical record review confirmed the use of the AED, the medical team present during the cardiac arrest, and the role the identified "man" played in responding to the cardiac arrest. (Parnia et al. 2014, p. 1803)

There are a lot of facts that need to be checked in these types of accounts to ensure that the information that a patient subsequently reports was not obtained through ordinary means (Greyson, 2010), and we will not go through that list here. In our judgment, from what is known about these cases, it is reasonable to draw the conclusion that genuine "apparently non-physical veridical perception" did occur (Rivas & Smit, 2013, p. 180). However, this does not mean that the reports necessarily support a separation between mind and brain. There are several alternative nonordinary explanations to consider. Given what we know about time-displaced remote viewing, the patients could have "seen" the events in the operating theatre either precognitively or postcognitively when their brains were fully functioning. That possibility is difficult to rule out (Baruss, 2003a). Just as we argued for the survival hypothesis over the super-psi hypothesis on the basis that such extraordinary super-psi abilities had not been found outside the context of mediumship, it is reasonable to argue in cases such as these that the hypothesis that perception occurred without brain activity is more likely than time-displaced remote viewing if the experiencer has no history of precognition or postcognition in other contexts.

Experiencers frequently report perceiving efforts on the part of medical personnel to resuscitate their bodies. These reports could just be imaginative reconstructions by experiencers of what they think happens when someone is resuscitated. But it is possible to check the accounts of patients who have been resuscitated who report having seen the procedures during an NDE against accounts from those who have been resuscitated who do not report having seen their resuscitations. Michael Sabom (1982) compared the accounts of 32 patients who recalled having perceived at least some parts of their resuscitation procedures against the attempts at describing resuscitation made by 25 control patients, who were cardiac-arrest patients who claimed to have not seen the resuscitation techniques that were used with them. Twenty-three of the 25 control patients provided descriptions of resuscitation, and 20 of the 23 "made a major error in their descriptive accounts" (Sabom, 1982, p. 85). On the contrary, those who had had an NDE did not make any major errors when describing the resuscitations that they had experienced.

However, the descriptions by those who had had NDEs were usually partial, which the experiencers explained as the result of being preoccupied with their amazement at the state in which they had found themselves and not having paid particular attention to the details of the resuscitation attempts (Sabom, 1982). Thus, these results should be interpreted with caution. Penny Sartori (2008) also found that those who recounted having seen the resuscitation procedures during their NDEs reported procedures correctly, whereas cardiac-arrest survivors without NDEs did not. In fact, 26 of 32 participants in her control group "had no idea of what was done to resuscitate them and could not even hazard a guess" (Sartori, 2008, p. 213).

Motivated by observations such as these, in several other studies, cardiac units have allowed the placement of hidden targets that resuscitated patients were asked to identify. In two studies, boards and shelves with images facing the ceiling were suspended in hospital rooms (Parnia et al., 2001, 2014). In another study, square cards with symbols and numbers on them were placed in the four corners of several rooms (J. Holden & Joesten, 1990). In yet another study, cardiac arrest was induced as part of a routine surgical procedure, and a computer displayed unusual visual images that could only be viewed from above the patient's body (Greyson, Holden, & Mounsey, 2006). Finally, in another study, cards with scenes on them were placed above cardiac monitors, out of view of the patients (Sartori, 2008). In the first four of these studies, out-of-body experiences did not occur during NDEs (Parnia et al., 2001), no patients with auditory–visual experiences during their NDEs had them when their bodies were in rooms with hidden targets (J. Holden & Joesten, 1990; Parnia et al., 2001, 2014), and patients experiencing induced cardiac arrest did not have NDEs (Greyson, Holden, & Mounsey, 2006). In the final study by Penny Sartori, eight participants reported an out-of-body experience in their NDEs, but none saw the targets (Sartori, 2008). Thus to date, hidden targets have not been verified, although there have only been eight reported opportunities to verify them!

This "hidden target" line of research is progressing today, so it is possible that a target will be identified tomorrow. However, it is also possible that these sorts of targets are uninteresting compared with the emotional content of NDEs, so that even when a patient experiences out-of-body perspectives during an NDE, she would not necessarily notice seemingly random symbols or images (van Lommel, 2013). One possible solution to this problem is to create targets that have been verified as being noticeable by those who are in a heightened ecstatic state without preparation or warning as to the existence of the target. One might assume that such targets would be more noticeable to individuals having out-of-body experiences in their NDEs, if such experiences indeed consist of some sort of travel of consciousness outside the body.

On the weight of the existing evidence, we think that at least some of the perceptions that occur during NDEs are veridical and that, quite likely, some of them occur during times that, according to the current knowledge of neuroscience, there is insufficient brain activity to support such conscious perception through the usual senses—specifically, a lack of cortical activity (Agrillo, 2011; van Lommel, 2006).

MIND WITHOUT A BRAIN

How does the mind think when it is not attached to a brain? What are the characteristics of a mind without a brain? These are questions that we need to address if we are to seriously consider the possible existence of an independent mind. It is easy to pose such questions, but what empirical data are we going to use to answer them?

One way forward is to go back to mediumship research. The idea is this: If mediums can obtain information from the deceased that matches known facts about the physical world, then perhaps they can also obtain correct information from the deceased about an apparently nonphysical world in which they reside. In a sense, mediums can be seen as imperfect observation tools, like microscopes, allowing us to see into a domain of reality that we cannot see with our ordinary vision (Kardec, 1874). The problem, of course, is that we cannot directly validate what they tell us, so that we cannot check to see how clearly these "lenses" are bringing into focus another realm of being (Baruss, 1996, 2007b).

There is another probe that we could use for obtaining information from the world of minds without brains, and that is *instrumental transcommunication* (ITC), the ostensible communication by discarnate entities through the use of electronic equipment (Baruss, 2003a). Michael Shermer's serendipitously resuscitated radio at his wedding, which we discussed in Chapter 4, would be a simple form of ITC. ITC also includes apparent voices on tape, unexpected text on computer screens, meaningful anomalous messages on smartphones, and so on. There is a large body of ITC research, but almost all of it has been done outside of the academic environment, and almost none of it has been published in academic journals or books, so it is difficult to aggregate and evaluate the knowledge that has been gained from that research (Alsop, 1989; Baruss, 2001, 2003a, 2007a, 2013a; Connelly, 2001; Foy, 2008; Fuller, 1985; Roach, 2005).

We could also go backward in time, in the sense of trying to find out what happened to people before they were born. If our minds survive death, then it makes sense that our minds also existed before we were born, and that our present lives are simply interludes in some sort of mental existence elsewhere. If so, then what were our minds thinking before we came here? What were our thoughts like? One way to answer that question is to study what children say about what happened to them before they were born (Bowman, 2001; Hinze, 1997; Masayuki & Akira, 2014; Stevenson, 1997a, 1997b). Also, just as there are cases of spontaneous after-death communication, as we summarized in Chapter 4, so it appears there can be spontaneous *prebirth communication* whereby children who are not yet conceived or born apparently show up in dreams or visions or in feelings of presences, sometimes with information about the state in which they find themselves (Hallett, 2002). Another way of examining prebirth communications is to deliberately regress people back to a time before their birth, using either hypnosis or some form of guided imagery, and ask them to describe the environment in which they find themselves during the regression (Baruŝs, 2003a; Kwilecki, 2014; Newton, 2009). Of course, in all of these cases we have the obvious problem of trying to determine how much of any of these reports could be true. A scientific attitude requires that we take such reports seriously but then try to assess their veridicality. Any information obtained in these ways could not be verified with a single example, but if multiple cross-cultural reports were to provide commonalities, this would be an interesting starting place.

One example of a promising approach is to infer the properties of an independent mind from the information provided by discarnates as they are portrayed by mediums. For instance, recall the medium who claimed he was being informed by chess master Géza Maróczy which moves to make in the chess game we discussed in Chapter 4, played in the style in which the living Maróczy played. On the basis of this single report, one tentative conclusion one might draw is that the cognitive skills acquired while alive are not lost at death, but neither are they necessarily augmented, given that the apparent Maróczy did not have an updated understanding of opening theory and lost to the living Viktor Korchnoi, who did. Similarly, the apparent Maróczy was asked by Wolfgang Eisenbeiss, via Robert Rollans, "whether the name 'Romi' meant anything to him" (Eisenbeiss & Hassler, 2006, p. 74). The apparent Maróczy claimed, through the medium, that there had not been such a chess player, but rather someone named "Romih," whom he had known in childhood and played against in the year 1930 at a tournament. Intriguingly, tournament records show "Romih" with the "h." Apparently, while living in Italy sometime after the 1930 tournament, Romi had changed his Slavonic "Romih" to the more palatable "Romi," by which he had been subsequently known. Eisenbeiss had not known this at the time of asking the question, so the answer had come as a surprise (Eisenbeiss & Hassler, 2006, p. 74).

This turn of events challenges the super-psi hypothesis by the demonstration of information that was specific to a discarnate's perspective rather than what could reasonably be the medium's perspective. It also suggests that

Maróczy's postlife memory had not automatically been updated by events that had occurred after his death. In other words, from this case it would appear that discarnate minds retain the cognitive skills and memories that they had while alive, but that is all. Systematically studying similar cases could allow us to determine whether this conclusion holds across multiple apparent discarnate personalities.

In seeking information about the nature of consciousness in the afterlife, the problem is not that there is no useful information out there but, on the contrary, that there is way too much. In fact, there is so much information that we cannot effectively summarize it, let alone evaluate it, for the purposes of this book. For instance, in the last several decades, there has been a great deal of public interest in what minds are doing before they are born into bodies and, in particular, why they chose to have the lives that they did, under the assumption that such choice is possible (Kwilecki, 2014). For example, according to his promotional material, Michael Newton, who has used a method of hypnotic regression to ostensibly take people back to the time before their birth, has sold almost 1 million copies of his books, which he has claimed have been translated into more than 30 languages (Newton, 2009, back cover). From a materialist point of view, an individual mind existing before or after life is impossible, so there is no need to study this phenomenon. So, inside academia little is said about the existence of mind before life and after life, whereas outside of academia there appears to be enormous fascination with such subject matter. This results in a schism between what happens in the academy and the rest of society (Bowie, 2013) so that the public understanding of "life after death" proceeds largely unchecked by the critical evaluation that authentic scientific investigation could provide. Academics should know what is being said about the afterlife simply because there is widespread public information about it that is bound to affect people's behavior.

MIND IN THE AFTERLIFE

In spite of the plentifulness of books about the afterlife, the authors could find only a single analytical summary of the material in those various books. Psychologist David Fontana (2005) created one by looking for common features in 32 sources and accepting such features only if they "present a picture that makes some sense if we assume that even in this life mind is non-physical and distinct in some understandable way from the material world" (p. 446). Commonalities in his sources could be due to objectivity of descriptions of the afterlife or, alternatively, biases among the living who are producing the accounts. Here we look briefly at two of the themes that emerged for Fontana: the notion that our minds retain their individuality after death, and the idea that our minds can directly influence the afterlife environment in which they find themselves. This discussion will bring up several related issues. While relying primarily on Fontana's book chapter to critically discuss these themes, we will also draw on a synthesized understanding of this material as reflected in the sources concerning the afterlife that we cite in this book.

The first notion is that the mind survives, not in some diffuse form, but with a person's individuality intact. That includes ingrained motivations, emotions, conditioned ways of thinking, and so on. So what is different? Well, the obvious difference is that there is no physical body. If there is no physical body, then where is this individualized mind operating? We are so used to the reductionist thesis that mind must supervene on some material machinery that our tendency is to look for some sort of substrate for the discarnate mind as well. There are at least two ways to approach this question.

One way is to relent to the reductionist urge and to restore some sort of "material" by assuming that there is a "body" of some sort that coexists with a person's physical body while she is alive and that leaves when she dies. Historically, different names have been used for such a body, one of which has been that of *double* (Guiley, 1991, p. 154; Muldoon & Carrington, 1929, p. xv). For instance: "During the whole of a man's earthly life he is accompanied by the double or unifying body. It is the link between the deeper mind and the brain, and has many important functions" (ostensibly Frederic Myers channelled by Geraldine Cummins; Cummins, 1932/2012, p. 46). The "material" of which this double is made could be some sort of subatomic stuff, or it could be dark matter or dark energy, or perhaps something that we have not yet found.

Having struck on the idea of an inner body that can leave the outer, physical, body, we can iterate the process as many times as we choose so that we can imagine there are bodies within bodies, like a matryoshka doll, made of ever finer gradations of "matter" (Baruss, 1996). This corresponds to the notion that there are levels of the afterlife. The idea is that, after death, we start by existing in the levels of reality closest to those of physical manifestation on earth and move toward more sublime levels (Baruss, 1996; Fontana, 2005).

An alternative view is that the double is not made of anything. That all such bodies are appearances only, without any actual substance. For instance, those in the afterlife are frequently perceived as wearing clothing. What is the point of clothing in the afterlife? And, in fact, is there anything actually underneath the clothes? Fontana (2005) gave the example of an ostensibly physically materialized being who said that "it was indeed easier to material-ize robes than the whole body, and drew back the hem of her robe to show that she had no feet" (p. 450). In other words, just as it is apparently easier for a materialized apparition to show up physically as clothing rather than an actual body, so it could be easier for deceased minds to present themselves mentally as being clothed rather than naked. Or one could just not bother trying to look like a person in the first place. For instance, based on his interviews with those who have had NDEs, Philip Berman has said that "Of the many near-death experiencers I have met, most felt they took on a new body of some sort, tending to describe that body as a cloud, a sphere, or some form of light" (Berman, 1996, p. 74).

Another way to think about the empty double is to consider what happens in dreams. We have bodies in dreams that we use to interact with our dream environments. What is the substance of our dream bodies? Of what is the dream environment made? One night, in a lucid dream, one of the authors of this book, Imants Barušs, found himself in a well-lit, empty room. He deliberately looked at the nature of his surroundings. They were as real as the surroundings in his ordinary waking state. He decided to enact Samuel Johnson's famous refutation of George Berkeley's immaterialist doctrine, in which Johnson kicked a stone to demonstrate the objective existence of the physical world. Barušs did not have a stone to kick, so he walked over to the wall to his right and pounded it hard with his fist. It was solid. No doubt about that. And by Johnson's argument, the wall therefore had an existence independent of Barušs's perception of it. Of course, Johnson's argument is nonsensical. The dream wall need not be made of anything that persists when no one is observing it (Barušs, 2012). The idea is that the situation in which we find ourselves after death could be the same as the situation in our dreams. The double, along with the landscape in which the double finds itself, need not be made of anything (Fontana, 2005).

The analogy with dreams could be more than an analogy. It is possible that if there is a double, whether substantive or just functional, then death might not be the only time that this double separates from the physical body. In fact, this separation could occur whenever we fall asleep, with dreams being the registration of the experiences that we are having in whatever domain it is in which our doubles find themselves. Or, perhaps more fittingly, out-of-body experiences, such as those that occur during NDEs, could be actual travels of the double outside of the physical body (Baker, n.d.; Barušs, 1996, 2003a; Monroe, 1972, 1994; Muldoon & Carrington, 1929; cf. Alvarado & Zingrone, 2015). Of course, even if veridical perceptions occur during these times, out-of-body experiences could just be products of brain activity. And in cases in which there is no cortical activity as measured by an encephalogram, brain activity could possibly be occurring at subcortical levels (Braude, 2003).

The second notion that we want to consider here is that a person shapes the afterlife environment directly with her thoughts. This is ostensibly done in conjunction with others who have similar thoughts. For instance, if the deceased Frederic Myers as channelled by Geraldine Cummins is to be believed:

> On higher planes of being your intellectual power is so greatly increased that you can control form; you learn how to draw life to it. As a sculptor takes up the formless clay and shapes it, so does your mind draw life and light to it and shape your own surroundings according to your vision. (Cummins, 1932/2012, p. 12)

And, indeed, the assertion has sometimes been made that people gravitate toward environments in the afterlife for which they have an affinity (Baruss, 1996). This is also consistent with the levels approach. For instance, connoisseurs of fine wines would find themselves in the company of others with similar interests and cocreate experiences of enjoying wine drinking. Of course, that raises the question of how such wine drinking even makes sense without the appropriate biological mechanisms for the sensations of taste and for inebriation. Nonetheless, the idea is that whatever went on during physical life can go on in the afterlife as a creation of the imagination. In addition to eating and drinking, that includes sleeping, having sex, and going to work every day doing whatever it is that one did while one was alive. Such behavior can continue until such time as a person gets tired of it and moves on to "planes" of existence with less resemblance to physical manifestation (Baruss, 1996; Fontana, 2005).

If we start with an assumption that our individual minds continue to work after our bodies die, then this levels notion raises several issues. The first is that it takes more than death to escape one's conditioning. While alive, we already seek out confirmatory data and discount evidence that is contrary to our beliefs, thereby creating communities of like-minded individuals. The pervasiveness of materialism in large sectors of the academy is a good example of this. Such aggregation is thought by some to be exacerbated in the afterlife, where the effects of one's thoughts on one's environment are apparently more immediate, which would make it even more difficult to escape the limitations of one's thinking (Baruss, 1996). If this were the case, different discarnate communicators would be expected to give different accounts of the nature of the afterlife, adding to the confusion that already exists. For instance, discarnate communicators pontificating on the occurrence or nonoccurrence of reincarnation could depend on the faction to which they belong after death (Fontana, 2005). And, of course, we have to remember that the information is being relayed through mediums who have their own biases so that such differences could have a more prosaic explanation.

A second issue that the "levels" notion raises is that of the nature of memory in the afterlife. Given that memory is necessary for us to have individual identities, some sort of memory purportedly persists, at least for a time, in the afterlife. If this is the case, how is that memory realized? If Géza Maróczy really can remember the skills associated with playing chess as well as the names of his competitors and other facts about his life, then where are those data stored? One possibility is that there are two different types of memories, namely, the memories somehow encoded in a person's physical body and the memories that are somehow encoded in the double, along with some sort of communication between them. So it could be argued that a person with severe dementia has not lost her self-identity because the memories necessary for self-identity are not in the physical body in the first place. Perhaps someone with dementia has already partially disconnected from her physical body (Fontana, 2005). In such cases, terminal lucidity could be explained as a brief reconnection of the double with the physical body, although that introduces a new problem, namely, the manner in which a nonphysical mind can affect a physical body when the ordinary apparatus for that connection may be impaired.

A third issue concerns time. What is the nature of time in the afterlife? Is this time the deep time revealed in some NDEs whereby an entire lifetime can be reexperienced apparently in an instant, as we discussed in Chapter 3? Do the experiences of discarnate entities have a temporal structure of an occurring present bracketed by a past and a future? It appears that they would need to for the ordinary activities of physical life to be adequately simulated (cf. Hamilton-Parker, 2001), and certainly to play chess or taste wine! It makes sense that the qualia of sipping wine would occur before the qualia of swallowing it. However, there are also apparently cases of people who do not know that they have died and for whom time seems to have stood still for decades while they continued to engage in whatever activities they were engaged in at the time of their death (Assante, 2012). One way to understand this is to suppose that the nervous system forces a temporal order on events that are not necessarily linearly ordered. Time, as we conceptualize it, could be "largely meaningless" in the afterlife and could "be mixed, jumped, reversed, looped, condensed, and expanded, or it can cease altogether" (Assante, 2012, p. 150). But then in what sense are minds still having the same experiences after death that they were having while they were alive? It is possible such life-like experiences are actually a small subset of the experiences of discarnates, but they are the only ones that we can understand, given the linear nature of subjective apparent time.

A fourth issue raises a potentially more serious concern, bringing us back to the material about unwanted intrusions we touched on in Chapter 4. Suppose that we are not just wine connoisseurs but alcoholics, and we die while addicted to alcohol. The idea that our cravings are not initiated from the physical body but from a double suggests that when we die, our cravings do not cease but persist after the body's dénouement, so that we become *hungry ghosts* (Fontana, 2005, p. 465). We still crave alcohol, or whatever it is that we wanted when we were alive, and so we interfere in the lives of the living in an effort to satisfy our desires. This is consistent with Ralph Allison's case of Elise, who had an alter named Shannon, from Chapter 4. In that case, the discarnate Dennis ostensibly satisfied his postmortem need for sexual intercourse by taking over the bodies of Shannon's lovers. We note, however, that a need to take over the body of a living being to experience sensual pleasure conflicts with the notion that we can experience whatever we want in the afterlife, so that either the idea that we have control over afterlife experience is false, or the idea of hungry ghosts is false, or both are true and it is just that the hungry ghosts have not figured out how to get what they want in the afterlife so they try to get it from the living. For Dennis, his infatuation with Shannon ostensibly led to the expression of physical sexual intercourse rather than, or possibly in addition to, noncorporeal sexual intercourse. The point is that the tendencies of the deceased could continue into the realm of the living in ways that affect the living.

We have tried to talk about the separation of the mind from the brain on the basis of anecdotes, a few formal reports, and several theories, but the reader can see the paucity of actual data. Going forward, it would be helpful if those trying to do research in this area would not be punished for doing so, as we noted in Chapter 1, and instead could receive support in the form of professional respect, research grants, and the opportunity to publish their work in mainstream academic journals. These lines of investigation need to move forward more vigorously, with the necessary balance of rigor and open-mindedness. Meanwhile, we leave aside theorizing about the separation of the mind from the brain until Chapter 8. We now move ahead to explore the research about another topic that leads toward the conclusion that consciousness can act independently of the brain and the body, namely, "Direct Mental Influence," in Chapter 6.

6

DIRECT MENTAL INFLUENCE

Physics is very muddled again at the moment; it is much too hard for me anyway, and I wish I were a movie comedian or something like that and had never heard anything about physics.
—Wolfgang Pauli (as cited in Bynum & Porter, 2005, p. 483)

In June of 1972, physicist Hal Puthoff invited the artist Ingo Swann for a week-long visit to Stanford Research Institute. Swann had previously participated in experiments of direct mental influence, and Puthoff wanted to see a demonstration of such abilities for himself. Without Swann's prior knowledge, Puthoff had organized access to a "well-shielded magnetometer" that was used for physics experiments and that was "located in a vault below the floor of the building." Swann apparently managed to "perturb the operation of the magnetometer" and then went on to draw a "reasonable facsimile" of the interior of the machine (Puthoff, 1996, p. 65). In Chapter 2, we considered the second of those abilities, namely, perceiving something that is happening without physical access to it. We can think of that as the *input* side of the relationship between mind and physical manifestation. The *output* side would consist of the ability to apparently influence something directly with the mind—in this case, the activity of a magnetometer. The output side is our subject matter for this chapter.

http://dx.doi.org/10.1037/15957-007
Transcendent Mind: Rethinking the Science of Consciousness, by I. Baruss and J. Mossbridge

As we have seen, there is a plethora of evidence of various sorts for anomalous information acquisition. And, indeed, anyone who wishes to do so can easily see a demonstration for herself by getting a good medium to talk for an hour or so, for instance, although that is not, of course, a formal experiment. But what about the output side? Where is the evidence for the direct influence of mental activity on physical manifestation? Here, demonstrations and supportive data seem elusive. In fact, by one estimate, the effect size for remote perception is about 10 times greater than it is for remote influencing (Targ, 2012). However, as we pull back the chaff, the evidence becomes clearly visible. So let us look at it.

In Chapter 4, we started by investigating reports of spontaneous phenomena and then examined the results obtained from deliberately inducing the same phenomena. Let us turn that around this time, so that we start by looking at deliberately induced phenomena using various random event generators, and then turn to a series of spontaneous events in which there appears to have been some direct mental influence. As we do so, we will consider increasingly more interesting phenomena so that the reader's boggle threshold is likely to get a good stretch in this chapter.

RANDOM MECHANICAL CASCADE

Let us start with an experiment that was carried out over several decades at the Princeton Engineering Anomalies Research (PEAR) laboratory at Princeton University. Researchers built a 6- by 10-foot box with a clear acrylic face, nicknamed Murphy, and placed it against a wall across from a couch. The upper part of the box contained an array of 330 nylon pins, and the lower part consisted of 19 vertical collecting bins. Nine thousand polystyrene balls, each three quarters of an inch in diameter, were sequentially released from an opening at the top of the box so as to fall through the array of pegs before landing in the collecting bins at the bottom. The release and cascade of the 9,000 balls constituted what the experimenters called a *run*, which took about 12 minutes. At the top of each collecting bin was an optical electronic counter that registered the presence of each ball as it entered the bin and an LED display at the bottom that gave a reading of the number of balls in the bin at any given time. That information was also saved to a computer, manually recorded in a logbook, and photographed at the end of each run. The distribution of balls in the collecting bins would naturally approximate a normal distribution with a mean of bin 10, given that there were 19 bins, and a standard deviation of about 3 bins (Dunne, Nelson, & Jahn, 1988).

The idea was that during each run a person, called an *operator*, would sit on the couch about 8 feet from the machine and mentally influence the activity of the balls by trying to make them go left or go right, depending on the prestated goal of the run. There was also a baseline intention in which an operator simply allowed the balls to fall without trying to influence them. The combination of a left-going intention, a right-going intention, and a baseline run constituted a *session*. A *series* was made up of 10 or 20 sessions. Because of changes to the distribution of balls in the bins caused by various physical variables such as temperature, humidity, wear on the pins, and so on, no effort was made to compare the resultant bin counts to theoretical distributions. Rather, the results of the right-going intentions were compared with the results of the left-going intentions within sessions (Dobyns, 2015; Dunne, Nelson, & Jahn, 1988).

When one of the authors of this book, Imants Barušs, took the students in his consciousness class on a field trip to the PEAR laboratory in February of 1993, he had an opportunity to formally participate in this experiment as Operator 190. Sitting by himself on the couch some 8 feet from Murphy, he intended the balls to go left or right, in different runs, and over time he got a clear separation of the left-going intention from the right-going intention in the correct direction. Indeed, that was consistent with the collective results of this experiment for individual people sitting on the couch attempting to affect the machine. Over the course of 87 series, the z-score, that is, the number of standard deviations away from the expected mean, of the shift in the average difference between the left-going and right-going intentions was $z = 3.89$, which was statistically significant with a probability of less than 5 in 100,000 that the results occurred by chance (Jahn, Dunne, Nelson, Dobyns, & Bradish, 1997). In other words, operators appeared to have been able to shift the balls in the intended direction in a statistically significant way. So, based on laboratory evidence with multiple operators, Ingo Swann's demonstration was not an isolated instance of direct mental influence.

With Murphy, we have a machine that emulates the deterministic activity of the billiard balls in one of our versions of materialism. In place of billiard balls, we have polystyrene balls, and, in addition to hitting each other and the walls of the box, we have them hitting pins, but otherwise this is about as close as we are going to get to a billiard ball model of reality that is supposed to run in a deterministic manner, impervious to mental influence.

But it is unlikely that these "billiard balls" were ever deterministic in the first place. As we saw in Chapter 1, materialists believe that quantum phenomena remain encapsulated in some microdomain incapable of contaminating people-sized events, so according to them, the actions of Murphy can then safely be described using just classical mechanics. But it turns out there is no stopping the upward creep of quantum weirdness. Calculation of the amplification of the differences produced by the multiple interactions of a ball as it falls through Murphy's array of pegs has revealed the possibility that initial microscopic differences as the ball is released from the aperture at the top are within the limits of quantum uncertainty. In other words, the random behavior of the balls as they fall through the array is "arguably quantum-mechanical" (Dobyns, 2015, p. 231). Thus, it is possible that, ironically, not even real billiard balls follow the billiard-ball version of reality.

RANDOM EVENT GENERATORS

From what we have said already, it is not clear that there can ever be any deterministic physical processes. Nonetheless, to avoid mechanisms that can putatively be explained deterministically, much of the history of research into direct mental influence has been conducted with *random event generators* (REGs), sometimes also called *random number generators*. These REGs use quantum mechanical randomness as their data source. For instance, Helmut Schmidt (1971) used radioactive decay as a source of binary random events. This was the analogue of flipping a coin that could land either heads or tails so that a random sequence of "heads" and "tails" was generated. In Schmidt's research, a run consisted of a sequence of 128 events, lasting about 2 minutes. The signal from the REG was sent to a display panel consisting of a circle of nine lights, one of which was always lit. If the REG produced a "head," then the light that was clockwise to the one that was lit would become lit instead. If the REG produced a "tail," then the light that was counterclockwise to the one that was lit would become lit instead. A participant in an experiment would try to get the lights to move in an overall clockwise direction. We will discuss the results from his experiments after addressing two critical factors that can influence direct mental intention experiments: the masking of skilled performers by nonskilled performers and psi-missing.

An alternative, used at the PEAR lab, was to sample the quantum-mechanical random noise from a diode, which was converted into a sequence of "random digital pulses" that could either be positive or negative (Dobyns, 2015, p. 220). In one trial, a sequence of 200 pulses would be compared with a string of alternating positive and negative reference signals and the number of matches would be counted, giving an integer between 0 and 200 with an expected value of 100 and standard deviation of about 7. Such trials would be accumulated into a *run*, and runs would be accumulated into *series* (Dobyns, 2015, p. 220).

So what happened? Well, using the PEAR protocol for 522 series gave $z = 3.81$ with a probability of occurrence by chance of 7 in 100,000 (Jahn et al., 1997). In other words, it appeared there was an effect. But then it got messy. A consortium of three research centers, including the PEAR laboratory, failed to replicate such results for a total of 750 series concatenated from all three laboratories, giving $z = 0.60$, which is not statistically significant (Jahn et al., 2000, p. 509). The machines did not move in the intended direction to a statistically significant degree, though they had apparently done so previously. What happened?

There are two main research goals that a researcher can have when investigating the existence of anomalous phenomena. The first is to determine whether a particular anomalous phenomenon actually occurs. Such a goal motivates an *existence study*, which only aims to assess the existence of a phenomenon. The second research goal is to find out which variables are responsible for the occurrence of a particular anomalous phenomenon. This goal motivates a *mechanism study* (cf. Bierman & Houtkooper, 1975). The two are related, of course, in that we need to know something about the parameters that could lead to the occurrence of an anomalous phenomenon to determine whether it exists. However, at the most basic level, where anomalous phenomena depend on the participation of single individuals, we want to include in our study only those individuals who seem to demonstrate the phenomenon. Later on we can figure out why they can demonstrate it when others cannot. In other words, if one wishes to determine whether any human can play the piano, then one had better try to find a person who can actually play the piano. Once this person has been found, we can begin to explore the necessary and sufficient factors required for piano playing.

Recall that in Chapter 4, we noted that in recent research with mediums, mediums have been pretested to see if they can get correct information. If they can, then they participate in formal existence studies. If they cannot, then they are left out of formal existence studies. There was no pretesting of participants in any of the PEAR studies, so that it was not clear which participants could or could not affect the machines in the first place. In fact, an examination of the original PEAR REG data led to the conclusion that the original anomalous results were due to a "talented" 15% of the participants (Dobyns, 2015, p. 233). Furthermore, in a somewhat different reanalysis of the original data, it would appear that only two talented participants of the total of 89, who contributed nearly 25% of the data, were responsible for the statistically significant effect. Meanwhile, in the replication performed by the consortium, the extent of contribution of each participant was standardized so that each participant contributed an equal number of runs. In this case, the contributions of a small number of gifted individuals would have been too limited to have made the necessary difference, resulting in the overall nonsignificant effect (P. Bancel, personal communication, June 11, 2015; Varvoglis & Bancel, 2015).

One of the alternative reasons given by the authors of the consortium study for the failure to replicate the primary results was that "certain subjective psychological conditions, essential to generation of the anomalies, were not properly recognized and/or incorporated in the replication" (Jahn et al., 2000, p. 517). One such psychological factor could be psi-missing. As we noted previously, *psi-missing* refers to a situation in which people who are instructed to intend to produce a specific anomalous effect actually end up with data that significantly avoid the effect they were asked to produce. For instance, someone who is convinced that direct mental influence is impossible could conceivably nonconsciously try to prove to herself that she is correct by attempting to create an REG output in opposition to the instructed output. If she is successful at a rate beyond chance, this would ironically suggest that she was capable of influencing the REG.

So how many of the participants are psi-missing? Obviously, such participants are going to have a cancelling effect on the participants who are *psi-hitting*. Using the protocol for his studies that we previously described, Helmut Schmidt (1971) looked at the performance of 18 readily available participants. Only three of them, or 17%, could get the light to go in the clockwise direction. Note that this is pretty much the same percentage as the percentage of proficient participants found in one analysis of the PEAR database. Most of the participants had a tendency to move the light in the counterclockwise direction. So Schmidt took a group of 15 participants who had a "negative scoring tendency" for another study (p. 757). This time the light moved in the intended direction for only 49.1% of trials, which is significantly below the expected value of 50%. In fact, the performance for the second half of participants' runs decreased from an average of 49.5% to 48.7% "as though [the participants] became more and more frustrated with the task of influencing a randomly moving light" and that frustration expressed itself as increasingly greater psi-missing (Schmidt, 1971, p. 757). In this case, the explanation for consistent psi-missing is likely not one of nonconscious desire to prove oneself right. One alternative explanation is that direct mental influence over matter may, for some people, not benefit from a frustrated or emotional approach to the task.

After finding this result, Schmidt (1971) pretested potential participants and chose two for a further study. One of those participants scored exceptionally high, and another scored exceptionally low during the pretest. As Schmidt expected, they continued this same behavior for the formal confirmatory test consisting of a prespecified 50 runs of 128 trials each. The participant scoring high was able to get 52.5% of the 6,400 trials to go in the clockwise direction, whereas the participant scoring low was able to get 47.75% of the 6,400 trials to go in the clockwise direction. The probability of such an occurrence is less than 1 in 10 million or less than $p = .0000001$ (Schmidt, 1971). Notice that the average score for the two participants is pretty close to zero, so that if their contributions were to be combined, we would think that there was no evidence for direct mental influence.

There is another important parameter that we need to consider. According to some researchers, "there is no such thing as a gifted participant as such, but rather how well a participant scores on a psi task depends on the person who does the testing and the nature of the experimental conditions" (Roe, Davey, & Stevens, 2006, p. 240). This is usually referred to as the *experimenter effect* (M. D. Smith, 2003). An alternative way to think about the experimenter effect is to conceptualize it as an *entire-world* explanation of the results of an experiment. A participant is apparently having some sort of direct mental influence on a machine. But now a second person comes along and also tries to influence the machine at the same time. And a third person. And a fourth person. And so on. Each individual's motivation, attitude, ability to have an effect, and so on could modify the outcome. Also, it was found at the PEAR laboratory that one did not need to be physically present to demonstrate the intended effects. Further, one did not need to try to influence the machine at the time that it was running to demonstrate the intended effects (Jahn et al., 1997).

So, multiple people, spatially and temporally removed from the random events themselves, could have an effect in either the intended or unintended direction. In particular, the experimenter could have an effect, anyone who has heard about the experiment in the past or will hear about it in the future could have an effect, and anyone who reads about an experiment in an academic journal or a book could have an effect (Baruss & Rabier, 2014; Bierman, 2001). In other words, the idea is that we are already living in a world in which we are always influencing everything of which we become aware whether we are explicitly aware of doing so or not. And one might suppose that our usual way of influencing events is to keep them within the bounds of what we regard as "ordinary" so that those who are trying to demonstrate the occurrence of anomalous phenomena are fighting against a general damping effect. These factors could interact with whatever other sources of effects exist in the universe, such as the nature of the system that is being affected, solar storms, and so on. Whether this entire-world explanation holds is not clear, but what is clear is that the so-called experimenter effect is something that needs to be carefully empirically investigated more so than it has been until now.

TWO-SLIT EXPERIMENT

We will consider one more variation on these direct mental influence experiments. But first, let us consider the two-slit experiment, which we introduced in Chapter 3. We considered a beam of photons, fired one at a time, at a barrier with two slits in it. When we could tell, in principle, through which of the two slits a photon emerged, then it would, indeed, emerge from one or the other of the slits. When we could not tell through which of the two slits that photon emerged, then we got an interference pattern. Then we considered a delayed-choice version of that experiment, in which a decision about how to detect the photons made after the photons had gone through the slits seemed to influence the path of the photons.

Okay. This result already seems anomalous. But what happens if we set up this device and then just *imagine* that we are looking at the two slits? If there is direct mental influence on matter, perhaps imagining we are looking at the slits is all that is required to reduce the presence of the interference pattern. This idea was tested in a series of three separate experiments. When participants were told to "concentrate," they were to "focus their attention on the two slits located inside the optical system," referred to as the *attention-toward* condition. *Optical system* is the name for the photon gun, barrier with two slits, and the detectors. By necessity, for the detection of the interference patterns, the optical system was contained in a box that was optically shielded. This means that participants could not directly look at the system; they just had to imagine that they could. When they were told to "relax," they were to withdraw attention from the device, referred to as the *attention-away* condition. In the attention-toward condition, participants were given auditory feedback in the form of volume changes in a "droning tone" that indicated to them how successful they were at modifying the behavior of the device (Radin, Michel, Johnston, & Delorme, 2013, p. 555). When the patterns on the recording device for the attention-toward condition were compared with the patterns for the attention-away condition, it was found that there was a collective deviation across all three experiments in the expected direction of $z = -6.81$, which has a probability of less than 1 in 208 billion. Meanwhile, when the same equipment was used without participants present, there was no difference between the attention-toward and attention-away conditions. In other words, when participants imagined looking at the two slits, the interference pattern decreased relative to when they were not imagining looking at the two slits (Radin et al., 2013).

How might the experimenter effect play into these results? According to quantum theory, observing the slit through which a photon passed would destroy the interference pattern, so the experimenters, who were aware of this idea, would have expected the observed effect: the reduction in the interference pattern when participants imagined looking at the slits. But what if the experiment is repeated, and positive feedback is now given to the observers every time the interference pattern gets stronger? And what if the experimenter thinks the participants are getting the same type of feedback as in the original experiment, so that the experimenter expectation is the same?

It turns out that, by mistake, the same research group that did the remotely observed two-slit experiments discussed previously performed exactly this experiment—"by mistake," because they did not realize that the computer code controlling the experiment actually reversed the direction of feedback to the participants. Thus, participants were being reinforced when they made the interference pattern stronger rather than weaker. Meanwhile, the experimenters thought that the experiment was working in the same way it used to work—they thought the feedback reinforced participants for making the interference pattern weaker. The results? The attention-toward periods produced stronger interference patterns compared with the attention-away periods, following the feedback, not the experimenters' expectations (Radin, Michel, & Delorme, 2015). This fortuitous mistake allows us to see that, at least in this case, the experimenters' expectations were outweighed by the feedback given to the participants.

What does this mean? It means that at least in this case, the experimenters did not bias the results through direct mental influence more than the participants did. However, because the participants were not certain what the feedback represented, the participants' expectations were not specific enough to bias the results in one theoretical direction or another. One interpretation is that the participants did whatever they needed to do, ostensibly using direct mental influence, to continue to receive positive feedback. And in this case, what they needed to do was to produce the opposite of the result hypothesized by quantum theory: a strengthening of the interference pattern when they were imagining looking at the two slits. In this particular case, it appears that the intention of the participants outweighed the expectations of the experimenters.

REMOTE HEALING

It is one thing to try to have direct mental influence over a machine of some sort as we have discussed thus far in this chapter, but what about influencing a person? In particular, what about praying for healing? The potential influence of prayer is not just a matter of theoretical interest. In one study, it was found that 57% of over 2,000 social workers surveyed reported praying in private for their clients. In another study, it was found that 39% of 1,900 cancer survivors had others pray for them. And in yet another study, it was found that "the use of prayer for health concerns has continually increased in the United States" from 2002 to 2008 (Schlitz, 2014, p. 97). There is also a dark side to this, in that "5 percent of Americans have prayed for harm to come to others," as revealed in a 1994 Gallup poll (Dossey, 1997, p. 1; see also Clifton, 2014).

The results from experiments testing *remote intercessory prayer* have been mixed, with some initial studies finding positive effects (Byrd, 1988; Harris et al., 1999) followed by several prominent large-scale studies with null results (Benson et al., 2006; Krucoff et al., 2005) or possible negative effects (Benson et al., 2006). There has been considerable analysis of the large-scale failures to replicate (L. M. McTaggart, 2007), with some of this analysis centered on the variability across different types of prayer. "Prayer is actually a proxy for a wide constellation of beliefs and behavior" (Ladd & Spilka, 2014, p. 33), with little research having been done on the phenomenology of prayer (Dein & Littlewood, 2008, p. 40). If we broaden the scope of attempted remote intercessions beyond those that are identified as prayer, then "taken as a group, laboratory or hospital experiments are quite variable. Consequently, most researchers agree that there is strong evidence for various kinds of distant and spiritual healing, but the results depend strongly on who is doing it" (Targ, 2012, p. 153). This is consistent with what we have already found about direct mental influence. Perhaps some people can do remote healing, whereas other people are either unsuccessful or have adverse effects. And their effectiveness also likely depends on exactly what it is that they are doing. In other words, some "techniques" may be more successful than others.

Two recent comprehensive meta-analyses of "noncontact healing studies," which included the aforementioned large-scale studies with null results but also included studies in which healers were in close physical proximity to those being healed, found that overall there were positive effects of healing intention on biological systems. One of the meta-analyses was done for non-whole human biological systems such as cell cultures, nonhuman animals, and plants and seeds, and a second one for whole humans. Strict inclusion criteria were determined beforehand, and ratings of methodological quality performed by judges who did not know the outcome of the experiments were used in determining which studies to include in the meta-analyses. The 22 nonwhole human studies meeting strict quality criteria gave a weighted effect size of $r = .12$ with 95% CI [0.09, 0.14]. Because the confidence interval does not include zero and is positive, this is considered a statistically significant, positive effect. And the 27 whole-human studies meeting strict quality criteria gave a weighted effect size of $r = .22$ with 95% CI [0.19, 0.25] (Roe, Sonnex, & Roxburgh, 2015). Again, the result is statistically significant and positive. In other words, it appears that remote healing really happens.

The authors of these meta-analyses expressed a concern that in spite of care taken with blinding in proximal human noncontact studies, some of the blinds may have inadvertently been broken so that a participant could tell whether she was receiving healing. As a consequence, some of the positive results may have been due to expectancy. This was one reason that the authors had also done a meta-analysis for nonwhole human biological systems, where expectancy effects should be absent. Those results were also statistically significantly positive, suggesting that the results overall in the whole human studies cannot simply result from expectancy effects. Among their recommendations, the authors stated that healers included in noncontact healing studies should have already demonstrated success with a particular condition "or should be able to show that previous success should generalize to the current situation" (Roe et al., 2015, p. 18). In other words, healers should be pretested to make certain that they are able to produce the desired effect before being included in an existence study.

THE PAULI EFFECT

The physicist Wolfgang Pauli was humorously credited with causing various accidents around him. "Machines would stop running when he arrived in a laboratory, a glass apparatus would suddenly break, a leak would appear in a vacuum system, but none of these accidents would ever hurt or inconvenience Pauli himself" (Peierls, 1960, p. 185). In a parody of the Pauli effect, a chandelier had been rigged to crash when Pauli showed up at a reception, but when Pauli arrived, the rope jammed and the chandelier failed to crash as planned. Ironically, this was "a typical example of the Pauli effect!" (Peierls, 1960, p. 185).

People who have had near-death experiences sometimes seem to be dramatically changed afterward, including having Pauli-type effects occur around them. "A surprisingly large proportion of these persons discover, for instance, that digital wrist watches will no longer work properly for them, or they 'short out' electrical systems in their cars, or computers and appliances malfunction for no apparent reason, and so on" (Ring & Valarino, 1998, p. 129). Such phenomena appear to have been "switched on" along with other phenomena, such as apparent remote perception and apparent remote healing (Atwater, 2007; Moody, 1975; Ring & Valarino, 1998). Careful investigation is necessary to determine whether these occurrences are actually anomalous. But to the extent that some of these are instances of anomalous phenomena, the Pauli-type effects could be regarded as a form of poltergeist activity.

POLTERGEIST ACTIVITY

Poltergeist activity consists of the anomalous movement of objects or the presence of anomalous sounds that cannot easily be explained. For instance, in what has been called the "Sauchie case" (Irwin, 1994, p. 190), which began in 1960, a heavy sideboard reportedly moved out about 12 centimeters and then back again, a full linen chest weighing about 23 kilograms apparently moved by itself parallel to a bed, and a school desk supposedly rose about 2 centimeters from the floor before settling down again. Percipients reported the sound of a bouncing ball and, on other occasions, loud knocks. These events seemed to be associated with the presence of an 11-year-old girl, Virginia Campbell, who had been dislocated from her family in Ireland to live with her older brother in Sauchie, Scotland. There were multiple witnesses who reported these events, including a minister, a schoolteacher, and a physician (Irwin, 1994).

Well, this sort of thing could be well on the other side of our boggle threshold, so let us just pause to consider some of the reactions that we could have to reading this. One possible reaction is that we should not be talking about this in the first place. That sort of reaction would be consistent with prevalent groupthink about poltergeist phenomena. This reaction suggests its opposite, a need to have an open discussion about these phenomena.

A second reaction could be that these sorts of things obviously do not happen. School desks cannot levitate. In fact, fraud is the most common natural explanation for these phenomena and appears to explain 8% to 26% of cases, depending on how poltergeist activity is defined and who is counting (Irwin, 1994; B. Williams & Ventola, 2011). But fraud is easy for an investigator to control, as long as an investigator is given access to the area where the poltergeist activity is taking place (cf. B. Williams & Ventola, 2011).

If not fraud, then reports of poltergeist activity could just be mis-attributions of well-understood natural phenomena. And there are instances in which apparent poltergeist activity turned out to be misinterpreted natural events (Irwin, 1994). But such naturalistic explanations do not exhaust the list of cases. For instance, some of the movements of objects through the air do not follow ordinary trajectories. Witnesses have described them as "floating, fluttering, falling in a zigzag pattern . . . curving around sharp corners . . . [or] changing their speed while in motion" (B. Williams & Ventola, 2011, p. 9). Of course, these could be misperceptions, hallucinations, mis-rememberings, and that sort of thing. The problem with the misperception or misremembering explanation is that witnesses are not always just addle-brained true believers. Some witnesses have been reasonable, educated observers with intact mental faculties, such as in the Sauchie case (Healy & Cropper, 2014; Honorton, 1993/2015; Pilkington, 2015; Pratt & Roll, 1958). If misperception or misremembering of any sort is going to be used as an explanation, then there needs to be evidence that such misperception or misremembering actually occurred. It is contrary to the scientific method to insist that they must have occurred in the absence of any evidence for them or any reason to suppose that they occurred other than our own psychological need to discount these phenomena. The bottom line is that we are left with a residue of cases that appear to be truly anomalous.

A third reaction could be that these sorts of things obviously did not happen, because they are contrary to the known laws of physics. Well, this is just an instance of confirmation bias. If we are only willing to consider those things that are in accord with our ideas about the nature of reality and dismiss everything else that is not, then we hold a bias that confirms our ideas about reality. In this case, we can never learn anything surprising about nature.

If it is true that poltergeist activity violates known laws of physics, then those laws of physics are wrong and we need to get rid of them or understand how to make appropriate exceptions. As we pointed out in Chapters 1 and 3, physics is in a state of flux today, so much so that it is possible that empirical data from poltergeist activity could actually be useful for distinguishing between different theories. However, it is not clear that poltergeist activity actually violates even the physical laws that are already understood. In fact, for one, "Wolfgang Pauli saw a link between quantum mechanics and 'poltergeist'-style mind-matter interactions" (Sommer, 2014, p. 40), suggesting that these phenomena could well be encompassed within the physics that we already have.

One of the explanations for poltergeist activity is a psychological explanation whereby the production of the anomalous phenomena are seen as a manifestation of unexpressed frustration on the part of someone around whom these phenomena occur. In such cases, the phenomenon has sometimes been called *recurrent spontaneous psychokinesis* (Irwin, 1994; B. Williams & Ventola, 2011). For instance, this explanation would hold that Virginia Campbell in the Sauchie case was frustrated by something, perhaps the separation from her ordinary surroundings, and expressed that frustration through the anomalous sounds and movement of objects around her. In other words, poltergeist phenomena result from spontaneous direct mental influence on the environment of some people who are capable of creating such effects. The obvious way to test this would be to put such people in a lab to see what they can do. That has been done, and the answer is that in a laboratory they are usually ineffective. However, the psychological mechanism through which poltergeist phenomena occur could be different from that which is required in a controlled lab experiment (Irwin, 1994).

Poltergeist activity is usually categorized as one of two types, either *person centered* or *place centered*. That is to say, the phenomena appear to be either attached to a person or to a place. The subconscious mental influence theory works, to some extent, for the person-centered cases, but not as well for the place-centered cases (Irwin, 1994). The place-centered cases could be explained by an alternative *spirit hypothesis*, whereby poltergeist phenomena are the result of discarnate entities. This hypothesis is supported by the finding that apparitions are reported in 23% to 29% of poltergeist cases (Irwin, 1994). So, according to the spirit hypothesis, it is not the living who have direct mental influence over physical manifestation but whatever discarnate entities might be out there. In other words, the idea is that discarnate entities can affect physical manifestation through their direct mental influence.

How well does the spirit hypothesis work? Well, note that we have already seen purported instances of such phenomena in Chapter 4: the spontaneous playing of Michael Shermer's wife's grandfather's radio on the day of Shermer's wedding (Shermer, 2014), the smell of cumin coffee associated with the deceased that was reported by the granddaughter of the deceased (Haraldsson, 2012, p. 35), pictures of the deceased glowing or vibrating (Assante, 2012; Barbato, Blunden, Reid, Irwin, & Rodriguez, 1999), and so on. These can all be considered to be poltergeist activities, although they could also just be examples of the same kind of psychokinetic phenomena that we considered earlier.

A sinister aspect to poltergeist phenomena has also been reported. Some individuals have reported flying stones, sometimes hot to the touch. Also, sometimes stones have apparently hit those who have been present, although apparently they have rarely hurt anyone. Stones have also been seen to "float" so that they seemed to have had less force than expected when they did strike (Healy & Cropper, 2014; Irwin, 1994, p. 193). Reportedly, some objects have burst into flames, including objects that would have been difficult to incinerate, such as wet towels. More concerning, in 15% of 500 cases, people have reported having been bitten, scratched, or pinched. Pinching was also reported in the Sauchie case. In the most serious cases, percipients have reported persecution with religious aspects to it (Irwin, 1994), such as those that we have already discussed in the context of unwanted intrusions in Chapter 4. Again, some of these cases are likely the result of misperceptions, hallucinations, misrememberings, and so on, but we need to carefully examine those for which there is good objective evidence that they occurred.

Suppose for a moment that the potential to affect physical manifestation through direct mental influence is an ability that only some discarnate entities possess. We saw from the REG data that only about 2% of participants have an effect. One could speculate that these are participants who have an entity "attached" to them that has the necessary ability and that those who show psi-missing have a mischievous entity that deliberately misbehaves. Or perhaps all of these variations could occur. Individuals could have a direct mental influence, discarnate entities could have a direct mental influence, individuals could knowingly or unknowingly assist discarnate entities to create effects, and discarnate entities could assist living individuals to have effects with those living individuals either knowing or not knowing that they are being assisted. An example of the last of these would be the invocation of the assistance of a divine being for the purposes of healing, such as in some cases of intercessory prayer.

A FICTITIOUS GHOST

Let us take a few more twists on these phenomena. In the 1970s, members of the Toronto Society for Psychical Research decided to try to create a collective hallucination of a fictional ghost whom they named "Philip." They gave Philip a fabricated biography as an Englishman in the 1600s who died after flinging himself from the parapets of his manor after his lover had been burned at the stake. The members of the group saturated themselves with the details of Philip's fictional life and, once a week, meditated together with the intention of creating a collective hallucination. By the end of 1 year, the group was down to eight members, and not much had happened (835850 Ontario Limited, 1974; Owen, 1976).

On the basis of research results by Kenneth Batcheldor in England, the Toronto group decided to change its tactics. Instead of meditating, they sat around a "plastic-topped card table, with folding wooden legs, strengthened at the corners by metal stays," engaged in conversation, told jokes, sang songs, and recited poetry (Owen, 1976, p. 30). Around the third or fourth week, the members of the group felt a rap within the top of the table. Additional raps occurred "as if someone had struck the table a light blow." The raps became louder until they could be "*heard* by everyone in the group" (Owen, 1976, p. 26, emphasis in original). This is not what they had expected, but it was consistent with the results of Batcheldor's work (Mishlove, 1993; Owen, 1976). Then the table ostensibly started to tilt and to slide around the floor, sometimes swiftly and violently, and sometimes outpacing the members of the group who were trying to keep up with it (835850 Ontario Limited, 1974; Meyer zu Erpen, 2013; Owen, 1976).

Again, this experiment could well take us to the other side of our boggle threshold. We might assume that the raps were caused by the knocking of water pipes or other ordinary events, that the participants were mistaken about the table movements and the table did not really move, and that this report just "smacks of fraud." But in this case again, the quality of documentation is good, including film footage of the table movements recorded in good lighting; these table movements included those that could ostensibly not be reproduced by trying to fake them (835850 Ontario Limited, 1974). Furthermore, there have been several replications of the Philip experiment using other fictional characters, with some degree of success (Meyer zu Erpen, 2013). So, let us continue.

The members of the Toronto group had not been sure how to deal with these unexpected anomalous events, when one of them wondered aloud whether Philip could be responsible for what was happening. That was immediately followed by a "very loud rap from the table top" (Owen, 1976, p. 28). The members of the group set up a code: "One rap meant yes, two raps meant no" (Owen, 1976, p. 28). In this way they queried "Philip" and received responses from "him." The members of the group found that if they had unanimous agreement among group members for the answer to a question, then they would get a loud rap. If there was uncertainty, then there could be a delay before receiving a rap. If someone mistakenly asked a question that could not be answered with "yes" or "no," then scratching noises would ensue (Owen, 1976, p. 41). On one occasion, when the raps had become feebler and somewhat indefinite, one of the group had ostensibly said, "Philip, if you won't talk to us, we can send you away and get somebody else!" Reportedly, this had been followed by silence, and it had taken most of the evening to get the raps back (Owen, 1976, p. 49).

In the case of Philip, we have the manifestation of typical poltergeist phenomena ostensibly produced by a fictional ghost. In other words, we are back to the psychological theory for poltergeist activity, in that the activity of the ghost can be thought of as a manifestation of the psychological dynamics of the members of the group. But there is another possibility. If these phenomena were genuinely anomalous, it may be that we can create mental *thought-forms* that can take on a life of their own and interact with us as though they were independent entities (Barušs, 1996). In other words, our psychological productions could become objectively available, not just to those who produced them but to others as well. The raps and table movements created by the Philip group were reportedly witnessed by others, although at least some of the members of the group appear to have been needed to be present for the phenomena to occur (Owen, 1976).

MACRO-PK

The movement of objects by mental intent alone is sometimes referred to as *psychokinesis* (pk). Effects on noise-emitting diodes and other electronic devices are sometimes regarded as *micro-pk*, whereas people-sized effects are known as *macro-pk*. Poltergeist activity can be thought of as a form of macro-pk, either by those who are physically present or by discarnate entities. And there are cases of individuals who reportedly have been able to deliberately create large-scale effects.

One such well-documented individual is Susan Padfield, who demonstrated for multiple observers that, in a laboratory and apparently using only her intention, she could move a light mobile that was suspended inside a glass bottle and kept on a vibration-free platform 5 to 6 feet away from where she was standing. Either she would state the intended direction and number of degrees of rotation beforehand or the experimenter would ask her to intend to rotate the mobile in a given direction, by a given angle. According to her report, she did this every week for 9 years and was successful around 70% of the time. She repeated these remarkable results at the Stanford Research Institute, where she was only able to see the setup, which was in a separate room, via a closed-circuit television monitor. About her experience of these macro-pk demonstrations, Padfield stated, "I must emphasize here that I feel myself to be a part of these processes and these events and not in any way separate from them. I am a part of the events, of the sequences, not merely observing them" (Padfield, 1980, p. 167). She later went on to explain that she did not feel that she commanded or communicated with the device, but that she merged with it and saw its future state (Padfield, 1980).

Another individual with apparent macro-pk abilities for whom there is good documentation is Thomaz Green Morton Souza Coutinho, who at one time lived in Brazil. The following was a "trick" apparently demonstrated by Thomaz. A person would take a Brazilian 500-cruzeiro note and cut it into four equal pieces with a pair of scissors. She would place the pieces on top of one another, fold them over several times, and clench them in her fist. There would then be a pause. Then Thomaz would say "Ra!" and the person would open her fist to find that the 500-cruzeiro note had been seamlessly reconstituted, except that some of the pieces would be back to front and reversed from left to right (Pulos & Richman, 1990, p. 93).

In Chapter 3, we considered the notion of time and the ways in which time can change in altered states of consciousness. Assuming the reports are accurate, it seems as if Thomaz was ostensibly able to accelerate the occurrence of biological phenomena a number of times in the presence of observers. Perhaps the most interesting of these accelerations were four occasions on which infertile chicken eggs hatched into baby chicks within minutes in Thomaz's presence. The first of these four incidents took place in 1982 before a number of witnesses that included a psychiatrist, a physician, a judge, and the American journalist Gary Richman. There is a written account by Lee Pulos, a clinical psychologist, and Richman, along with a sequence of seven black-and-white photographs of the events that occurred (Pulos, 1995; Pulos & Richman, 1990).

A reader could react by thinking that these sound like magicians' tricks and that the psychiatrist, physician, judge, and journalist whose photographs we have were all duped. However, Gary Richman lived and travelled with Thomaz for over 8 months, interviewed 200 people, 90% of whom had witnessed these phenomena for themselves, and "scrutinized the surroundings for alternative causal mechanisms" (Pulos & Richman, 1990, p. xvi). No evidence for magician's tricks was found. It is also not clear how any magician could produce some of these phenomena under the conditions that were present during their occurrence. We need to be careful here not to make a

Type II error, whereby we dismiss data too readily. What would make more sense would be for qualified scientists to engage in a field study or to bring Thomaz into a lab to examine these phenomena for themselves.

Thomaz asked for 15 eggs to be purchased at the local market and brought to him. Once these had been placed on a table in front of him, he appeared to enter an altered state of consciousness, in which his eyes were "open but unfocused." One by one, he slowly held each of the eggs against his forehead before cracking them and spilling their contents into a flat bowl. He then hyperventilated with "puffed" chest and "taut and crimson" face, and stretched his arms with "palms down over the eggs." Within 5 minutes, the yolks solidified and darkened until the "fetal forms of baby chicks could be identified" (Pulos & Richman, 1990, p. 173). At 7 minutes, "the internal organs of the embryos could be seen through thin membranes." And at 9 minutes, the cheeping of baby chicks could be heard. Nine of the 15 eggs hatched, four survived longer than 3 days, and a couple of them, from this series of experiments, lived in the backyard until they were eaten for dinner (Pulos & Richman, 1990, p. 181). An effort to replicate this experiment in January of 1983 before an Australian film crew resulted only in the "development of well-discernible internal organs in the chickens' embryos" but no hatched chicks (Pulos, 1995, p. 5).

For some readers, it may be easier to imagine anomalous inorganic processes, such as the case of the "gold leaf lady," a woman for whom brass foil would appear within minutes on her skin in patches sometimes measuring 4 by 5 inches or more that sometimes left red marks on her skin when removed. In some cases, foil would have appeared on her skin in formal experiments after a physician had searched her body before she was videotaped. The brass could also appear on her clothing, on other objects around her, and in sealed containers. On laboratory analysis, it looked like ordinary commercial brass of about 80% copper and 20% zinc (Braude, 2007). It is difficult enough to understand how something of that sort could occur, let alone how live chicks can manifest from unfertilized eggs and run around within 14 minutes. How can entire bone structures, muscle groups, nervous systems, and so on, emerge from egg yolks so quickly in such a way as to support life? So we might have the tendency to automatically reach for the default triad of lying, cheating, and mental illness. But it is precisely because of the degree to which this example challenges our ways of thinking about reality that it could prove to be instructive.

Accelerated biological processes sometimes come up in the context of spontaneous remission from disease. Such remission sometimes occurs in the context of near-death experiences, such as that of Anita Moorjani (2012). Anita had lymphoma, a type of cancer. The disease progressed to the point where she needed to use an oxygen tank to be able to breathe, she could not lie down as she would drown in her own body fluids, she had skin lesions throughout her body, she could rarely sleep, her digestive system could not absorb nutrients so that her body consumed itself and she became a skeleton, her muscles disintegrated, and she could no longer walk. One morning her face, arms, legs, hands, and feet swelled up, and she went into a coma. A doctor told her husband that it was too late to save her.

Anita, however, felt fine. More than fine. She felt that she had awakened to a consciousness that extended across space and time so that she "encompassed—no, *became*—everything and everyone" (Moorjani, 2012, p. 64). "Although I try to share my near-death experience here, there are no words that can come close to describing its depth and the amount of knowledge that came flooding through" (Moorjani, 2012, p. 71). So she used the following metaphor. She asked us to imagine a dark warehouse in which we are wandering around with a single flashlight. Suddenly someone throws a switch and all sorts of lights, neon signs, and fireworks come on, illuminating the varied fascinating contents of the warehouse. She said that "even when the switch goes back off, nothing can take away your understanding and clarity, the wonder and beauty, or the fabulous aliveness of the experience" (Moorjani, 2012, p. 72).

Anita said that she also knew that if she chose to go back into her body, then she would heal within days. She said, "I understood that my body is only a reflection of my internal state. If my inner self were aware of its greatness and connection with All-that-is, my body would soon reflect that and heal rapidly" (Moorjani, 2012, p. 75). According to the medical records at the hospital in which Anita was treated, within several days there was a 70% reduction in the size of her tumors. Peter Ko, a physician investigating her case afterward was apparently curious how billions of cancer cells could leave her body so quickly, because the internal organs that would normally have to process those cells were failing (Moorjani, 2012).

In Moorjani's case, the macro-pk of disappearing cancer cells was not something that she deliberately manipulated with her mind. She just thought that her body would follow her subjective conviction that if she continued to live, she would be well. This is reminiscent of Padfield's report of merging with the mobile in the glass bottle and simply seeing its future state. From these cases, here we take the more general concluding idea that although it is not clear what the mechanism is for these types of mental influence, they may involve the activity of deep, nondual aspects of consciousness that we are only beginning to explore as a species. As we discuss in the next chapter, careful exploration of the subjective features of consciousness could be the key to making progress in understanding the nature of consciousness and its relationship with physical manifestation.

7

REINTEGRATING SUBJECTIVITY INTO CONSCIOUSNESS RESEARCH

Introspective observation is what we have to rely on first and foremost and always. *The word introspection need hardly be defined—it means, of course, the looking into our own minds and reporting what we there discover.*
—William James (1890/1981, p. 185; emphases in original)

In the early 1900s, John Watson wrote an influential essay, "Psychology as the Behaviorist Views It." He laid bare what would become the methods by which most research psychologists and some clinical psychologists did their work until the 1970s, although his influence extends to the present day. As psychology had struggled for acceptance among the ranks of the natural sciences, Watson's words did not fall on deaf ears. He asked psychologists to consider consciousness a private function that is used for thinking and perceiving but that is of no use in understanding the behavior of humans or other animals. Watson also expressed disgust at introspection as a method for understanding consciousness, stating:

> Human psychology has failed to make good its claim as a natural science. Due to a mistaken notion that its fields of facts are conscious phenomena and that introspection is the only direct method of ascertaining these facts, it has enmeshed itself in a series of speculative questions which,

http://dx.doi.org/10.1037/15957-008
Transcendent Mind: Rethinking the Science of Consciousness, by I. Baruss and J. Mossbridge

while fundamental to its present tenets, are not open to experimental treatment. (J. B. Watson, 1913, p. 176)

Watson was wrong that conscious phenomena are not open to experimental treatment using introspection. But it is the case that introspection can produce results rife with errors and thus can fail as a method for rigorously testing psychological hypotheses. Although there are ways to develop introspection so it can be used carefully and with some confidence, as we shall discuss next, Watson did not appeal to these methods. Not only did he not appeal to them, he actively encouraged scientists to ignore them. He asked psychologists to assume that it is reasonable to "dispense with consciousness in a psychological sense" (J. B. Watson, 1913, p. 176), arguing that this assumption would lead to viewing consciousness as simply a tool with which to do research.

> The separate observation of "states of consciousness" is, on this assumption, no more a part of the task of the psychologist than of the physicist. We might call this the return to a non-reflective and naive use of consciousness. In this sense consciousness may be said to be the instrument or tool with which all scientists work. Whether or not the tool is properly used at present by scientists is a problem for philosophy and not for psychology. (J. B. Watson, 1913, p. 176)

The point that consciousness is a tool used by all scientists is of course correct; no meaningful observations are possible without a conscious observer to assign meaning (e.g., Velmans, 2009). But it is logically untenable to propose that scientists should not bother themselves to determine whether a tool used by every researcher is used properly. Despite that glaring logical flaw in Watson's argument, this particular pronouncement may have come as a relief to psychologists. The careful use of the tool of consciousness to investigate any phenomenon and draw accurate conclusions requires insight, time, and training in understanding, neutralizing, and transforming one's own beliefs, biases, and flaws.

Research would be faster if we could skip the work of learning to clearly see and effectively transform flaws in our observation and thought processes. However, we cannot skip this step if we want our observations and insights to have any validity. Strangely, current research training in any science, including psychological research, leaves much to be desired in the area of training in critical thinking and effective first-person observation. Although the best undergraduate and graduate programs in scientific research do teach some critical thinking skills, these programs generally do not teach students how to examine and transform their own biases. In the current context, the most obvious result of this problem of unacknowledged bias is that we have scientists espousing materialist worldviews that are not reasonable if one takes into account the accumulating data from physics and psychology, as we discussed in Chapter 1.

In the present chapter, we argue that the difficult work of honing one's subjective observation skills must be done by every scientist, and especially by consciousness researchers. Then we describe some pathways to doing it. We discuss what we feel should be taught to every student within the science curriculum, early in her training: that when attempting scientific observation, it is not possible to ignore the development of first-person tools such as introspection. We explore how people have used controlled introspection and have combined first-person observational techniques with third-person observational techniques to investigate consciousness, and we describe methods that scientists and clinicians alike can carefully use for becoming skilled first-person observers of conscious awareness. Finally, we discuss some intuitions about consensus reality that have been obtained by individuals with practice in intuition and meditation.

FIRST-PERSON OBSERVATION AT THE CORE OF SCIENCE

Francis Bacon, who championed empiricism as the root of the scientific endeavor, struggled to advance the idea that data should be primary in our understanding of nature. He worked to defend this idea against the dogma of his day, which dictated that theory and syllogistic reasoning trumped observation. Even so, he was well aware of flaws in the human mind that can bias observation. "For the mind of man is far from the nature of a clear and equal glass, wherein the beams of things should reflect according to their true incidence, nay, it is rather like an enchanted glass, full of superstition and imposture, if it be not delivered and reduced" (Bacon, 1842, p. 211).

As Bacon pointed out, first-person accounts of any event—not just our own conscious experiences—are prone to major flaws. Investigators of consciousness have stated that "methodological behaviorists were, in a way, correct in their assertion but fell short in their criticism" (Pekala & Cardeña, 2000, p. 55). Both subjective observations themselves and the conclusions we draw from them are influenced by our beliefs, biases, emotions, and past experiences. For example, visual illusions can fool us into thinking we have observed something we have not (e.g., Hoffman, 1998), including complete fabrications of absurd proportions, as when several observers agreed that a photo of a bird in a forest actually depicted a tiny human hunter about four inches tall (Kornmeier & Mayer, 2014).

Despite these problems with empiricism, there is no getting around the notion that subjectivity is a necessary tool for empiricists. One of the foreparents of psychology, Wilhelm Wundt, pointed out that scientific observation necessarily depends on the experiences of scientists (Lyons, 1986). The natural sciences have generally adapted to this problem by creating the ideal that first-person observations should be followed with third-person confirmation in the form of independent replication of the original observations. Although a person can replicate an observation for herself multiple times, natural scientists would be more satisfied with at least one third-person observation of those multiple replications. Regardless of the fact that the ideal of third-person replication is not always followed, the assumption that it can fix the problem of observation is also flawed, as "even our observations of behavior, brain activity, and events in the world belong to a human perspective and are within at least someone's experience" (Price & Barrell, 2012, p. 2). Independent replication consists of recording another first-person observation that could be subject to the same flaws as the original observation, which would be consistent yet nonetheless potentially incorrect.

Independent replication corroborates observations, not inferences based on those observations. In the case of a visual illusion in which two people observe that two lines of the same length seem to be of different lengths, it is not the case that the two lines are, on mutual agreement, suddenly of different lengths. The inference of different-length lines is not replicated; instead, what is replicated is the illusion itself. Of course, both observations and inferences can be flawed. But the point of independent replication is to attempt to take into account the possibility that a single observation could have been in error. The confusion between replication of observations themselves and replication of inferences based on those observations is a mistake that has been, unfortunately, replicated consistently.

Let us take the example of the scientific understanding of human reproduction. For decades, accurate observations of eggs and sperm under the microscope were used to infer that the egg was entirely passive in the process of fertilization, even though no information obtainable through microscopic imaging could possibly show the chemical role of ova in reproduction. This inappropriate inference followed in a long history of biased assumptions supporting the idea that all reproductive power belonged to the male (Tuana, 1988). A tool (observation through a microscope) was being used to support an inference (female passivity) without the tool actually having the power to test the inference. The illogical inference could be replicated across scientists, using the pretense of observational replication, regardless of the inappropriate observational technique. Beyond the inappropriateness of the tool, the logical flaws here may have gone unquestioned because, at least partially, of an unexamined cultural agreement among male scientists about the nature of women (Tuana, 1988).

Neuroscientists Donald Price and James Barrell (2012) pointed out the problem of unexamined bias explicitly within the context of consciousness research:

> After all, we could be deluded, biased, or simply engaging in a belief system when we arrive at our conclusions. That a critical component of scientific verification relies on subjective dimensions such as certainty and positive regard for a conclusion is not easy to reconcile with a predominant focus of Western scientific practice that implicitly assumes that the conclusions of science exist in a disembodied viewpoint—a view from nowhere. (Price & Barrell, 2012, p. 2)

Price and Barrell argued that "even understanding the material world requires that we look inwardly into the nature of our experience" (p. 3). It should be clear by now that looking inwardly into our experiences and the role of our biases is critical to honing our imperfect subjective tool for observing the world. And yet it should also be clear by now that our intuitions about how things work, based on our subjective experiences, are often incorrect. How can we move forward?

What is needed is to acknowledge that careful observation is a learned skill, a skill that must be honed in a community of individuals who know that our experiences are valuable, if not always accurate. However, there are cultural forces within science and outside of it that seem to keep us from learning how to do just that. One of the authors of this book, Imants Barušs, has described in depth how the theories of Carl Rogers and Martin Heidegger explain the ways people learn to habitually ignore their own experiences, and how this ignorance influences the authentic practice of science (Barušs, 1996). We summarize the discussion briefly here.

There are developmental changes in our ways of valuing experiences across the lifespan. For instance, infants value any experience that assists their immediate need, and they reject any experience that does not. This form of valuing is clearly problematic, as it does not take into account information from anyone else about what might be good for the infant, and the infant does not know enough to evaluate what is necessary. Fortunately, as we grow we learn an adult way of valuing, in which we take into account the needs, desires, and opinions of others. However, what happens in this process, for many of us, is that we can become overly concerned with attending to "introjections" from our parents as well as our communities, who are invested in ensuring that we are compliant with cultural norms. As a result, many of us forget that there is validity in our own experiences, and some of us even deny our own primary experience. In this process, our individual observations of our perceptions and thoughts are either not recorded or not remembered, and we default to the experiences and observations of others (Barušs, 1996).

According to Rogers, commonly held "introjections" include the beneficial nature of obedience—particularly obedience without questioning—
and the accumulation of money, appliances, and facts. Having lost the
locus of valuing within ourselves, we become subjected to the norms of
the community around us. Rogers calls this state "adult valuing." It would
correspond approximately to the inauthentic mode of existence described
by Heidegger. (Barušs, 1996, p. 12)

This inauthentic relationship to one's actual experience is a profound problem for both scientists and clinicians because both of these professions require
practitioners to attend especially well to their own observations and inferences, even if they are different from those of others. The problem becomes
even more profound in a situation like the current one, in which the dogma
of scientism demands young scientists to conform their observations and
inferences to the norm of materialism. And it becomes even more profound
still when we consider the case of those of us who are explicitly setting out to
examine consciousness itself, because obtaining third-person verification of
first-person observations about consciousness requires that all investigators
be adequately trained to observe their own experiences, something that is
lacking among Western consciousness researchers (Desbordes & Negi, 2013;
Varela, 1996).

Fortunately, there is hope here. Once attention is drawn to one's own
relationship with one's subjective experience, it is possible to move beyond
immature "adult" valuing. This is a developmental necessity for scientists
and clinicians working with consciousness. We must move into a *mature way
of valuing* in which "one learns to trust again one's sensations, feelings, and
intuitions, which may contain more wisdom than one's rational faculties"
(Barušs, 1996, p. 12). Mature valuation parallels an infant's way of valuing,
with the critical addition of concepts, memories, experiences, and the willingness to consider the viewpoints of others as votes rather than vetoes over
one's own experience.

Toward the end of this chapter, we more thoroughly examine ways in
which we can train ourselves to improve the accuracy of our subjective observations as well as the inferences we derive from these observations. But first,
it is worth developing a deeper understanding of the pitfalls of first-person
observation as well as approaches that have been used to address these pitfalls.

SOME PROBLEMS WITH SUBJECTIVITY IN PSYCHOLOGY

The fundamental problem with subjectivity in science in general is
that it can never be objective—there is no "view from nowhere" available
(Price & Barrell, 2012), despite such an objective view being the ideal. Bias,

fantasies, desires for fame, cultural pressures, and many other factors shape how we see things. However, as we have already pointed out, subjectivity is the only tool we have with which to make observations, whether in psychological research, clinical psychology, or in the natural sciences in general. So, instead of attempting to ignore the reality that scientists and clinicians are human and therefore flawed in their perceptions, the way forward is to learn what flaws are likely and how to identify them so we may attenuate their effects as much as possible. Here we give an overview of the pitfalls of subjective reports, specifically reports of psi experiences that cannot be corroborated by others.

One problem with trusting subjective reports of psi experiences that do not have additional witnesses is that the reporter could be delusional. Considering the unusual nature of psi experiences, many people have reasonable concerns that those who experience them are exhibiting signs of mental illness. Fortunately, there are several benchmarks that can be used to differentiate psi experiences from psychopathology (Berenbaum, Kerns, & Raghavan, 2000).

First, the prevailing beliefs of the culture in which the reporter finds herself can make a big difference—hearing voices in one culture may be considered mainstream, whereas in another culture this same experience would be cause for worry. However, as we have discussed, prevailing beliefs are sometimes incorrect, especially when it comes to relatively rare occurrences. So, additional guidelines are essential. Second, if an experience is pleasurable and does not create functional difficulties for the experiencer, then it has been argued that the experience should not be considered pathological unless it leads to behavior that hurts others or one's self. For instance, a vision leading to a religious conversion is not necessarily considered pathological, but if it leads to becoming a serial murderer, this vision would be evaluated differently. Third, if the experience can be controlled by the experiencer, one might argue that it is less likely to be pathological than uncontrolled psi experiences. However, if the experience cannot be controlled, this does not mean it *is* pathological. Fourth, if the experience is fleeting and not continuously occurring, it should not be considered pathological. Mental illness is usually relatively stable over time, whereas near-death experiences, hearing voices from God only in church, and periodic out-of-body experiences are phenomena that occur during circumscribed times (Berenbaum, Kerns, & Raghavan, 2000).

Even if we assume that an observer is not mistaken about her experiences, we still have more mundane problems that get in the way of interpreting subjective reports of unusual experiences. Perhaps the most consistent observation about interpreting subjective reports is that people are much more accurate at reporting *what* they are experiencing than they are at discerning *why* they are experiencing it (Pekala & Cardeña, 2000; Price and Barrell, 2012). For instance, in a series of three experiments, researchers subliminally or unconsciously primed behavior in their participants that was contrary to desired behavior. The unconsciously primed behaviors included not completing an experiment that was posed as a favor to a classmate, or eating more chocolate than a particular preset limit. Subliminal and unconscious primes influenced the behaviors of the participants who received them compared with participants who did not. Participants who received the primes confabulated the reasons for their "bad" behavior, generally claiming that they had decided to act in a way that they had previously established was not their aim (Adriaanse, Weijers, De Ridder, De Witt Huberts, & Evers, 2014). Such results have been used to justify the claim that introspection is so flawed as to be useless (Nisbett & Wilson, 1977). But logic dictates that we only conclude from these results that introspection about our mental processes can sometimes be flawed, not that introspection is necessarily always flawed (Barušs, 2003a).

Such examples of unacknowledged subliminal and unconscious influences may appear to be isolated to the laboratory, but few if any of us are actually capable of knowing why one feeling, desire, or perception is experienced and another is not experienced. Thus, the first rule of interpreting first-person reports is to treat "why" explanations as speculation, focusing on the phenomenal contents themselves. This is one rule that scientists and clinicians in all fields might consider teaching to their students: Have greater trust in the observations themselves, less trust in explanations and attributions. In all cases, whether examining reports of psychological states or of the density of star clusters, it is essential to be aware that culture, confusion, expectations, illusions, a desire for status, or just plain ignorance of all the factors can lead to inaccurate explanations of events that are, in themselves, accurately reported.

Even if we limit ourselves to investigating our own observations of, and reports about, what has happened in our experience rather than explanations of why it has happened, we are limited by multiple factors that cannot be avoided but can usually be addressed. These factors include, but are not limited to, lack of independent verification, forgetting, and distortion (Pekala & Cardeña, 2000). We will look at each of these in turn.

First, there is the problem of the lack of independent verification for our private experiences. In this case, we are referring to the seeming impossibility of a personal experience being replicated by someone else. This problem is only the tip of the iceberg, but it is this concern that sent Watson and other behaviorists scurrying away from trying to understand consciousness. The idea is that every private observation requires independent verification because (a) not everyone is good at reporting exactly what they experience, and (b) different individuals have different experiences of the same types of private events, like particular mood states or sensations. However, it is important to keep in mind that both of these problems are inherent in all kinds of observations, not just observations of private experiences. For instance, the mood set by conversation at a party, the feeling of the beat of a complex musical rhythm, and even the color of a dress are all observations of public events and objects that have no absolutely correct and "objective" associated observations. Meanwhile, there are certain private events that produce remarkable agreement across individuals, as we will see in the section titled Psychophysics that follows. For instance, the time that it takes to imagine a cube of a given size rotating through a particular angle is highly predictable across individuals, even though this is an event that has no actual occurrence in the physical world (Shepard & Metzler, 1971).

A second concern with subjective reports is unintentional forgetting. Between the time an event is experienced and the time at which it is reported, details of the experience can fall away or become distorted (James, 1890/1981). In addition to temporal delays that occur between having an experience and reporting that experience, another reason why people may unintentionally forget an experience is if the experience occurred in a different state of consciousness than the state in which a report is attempted. Identifying such *state-specific memories* is useful for both clinical practice and empirical research. Charles Tart (1972) boldly described how science could be accelerated if we combined observations about a single phenomenon across multiple states of consciousness, though his innovative recipe for scientific progress has not been followed. In terms of how to handle such state-specific memories that are likely to weaken with a transition to other states of consciousness, the best solution is to ask people to record their experiences while they are still in, or close to, the state in which they had the original experience.

A third major problem that haunts subjective reporting of private experience is distortion: We report events or characteristics of events that do not accurately reflect the experience itself. It is worth noting that distortion can also occur in reports of publicly verifiable events like descriptions of a chemical explosion, the evolution of a supernova, or the weather patterns in Libertyville, Illinois. Distortion can be caused by perceptual errors that originate with the limitations and expectations of our sensory systems, or it can occur as a result of cognitive or emotional factors. For instance, when reporting any experience, people can feel social pressure to adhere to what is considered "normal" or "accurate" by an authority, or alternatively what is considered "interesting" to one's peers. This kind of bias, which may or may not enter conscious awareness, results in reports that are flawed in one of two ways. These reports either support mainstream schemata although the original events did not, or they unintentionally or intentionally include fabricated events that violate mainstream expectations when the actual original events were mundane.

FIRST-PERSON METHODS IN PSYCHOLOGY

Okay, first-person reports are necessary to make progress in consciousness research, so we have to address concerns about independent verification of subjective reports. We have two options. We can compare across people to determine a "majority wins" vote or a weighted average of the reports. Alternatively or in combination with this group method, we can compare reports to some third, correlating measure, like physiological activity or behavioral variables that have already been established as correlating with subjective experience. "The line of separation—between rigor and lack of it—is not to be drawn between first- and third-person accounts, but determined rather by whether there is a clear methodological ground leading to a communal validation and shared knowledge" (Varela, 1996, p. 340). Three fundamental methods have been rigorously used to glean some insight into the substrate and content of conscious awareness. These are phenomenology, psychophysics, and psychophysiology (Pekala & Cardeña, 2000; Price & Barrell, 2012).

PHENOMENOLOGY

Phenomenology refers to the study of consciousness from a first-person point of view (D. W. Smith, 2013). It is based on the idea that the best way to know what someone has experienced is to ask her. Because explanations of experience fall short in their accuracy, as we have already noted, most present-day phenomenological studies rely primarily on reports about the contents of consciousness as opposed to suppositions about the processes underlying these contents. Two slightly differing phenomenological methods that we will discuss here are the experiential method and the descriptive experience sampling method (Price & Barrell, 2012).

When the *experiential method* is used to examine emotional states, a group of participants are asked to observe and report on their experiences of particular emotions. Then these reports are collected and compared across participants to find commonalities that define a given emotion. For example, in an attempt to answer the question "What are the common factors of jealousy?" Barrell and Richards (1982) asked each participant to recall a situation that induced jealousy, then asked her to report on her experiences. Across participants, the following common elements of jealousy were recorded:

1. I perceive or imagine someone having an experience with an object, event or person that we both desire.
2. I expect it to be difficult or impossible for me to have this experience.
3. I don't feel that the other person deserves this experience.
4. I have a desire for the other person not to have the experience. (Price & Barrell, 2012, p. 295)

Thus, in the experiential method, participants are asked to report on an experience after they have had it, introducing the problem of forgetting and state-specific memories. To address these concerns, researchers compare these first-person reports across participants to get third-person confirmation. As a result, this methodology might more accurately be said to describe memories rather than experiences. Regardless, this is a powerful method that can be used to examine memories of almost any universal human experience.

The *descriptive experience sampling* method is used by researchers who have a different aim. They wish to understand individual differences in the contents of awareness during very brief, randomly determined moments. Participants in descriptive experience sampling studies are given a beeper that makes an alerting sound multiple times per day for each of 3 to 10 study days (Price & Barrell, 2012). Once they hear the beep, participants are to write down everything they are experiencing at that moment. So again, participants are reporting memories of experiences, except this time the experience is more proximal than in the experiential method. According to Heavey and Hurlburt (2008), participants improve in the clarity of their reports over the study days. Furthermore, an interviewer asks each participant to describe what she was experiencing during the beep, and the interviewer helps the participant learn how to avoid explanations and interpretations in her reporting.

One interesting result that has arisen from the descriptive experience sampling method is that there are clear individual differences in the everyday contents of consciousness. Although some participants report primarily visual experiences and almost no experiences of hearing inner speech, some participants have the directly opposing experience (Price & Barrell, 2012). Also, the method can be used to assess the recent experiences of individuals who suffer from mood and other psychological disorders. A study examining the sampled experiences of individuals who checked "yes" to the item "I am sad all the time" on a depression questionnaire found that these people were actually feeling sadness during less than half of the sampled experiences (Hurlburt & Heavey, 2001). These data suggest that when a depressed individual experiences always being sad, this feeling may be driven by other factors aside from her direct experience.

Both the experiential method and descriptive experience sampling could be powerful tools for discovering commonalities and individual differences in memories of experiences beyond those in everyday waking consciousness. This avenue for future research remains open for exploration.

PSYCHOPHYSICS

Psychophysics, the study of the relationship between precisely controlled stimuli and prearranged behavioral responses to those stimuli, is derived from a behaviorist assumption that the mind can be treated as a black box. The idea that originally motivated psychophysics is that the secrets of sensation and perception can be discovered by carefully controlling sensory inputs and quantitatively analyzing behavioral outputs, then extrapolating how the mind perceives the world. On the basis of this model, which is similar to control systems engineering, psychophysics survived the behaviorist period and has developed into a method that offers the most replicable results in all of psychology (Price & Barrell, 2012). For instance, the equation for the curve that relates sound intensity to an individual's ability to detect a sound is remarkably stable across individuals who are not hearing impaired (Moore, 2012).

What is fascinating about psychophysics in the context of its history is that despite its machine-based inspiration, it is essentially careful phenomenology that is focused on sensation and perception. The responses corresponding to the stimuli necessarily involve the participant making meaningful observations of the stimuli. Making sense of the behavioral output requires the assumption that the participant has a mind that understands requests such as "turn this knob until those two bars appear to have the same length" or "press the button to indicate the sound that seems higher in pitch." It is as if experimental psychologists went into stealth mode during the behaviorist era by resorting to the most machine-like description of subjective human experience possible, then continued to explore human experience using this cover story (Price & Barrell, 2012; Velmans, 2009).

The behaviorist history of psychophysics does not make it any less useful in the understanding of consciousness. In terms of the sensory and perceptual aspects of consciousness, psychophysical methods have given us powerful insights into subjective experience. To take three examples, subjective scaling of painful experiences is remarkably consistent across people (Bellamy, Buchanan, Goldsmith, Campbell, & Stitt, 1988), setting up an expectation for a particular type of stimulus makes people less likely to perceive unexpected stimuli (Dai & Wright, 1995; Wright & Dai, 1998), and temporal experience is simultaneously punctate and integrated across moments (Viemeister & Wakefield, 1991). In addition, psychophysical methods have led to insights that have had far-reaching influences on fields other than experimental psychology, such as the introduction of *signal-detection theory* (Green & Swets, 1966), an analysis method that has been used across multiple domains to model the difference between observations of signals versus noise—all of this, from careful phenomenology dressed up in the guise of mechanistic psychology.

The principles of psychophysics have been used sparingly to examine the characteristics of psi. For example, in their meta-analysis of precognition experiments, Honorton and Ferrari (1989) showed that forced-choice precognition is progressively more accurate as the delay between a guess and feedback for that guess is shortened. This result is conceptually similar but in the opposite direction of a classical psychophysics result showing that the ability to detect a stimulus is improved as the delay between the stimulus and a subsequent masking stimulus is increased (Moore, 2012).

Let us look at another example of the use of psychophysics principles to understand psi. David Vernon (2015) conducted an experiment in which he probed the properties of precognitive abilities to determine whether repetition of a stimulus in upcoming trials would influence behavioral responses to that stimulus on a given trial. We already know that when a stimulus has been presented multiple times to a percipient, future responses to that stimulus speed up and become more accurate, suggesting that the mind becomes more efficient at processing that stimulus, an effect known as *repetition priming* (e.g., Scarborough, Cortese, & Scarborough, 1977). After replicating this effect in the temporally forward direction, Vernon partially replicated the effect in the reverse direction: Stimuli that would be presented multiple times in the future, after a trial, showed more accurate, but not faster, responses than stimuli that would not be presented multiple times in the future, after a trial. Further, the precognitive effect of future presentations was not apparent when a given stimulus would only be presented once more, whereas the forward-time effect of standard repetition priming was still apparent when even only one previous trial had been presented prior to a given stimulus. Because Vernon carefully controlled the number of times each stimulus was presented, we can extrapolate from these results that repetition priming from future events may be weaker than, but follow a similar pattern as, standard prior-event repetition priming. So the application of psychophysical techniques can provide insight into the mechanisms underlying psi. Such an approach is powerful, but it is also in its infancy.

PSYCHOPHYSIOLOGY

Psychophysiology is the study of how physiological measures are related to subjective experiences, to shed light on the mechanisms associated with those experiences. In the context of controversial and private subjective experiences, psychophysiological methods also provide a form of third-person confirmation of first-person experience. For example, as we saw in Chapter 3, some people have had conscious feelings of foreboding or excitement about a seemingly unpredictable event that occurs in the imminent future. Scientists working from a conventional perspective only began taking these experiences somewhat seriously after psychophysiology experiments demonstrated that certain physiological measures such as sweating, heart rhythms, and respiration correlated with these seemingly unpredictable events (e.g., Mossbridge, Tressoldi, & Utts, 2012).

Psychophysiological methods are useful, but this utility does not have any bearing on the question of whether physiology creates our conscious experience. It instead indicates that we can sometimes find close and enlightening correlations between physiology and experience, and those correlations may help us understand mind–body relationships. To that point, Francisco Varela (1996) introduced the idea of *neurophenomenology*—the field of psychophysiology that specifically examines neurophysiological data recorded while trained observers keep track of their phenomenal experiences.

Making no assumptions about the direction of any potentially causal relationship between mental experience and neurophysiology, we can still examine what is commonly a close relationship between mind and brain. For instance, experiments using Tibetan Buddhist meditators monitored with scalp electrodes have shown that these meditators with many years of intensive training seem to have greater brainwave activity than control participants specifically in a frequency range around 40 Hz, and that this change occurs with the reported onset of meditation (Lutz, Slagter, Dunne, & Davidson, 2008). This so-called gamma frequency range at around 40 Hz has been associated with conscious awareness of sensory information (Engel & Singer, 2001). So here we have a case in which the neurophenomenological approach is pushing both consciousness research and neuroscience in general to examine why and how oscillations in brain activity are related to awareness.

TOWARD AN INTEGRATED FIRST- AND THIRD-PERSON APPROACH

There are so many voices calling for a combined first- and third-person research approach in psychology in general and consciousness research in particular that it is difficult to catalogue them all. In *Science as a Spiritual Practice*, Imants Baruš (2007b) made the point that to make progress in science, one makes observations and continually tests them against both one's continued experience with the subject matter as well as the experiences of others who are undergoing a similar pursuit using similar means. He pointed out that this is the same approach used in authentic mysticism. In both science and mystical pursuits, dogma can prevail, so there is a necessity to return to the empirical roots of these traditions to understand the similarities of the underlying methods.

> This implies a return to empiricism: taking the *methods* for making penetrating observations of all kinds of natural phenomenon to be of the highest value, instead of assuming that the materialist *ideology* in its present formulation already provides a key to unlocking all the remaining mysteries of nature. (Wallace, 2007, pp. 41–42; emphases in original)

Alan Wallace (2007) spoke of building "contemplative observatories"—he hoped to develop scientists who are trained to investigate inner space just as astronomers know how to investigate outer space. Or, as described by Charles Tart (1998),

> You share your observations, theories, and predictions so that colleagues can test and extend them. You as an individual may have blind spots and prejudices, but it is unlikely *all* your colleagues have the same ones; so that a gradual process of refinement, correction, and expansion takes place and scientific knowledge progresses. While this process is genuine science, it is also a quite sensible way of proceeding in most areas of life. (p. 75; emphasis in original)

Of course, as we will point out again, observations of one's own experiences are not the only ones prone to error. All observations are in some sense subjective in that they require an observer, but some observations can be made pseudo-objective by obtaining intersubjective agreement (Velmans, 2009) or by correlating reports of subjective experience with physiological measures (Varela, 1996). This is the aim of first–third person integrated consciousness research: to carefully combine trained first-person observations with additional measures to better answer our basic questions about how consciousness works (Price & Barrell, 2012; Varela, 1996). The only addition to the standard scientific method here is the necessary and long-overdue acknowledgment that most researchers and clinicians have biases that can influence our observations and inferences, and that we must train ourselves to address these. Of course, this turns out to be a big addition.

DEVELOPING FIRST-PERSON OBSERVATION SKILLS

All is not lost. Applying critical thinking skills to our observations and inferences as we practice introspection can eventually facilitate awareness of at least some biases, whereas exposure to conflicting viewpoints and taking the perspective of others can help reduce at least the biases that manifest consciously (Beaman, Chattopadhyay, Duflo, Pande, & Topalova, 2008; Czopp, Monteith, & Mark, 2006; Pronin & Schmidt, 2013). In contrast, nonconscious bias is difficult to detect, by definition. Even those with excellent self-examination abilities cannot directly examine what is not conscious. One bias particularly relevant here is *ideological bias,* or the assumption that one's own views are the result of critical thinking but the views of others are based on ideology (Pronin & Schmidt, 2013). Both authors of this book have identified and neutralized their own ideological biases as much as they can, so as to be able to approach the subject matter of consciousness in as neutral a manner as possible.

Hidden or nonconscious bias can be examined using *implicit attitude measures,* which show that, for instance, participants are generally faster at responding to Black faces paired with negative words than to White faces paired with negative words, even when responses on explicit racism questionnaires indicate that these same participants strongly disagree with statements of overt racism (W. A. Cunningham, Preacher, & Banaji, 2001). Such implicit bias can actually be reduced using both exposure techniques and sleep training, a type of training in which sounds that are first played simultaneously with the material to be learned are then played again during slow-wave sleep (Hu et al., 2015). Bias scores, as measured by response times on an implicit attitude measure, were reduced after participants looked through slides showing photographs of members of stereotyped groups along with words that did not match the stereotype (e.g., a photo of a woman with the word *math*). Implicit bias scores were reduced further after sounds that had been associated with these slides had been delivered to participants during slow-wave sleep. So reinforcement of counterbias memories in an altered state of consciousness appears to reduce nonconscious bias. Such an approach might be useful for consciousness researchers who wish to reduce implicit biases toward theories or explanations that conflict with cherished hypotheses or emotional states.

But not all biases lead to scientific disaster, as long as they are discovered in time. In *The End of Materialism,* Charles Tart (2009) described how he thought a nonconscious bias against precognition ironically allowed him to uncover data in support of precognition. He was confronted with the reality of this bias while examining data from one of his telepathy experiments. In this experiment, a "sender" sat in front of an array of 10 lights. A random-number generator would determine which of the 10 lights would be lit next, and once that light was illuminated, the sender attempted to communicate the appropriate target light to a "receiver" who indicated on a similarly arranged panel of 10 switches which light she thought had been lit. The data supported Tart's hypothesis in that the suggested telepathy had occurred. Tart could have stopped there, but he recognized that other researchers had analyzed telepathy trials for precognitive telepathy by comparing the correct response for each trial (e.g., Trial 2) with the response given on the previous trial (e.g., Trial 1). He analyzed the data in this way to look for precognitive telepathy, even though he assumed he was just being thorough. To his surprise, he found a statistically significant effect.

Tart (2009) reflected that finding this precognitive effect is what made him aware of his bias against precognition, a bias that surprised him because he thought he believed the existing precognition data from other laboratories. "My bias is that at some deep level, I find the idea of precognition . . . so incomprehensible that I just never think about precognition in a serious way" (Tart, 2009, p. 136). He suspected that the reason he was able to do the analysis that led to seeing the evidence for precognitive telepathy in his data was because he found precognition so absurd that it did not threaten him. "In a sense I hadn't 'rejected' or 'defended against' the idea of precognition; the very idea was so nonsensical to me at a deep level that I hadn't needed to actively reject or defend against it" (Tart, 2009, pp. 136–137).

But Tart has recognized this bias in time. If he had not, he could have easily dismissed his newfound evidence for precognitive telepathy a bit later, when he discovered that what he had assumed was a random series of light patterns instead was not in fact random. It turned out that the particular sequence of lights he used could have been responsible for what seemed to be a precognitive telepathy effect, because after a particular light was lit, it was not likely to be lit again. This was a flaw in the randomization, and it happened to match a tendency in the participants to not choose the same light twice.

It would have been easy for Tart to assume that the precognitive telepathy results were due to the correspondence between the nonrandom sequence and the participants' responses. However, Tart thought critically about the situation, realizing that if the errant randomization had been to blame, then he could simulate the randomization error and calculate whether the results could be explained fully by it. He found that the patterns created by the randomization error and the participants' responses could explain some, but nowhere near all, of the precognitive telepathy effect. So, even if Tart is correct in assuming that the depth of his bias is what allowed him to do the analysis in the first place, the data were eventually correctly interpreted only because Tart carefully observed his own subjective state and used critical thinking to counter his own bias!

Introspection is a critical path toward identifying our biases, and introspection is one of the processes that occurs during some forms of meditation. For many Western scientists and clinicians, the benefit of meditation has been taken seriously as a research topic only in the past 2 decades. The shift in attitude toward taking meditation seriously as a path to gaining insight is probably due to research reports offering third-person data confirming the first-person insights of practiced meditators. For instance, meditators have reported that their experience during meditation represents a state of consciousness somewhere between wakefulness and sleep, and subsequent studies have indicated that brain activity during transcendental meditation indeed shares traits of both alert wakefulness and sleepiness (Cahn & Polich, 2006). Similarly, a type of meditation in which practitioners experience thoughtlessness, or *emptiness*, turns out to be correlated with lower brain activity overall (Hinterberger, Schmidt, Kamei, & Walach, 2014). Also, a type of nondual meditation in which practitioners report an integration of thoughts between those that normally segregate self from others also reveals a reduction in the separation of brain regions associated with those categories (Josipovic, 2014). Long-term meditators in some traditions report better attentional focus and more accurate perception, which has been supported by empirical data across multiple studies (Elliott, Wallace, & Giesbrecht 2014; Zanesco, King, MacLean, & Saron, 2013; for a review, see Lutz, Slagter, Dunne, & Davidson, 2008). On the basis of these data, it appears that empirical evidence already points toward how to hone our first-person observation skills. "Contemplative practices have been known for centuries. Western skeptics may attribute such practices to supernatural beliefs, but a better analogy may be to music training, where generations of adepts pass on a high-level skill" (Baars, 2013, p. 3). Before we discuss pathways to such training, we point out that self-examination is not without its risks. Such practices can, for some, lead to difficulties that may require professional clinical assistance.

How do we begin? Francisco Varela (1996) outlined one approach that Western consciousness researchers can use to begin to open up their phenomenal experience to careful investigation. According to Varela, the first step is to doubt one's own experience. One can doubt any stories that one has about what is happening both inside and outside of oneself, and one can practice reflexively turning each thought around to its source. Instead of focusing on the objects *in* the train of thought, one can focus on *the train itself*. What is it? Where did it come from? Where is it going? The second step occurs over time, as a result of practicing the first step. It is to attain intimacy with the experience of what is happening right now. Varela stated that making a habit of examining the contents of the present moment leads to intuitions and insights about what is actually present. Varela's third step is to learn to accurately describe what is experienced and to share this with colleagues. His fourth and final step is to attain stability in one's subjective observations by training oneself in disciplines that deepen one's attention as well as one's intuitions.

Some of us may already be well on our way through the steps outlined by Varela or through a similar process that demands careful self-examination combined with conferring with colleagues. For instance, anyone who has been in psychoanalysis is likely much better trained in monitoring her internal state than anyone who has not, and perhaps this is even more the case for psychoanalysts, who are required to go through psychoanalysis as part of their training. However, a major difference between psychoanalysis and meditation is that psychoanalysis has been geared toward insight, whereas meditation has highlighted awareness (Hoffer, 2015). In this context, *insight* is about understanding the mechanisms underlying experiences, whereas *awareness* is about clarity of experience on a moment-to-moment basis, without explanation.

As for scientists, it is worth considering that some of us may have been drawn toward research because we seek a so-called objectivity that allows us to explain and systemize the world, while we simultaneously avoid trying to understand our own subjective experiences or those of others. For instance, one research team found that a tendency to be drawn toward systemizing versus empathizing predicted which individuals entered careers in the physical sciences versus the humanities (Billington, Baron-Cohen, & Wheelwright, 2007). However, other scientists are periodically able to do their work in a state of mature valuing (Baruss, 1996). When in a state of mature valuing, as we do our work and test our "hunches," we may in fact also have access to extended capacities, beyond the systemizing mind.

> Is concentrative meditation so different from what a scholar or scientist does in order to solve a problem? She focuses her thoughts on the object of interest, brings to bear all pertinent information, and confines her thoughts to those which are relevant in order to understand the problem more deeply. Is it also possible that she exhausts the resources of the discursive mind and draws on a latent faculty? (Baruss, 1996, p. 68)

No matter whether we are in a state of valuing our subjective observations or not, the validity of our observations themselves can be improved by self-examination practices. Beyond benefits for physical health and longevity (Bond et al., 2007; Schutte & Malouff, 2014), some forms of meditation improve basic observational skills. For instance, *focused awareness* meditation improves attention and reduces habitual responding to stimuli, allowing practitioners to make more accurate observations and react to them with greater purpose (Lutz, Slagter, Dunne, & Davidson, 2008). Focused awareness meditation is a broad category, covering any meditative practice that requires one to continually return to a single object of focus.

> A widespread style of Buddhist practice consists in sustaining selective attention moment by moment on a chosen object, such as a subset of localized sensations caused by respiration. To sustain this focus, the meditator must also constantly monitor the quality of attention. At

first, the attention wanders away from the chosen object, and the typical instruction is to recognize the wandering and then restore attention to the chosen object. For example, while intending to focus on localized sensations around the nostril caused by breathing, one may notice that the focus has shifted to the pain in one's knee. One then "releases" this distraction, and returns to the intended object. (Lutz, Slagter, Dunne, & Davidson, 2008, p. 164)

Once practitioners are proficient in focused awareness meditation, an important next step for consciousness researchers could be to make the object of focus not an object at all, but instead the moment-by-moment experience of one's own conscious awareness (Lutz, Slagter, Dunne, & Davidson, 2008). Such *open monitoring* meditation is similar to Varela's (1996) second step. It allows practitioners to have a reflexive inner experience of the source of conscious experience.

An established practice of open monitoring meditation or similar training could be a useful requirement for participants in experiments using phenomenological methods. After all, such a continuous practice may train individuals to better observe their internal states. But unfortunately, experts in reflexive awareness disciplines like open monitoring have only been included in a few phenomenological studies (Desbordes & Negi, 2013). One way to address this problem is by incorporating meditation training into the training sequence for all consciousness researchers. Such a training requirement would help us learn how to identify appropriate participants for phenomenological studies. And it could allow us to use ourselves as participants in these studies. In fact, some graduate programs are already offering students training in meditation, and the mission of at least one major effort, the Mind and Life Institute, sponsored by the fourteenth Dalai Lama, includes introducing neuroscientists to meditation (Desbordes & Negi, 2013).

SELF-DEVELOPMENT FOR CONSCIOUSNESS RESEARCHERS

Self-examination, when taken seriously, can have life-changing results. And there is potential for both positive and negative changes. We have alluded to the fact that using self-examination to hone one's critical subjectivity is not without psychological risks. Navigating those risks can be difficult, especially in some types of self-examination during which defects of character may be laid bare in front of an increasingly accurate witness who now has fewer resources to defend herself.

Before starting a self-examination practice, it may be useful to get a sense of where one is on the hierarchy of needs (Maslow, 1969). Does one have a sense that one is self-actualized, in that one is at peace with one's identity and one's emotions, and one wants to move beyond these concerns? Some would suggest that this is the only stage at which a practice like meditation should be introduced (Epstein, 1990). This idea is based on the rationale that the human desire for self-transcendence is usually preceded by a need for self-actualization (Maslow, 1969).

Suzanne Segal (1996), a lifelong transcendental meditator, was pregnant and living in a part of the world that was foreign to her. So she was already facing the identity-annihilating experience of hosting another person in her body while she was in a place where she had to learn to speak and understand the language. One day, as she stepped onto a city bus, she was stunned to suddenly lose her experience of having a self.

> I lifted my right foot to step up into the bus and collided head-on with an invisible force that entered my awareness like a silently exploding stick of dynamite, blowing the door of my usual consciousness open and off its hinges, splitting me in two. In the gaping space that appeared, what I had previously called "me" was forcefully pushed out of its usual location inside me into a new location. (Segal, 1996, p. 49)

This experience gave rise to a terror that continued for years afterward, during which she was told by multiple experts that she was in a pathological state (Segal, 1996), which of course may have been correct. Perhaps Segal would not have felt so terrified by this extreme self-transcendent experience if she had been surrounded by individuals who understood what had happened to her. Over time, she realized that she was, in a sense, using the wrong third-person observers with whom to compare her first-person experiences. She was using third-person observers who were not trained in the same way she was. She was making essentially the same mistake as a chemist who checks with an archeologist about the veracity of her results. When she switched her choice of colleagues to contemplative adepts who were compassionate and knowledgeable about her state, her terror was reduced as she recognized that her selfless state was not necessarily pathological.

> The notion of "cure" involves trying to eliminate, stop, or change something that you, or more importantly your therapist, cannot accept as appropriate. But there was obviously no way the experience of individual identity was going to return, and it was now appallingly clear that the field of psychology hadn't the slightest clue about what was going on. (Segal, 1996, p. 104)

As Mark Epstein (1990) pointed out, if absolute peace with oneself is required before launching a meditation practice, meditation is of little usefulness because of the small number of potential practitioners. A more approachable goal is to carefully undertake a new self-examination practice among a community of compassionate individuals who are adept in that practice, just as new graduate students become apprentices to individuals who know something more about what happens in the course of clinical training and scientific research.

ACCURATE INTUITIONS ABOUT EVENTS IN CONSENSUS REALITY

Integrated first- and third-person research approaches using skilled contemplatives are of obvious use in consciousness research. Also, similar approaches can be used in other fields of research to obtain information about events in consensus reality that are not accessible to most of us in everyday waking consciousness. For instance, in 1980–1981, a group of six prescreened skilled intuitives were independently interviewed to gain their intuitive answers to questions about the disease processes underlying bipolar disorder (Grof & Kautz, 2010). Using a first–third person integrated approach, the researchers asked each of these participants to answer the same set of questions and reported answers that were common to more than one respondent. None of the six intuitives had been involved in psychiatry or medicine, so they did not answer these questions on the basis of their intellectual knowledge. Intriguingly, some of their answers were similar to what we know now about the disease. For instance, multiple intuitives suggested the involvement of thyroid hormones, which were later found to be implicated in certain subtypes of the disease. The intuitives also identified chromosomes 6 and 13, which later became known to be involved in some types of bipolar disorder (Grof & Kautz, 2010). However, one problem with reports such as these is that full documentation of the contents of the interviews is lacking. We do not know how many responses completely missed their marks without being reported.

What if we were to ask individuals with good intuition to work together to come to their conclusions, rather than simply combining insights after responses are recorded? The Intelligence Advanced Research Projects Activity (IARPA) in the United States has an interest in finding practical ways to improve intuition. They sponsored a large project in which they asked individuals, who had been selected online, to participate in "forecasting tournaments" in which they competed by using their abilities to predict answers to questions about world events, such as "Will Turkey ratify a new constitution by February 1, 2014," or "Will the official Euro to U.S. Dollar exchange rate exceed 1.40 before December 31, 2014?" (Mellers et al., 2015, p. 276). These are questions that could potentially be answered by educated guesses, and indeed that is what the authors assumed was going on. We point this out because once the possibility of precognition has been established (see Chapter 3, this volume), any task in which participants attempt to guess the future could be at least partially accomplished by using precognition. What we are interested in examining here are the characteristics of the top performers, because the top performers in these tournaments were asked to join communities specific to this task. They formed elite teams of "superforecasters." Every superforecaster was told that she was working with other superforecasters, and superforecasters in these groups posted their ideas and questions about each world event question online, participating in discussion forums and learning about the intuitions of their teammates. Working in these groups seemed to greatly increase the ability of the superforecasters to make correct predictions, as they improved much more over 2 years in the accuracy of their predictions than other forecasters who did not work in elite groups.

The researchers were surprised by the results of this study because even though all forecasters were specifically trained in cognitive prediction and antibiasing techniques, superforecasters exceeded expectations and also performed better than other groups (Mellers et al., 2015). The researchers found that superforecasters attempted to answer 40% more forecasting questions than regular forecasters did and followed more links to relevant news stories than other forecasters. Superforecasters also altered their opinions in an online record of their thought processes more often than other forecasters. Although superforecasters had higher IQ scores than other forecasters, it turned out that the frequency of updating one's beliefs was the best possible predictor of accuracy, and such updating commonly occurred as a result of interactions with other superforecasters. All of this suggests that superforecasters were those who may have begun with greater intelligence but who became superforecasters as a result of practice, willingness to interact with and consider the insights of their community, and a close relationship to their own experience as it evolved over time. We do not know about the beliefs of these superforecasters, but in separate research it was found that individuals with extraordinarily transcendent beliefs, such as the belief that altered states of consciousness are highly significant (see Chapter 1, this volume), are more likely to value the process of internal self-development (Lukey & Baruš, 2005).

As we noted previously, the IARPA-funded study did not differentiate between educated guesses and precognition. That is, teams of superforecasters may draw from information available in the present, using cognitive and intuitive skills, as well as in the future, using precognition. But one study of the prediction skills of 18 meditators has shown that contemplatives may have precognitive access to information about events in the future that cannot be predicted by information available in the present (Roney-Dougal, Solfvin, & Fox, 2008). The meditation styles of the participants included several forms, but 11 of them were contemplatives in related Tibetan Buddhist lineages. Specifically, the participants were shown four pictures, one at a time, and asked to rank each of the four pictures as to the likelihood that they felt it would be shown to them again, in the future. After all four pictures were shown, one of them was randomly selected and shown again. The results revealed a strong positive correlation between participants' years of meditation training and their ability to predict the upcoming image. The effect was strongest for Tibetan monks, suggesting that some forms of meditation may indeed result in the ability to obtain information about future events in consensus reality.

Why should this be the case? Given what we already discussed about some forms of meditation and their positive influences on perception and attention, it seems reasonable to suppose that some types of meditation may allow adepts, over time, to more accurately access consensus reality. In Chapter 3, we described how physicists seem to be unclear about whether time really exists and that certain well-tested physical theories, like Einstein's theory of special relativity, support the idea that all events exist simultaneously. So, it is possible that the ability of some contemplatives to precognitively access future events could be another reflection of the positive influence contemplative self-examination practices have on our ability to experience the world as it is, including the contemporaneous existence of the past, present, *and* future.

If at least some forms of meditation training can allow us to more accurately perceive consensus reality, this suggests that each of us, nonmeditators and meditators alike, has some potential ability to perceive and act on information that is not available to our conscious waking awareness. We know that the nonconscious mind perceives and acts on information all the time (e.g., Hassin, 2013). However, we are used to thinking of the nonconscious mind as being aware of subliminal information that nonetheless exists in the present moment. Is there also a part of our mind that is aware of the kind of information that is unavailable to most of us in the present moment? Is there a part of our mind that we can learn to access to discover answers to questions that are not known by anyone in the present moment, so as to make better decisions about our lives? If so, perhaps this part is what we can learn to hear as we quiet our mental chatter.

The Italian psychiatrist Roberto Assagioli (1965) called the part of our psyche that wisely informs our actions toward the best outcome in the future the *superconscious*. He saw it as the source of intuition and our connection with spirituality. For Assagioli, one crucial part of the process of psychological development could be construed as a series of steps toward synthesizing multiple aspects of the psyche, including the subconscious, the immediate "field" of conscious awareness, the personal "I", the superconscious, and the transcendent Self.

Importantly for our purposes, Assagioli voiced concern about the idea that the personal "I" or ego should be obliterated completely. "As I said before, 'we can benefit from and utilize every function and element of our psyche, provided we understand its nature and purpose, and place in it its right relation with the greater whole'" (Assagioli & Vargui, 1976, p. 1). Only in integrating these parts of ourselves can we understand reality, including our own consciousness (Assagioli, 2007).

This idea of syntheses is echoed by Evan Thompson's (2015) more recent writings about consciousness, in which he warned that self-development does not consist of ignoring or eliminating the self: "Rather, it consists in wisdom that includes not being taken in by the appearance of the self as having independent existence while that appearance is nonetheless still there and performing its important I-making function" (p. 366). According to Assagioli and Thompson, then, as we become more integrated we see ourselves as we are, rather than by totally identifying with or completely rejecting portions of ourselves. This is not unlike seeing consensus reality for what it is, rather than identifying with or rejecting portions of it.

So, at least some people can develop their ability to obtain correct intuitions about events that are not currently verifiable. What if we were to combine these intuitions using an integrated first- and third-person research approach? Is it possible we could begin to realize Charles Tart's vision, in which the same natural phenomenon could be glimpsed from multiple states of consciousness? Such an effort could potentially create a more accurate, fuller description of the natural world (Tart, 1972). This vision would impact not only consciousness research but also the progress of the world in general. For instance, Price and Barrell (2012) stated that if we could come to a third-person consensus on first-person accounts of the experience of unconditional love, we might be able to learn exactly what it takes to train ourselves to see others with compassion. They quoted the fourteenth Dalai Lama, who echoed the extraordinarily transcendent position (Baruss, 1990) when he said,

> You spend a large amount of the best human brain power looking outside—too much—and it seems you do not spend adequate effort looking within. Perhaps now that the western sciences have reached down into the atom and out into the cosmos finally to realize the extreme vulnerability of all life and value, it is becoming credible, even obvious, that the inner science is of supreme importance. (fourteenth Dalai Lama, as cited in Price & Barrell, 2012, p. 269)

8

TRANSCENDENT MIND

Science makes people reach selflessly for truth and objectivity; it teaches people to accept reality, with wonder and admiration, not to mention the deep awe and joy that the natural order of things brings to the true scientist.

—Lise Meitner (as cited in Bynum & Porter, 2005, p. 431)

Many of the chapters of this book contain material that is easiest to explain if we assume that consciousness is capable of existing in an extended or transcendent state in which it is not completely bound to the brain. When we triangulate the constellation of this material, the presence of mind beyond the brain comes into sharper focus. Is there a theory that allows us to fit together the different pieces that we have found? Clearly there is no point in entertaining materialist theories, so we will not do that here, but work from a postmaterialist perspective. Whatever theory we do come up with must be grounded in the empirical data that we have reviewed in the previous chapters.

In our search for a theory, let us start with an obvious choice, namely, that of *quantum mind*, the area of investigation of the interface between quantum theory and consciousness. Then we will move on to look at filter theories, after which we will examine the idea that consciousness could create the brain and matter in general. We will propose a flicker-filter model that will have

http://dx.doi.org/10.1037/15957-009
Transcendent Mind: Rethinking the Science of Consciousness, by I. Baruss and J. Mossbridge

to do for now. Finally, we will look at some implications of this material for research methods, clinical applications, and scientific progress.

QUANTUM MIND

Is quantum theory useful for trying to understand a greater mind beyond the brain? We think the answer is "not very," but it has prompted the development of postquantum theories of which the flicker-filter model, that we describe below, can be considered to be an example. This is not easy territory (Barušs, 2006, 2008b, 2008c, 2009, 2010; Tarlaci, 2010). Rather than trying to cover it exhaustively, we will just make a few comments.

Perhaps the first thing to note is that *quantum theory*, as we use that expression here, refers not a single theory but to a collection of theories describing the nature of subatomic phenomena. Each of the theories in that collection has problems. For instance, the fundamental equation of quantum mechanics is incompatible with the requirement from relativity theory that time and space be treated in the same manner. More recent quantum field theories, which fix that problem and provide greater accuracy of prediction for the outcomes of experiments, have been criticized for the cavalier manner in which infinite values are handled. And gravity is difficult to reconcile with either of them. In any case, they need to be patched up anyway, as we shall see in a bit. So the phrase quantum theory stands for a complex constellation of interrelated formalisms, each of which has its own problems (cf. Polkinghorne, 2002; Smolin, 2006; Zee, 2007).

The second thing to note is the obvious fact that quantum theories are mathematical in nature. It is not clear whether the mathematics describes anything that is objectively real or not (Ringbauer et al., 2015). What this means is that it is not clear that the terms of the mathematical formalism refer to anything objective "out there" in reality. Aside from the values of observables, do the mathematical constructions actually correspond to anything in the "real" world? Unlikely. This becomes clear when we consider that there are different mathematical formalisms that can be used for describing the same subatomic processes (Barušs, 2010; Coecke & Pavlovic, 2009).

But to even get to where we can consider ontological questions, such theories require a sufficient level of mathematical knowledge to be able to read them. And they usually come with their own notation, which further conceals the meaning of the mathematical formalisms for those who are unfamiliar with them. So there is a certain level of appropriate mathematical expertise that is required to understand these theories. We could try to discuss quantum theories without knowing the mathematical formalisms, keeping in mind that the mathematics might not correspond to anything in reality anyway. Again, that is problematical, as mistaken conclusions could easily be drawn without understanding the mathematics.

One example of such mistaken conclusions was provided by Alan Sokal (1996b), a physicist who wrote a paper about "quantum gravity" that was published in a humanities journal. In a separate article, published in another humanities journal, he revealed that the first paper had been a spoof, which could have easily been identified as such by anyone with a modicum of knowledge in mathematics or physics (Sokal, 1996a). For Sokal (2008), "clear thinking, combined with a respect for *evidence*—especially inconvenient and unwanted evidence, evidence that challenges our preconceptions—are of the utmost importance to the survival of the human race in the twenty-first century" (p. xi; emphasis in original). The result of the spoof was a vigorous debate about how science studies scholars go about doing what they do and a chilling of relations between some sectors of the humanities and social sciences and the rest of the academy (Bérubé, 2011).

Another consequence of Sokal's spoof could be the fear of criticizing physics from outside the discipline of physics. Why would that be a problem? Well, this brings us back to the subject matter of Chapter 1 of this volume. When unchecked by sufficient self-criticism, a discipline can run along a misleading set of train tracks held in place by groupthink.

A scientist could argue that this kind of dogmatic groupthink could never happen and that external criticism is unnecessary. She could argue that nature is the only critic that a scientist needs. The sciences are empirically based, so that scientists have no choice but to follow the evidence. Well, if that were the case, it would not have been necessary for us to write this book. It is precisely because conditioned ways of thinking have displaced empirical evidence that we need to restore the scientific footing of consciousness research. We have been applying Sokal's dictum of a return to logic and empiricism to consciousness studies. However, in addition, from what we have seen in this book, there are also dangers associated with reliance on naïve empiricism. To see this, let us comment as nonexperts on what appears to us to be going on in physics.

We think that physicists got to be physicists because they were interested in the way in which the physical world works. They went to school and learned a lot about physical nature and its underlying mechanisms. And when they themselves created new physics, they built new physical theories that tell us in greater, more accurate detail about how the physical world works. In all of this, there is an implicit understanding that the "physical world" is "out there" (cf. Sokal, 2008).

So, what happens to consciousness in this process? Well, as we have made it clear throughout this book, consciousness is not "out there" but "in here" in the form of existential qualia, subjective experience, and first-person mental events of various sorts. What do physicists do with those? How about ignoring them? After all, they are not part of the job description of figuring out the physical world.

> I get a lot of e-mails about consciousness. To most of them I reply that whereas there are real mysteries about consciousness, they're beyond what science can tackle with present knowledge. As a physicist, I have nothing to say about them. (Smolin, 2013, p. 267)

Well, science can tackle consciousness, but believing that it cannot is one way of disregarding it. Perhaps this is not the case for Lee Smolin, but it seems to us that for many physicists, consciousness is a nuisance to be disregarded as much as possible in any explanation of the nature of the universe.

However, we have seen in this book that the effort to isolate consciousness from the physical world is bound to fail. We described in Chapter 3 that when photons pass, one at a time, through a plate with two slits in it, they land on a detecting screen on the other side of the plate in a pattern of light and dark bands in such a way that suggests that each photon had emerged from both slits at once, creating an interference pattern of waves. If we introduce some way in which we could, in principle, determine through which of the two slits a photon emerged, then the pattern of light and dark bands disappear, and the photons land on the detecting screen across from one or the other of the slits. The manner in which we could, in principle, figure out through which of the two slits a photon emerged can be indirect, as has been shown by so-called quantum eraser and delayed-choice quantum eraser experiments (M. Holden, McKeon, & Sherry, 2011; Peng, Chen, Shih, & Scully, 2014).

In the epigraph at the beginning of this book, we quote Richard Feynman saying that nature is absurd. Sometimes our common sense ideas about what reality must be like conflict with empirical evidence. How is it that the behavior of light changes depending on whether we can, in principle, know through which of two slits a photon passes? When we can know, the photon chooses one or the other of the slits. When we cannot know, the photon chooses both slits at once. Well, we need to be careful here. So far with the two-slit experiment, we just need an adequate "observer" for which "knowledge" need not be knowledge in an experiential sense. But now, let us increase the absurdity of the situation in a way that explicitly brings in consciousness. As we saw in Chapter 6, if we direct our attention, in our imagination, to the two slits in the two-slit device, then the photons react as though we could tell through which of the two slits they had emerged. When we do not direct our attention in our imagination to the two slits, then the photons behave as though we cannot tell through which of the two slits the photons emerged. And, in one more absurd twist, as we saw in Chapter 6, we can also create the reverse effect. If we are given reversed feedback, now attending to the two-slit device can lead to having the photons react as though we do not know through which of two slits they will emerge and when not attending, they react as though we do!

One of the assumptions that many physicists appear to make is that they are "discovering" a physical world that is independent of what they already think it should be like. And there are certainly sufficient examples of scientific discoveries that are contrary to expectation to have at least some confidence in that assumption for much of physics. But the unexpected reverse finding of the two-slit experiment, as an example of a scientific discovery contrary to the expectation of the experimenters, has implications for the process of scientific discovery. Taken together with the other evidence in Chapter 6, such results suggest that we not only "discover" but also "create" what we find, although the proportion of creation to discovery remains to be established. Regardless of the proportion of creation to discovery, the mere admission that even to a small extent we create the effects that we find is revolutionary. Subatomic particles are "discovered" using elaborate machines that purportedly amplify the decay products of the collisions of subatomic particles (Daintith, 2014; Della Negra, Jenni, & Virdee, 2012). To what extent are the expectations of scientists, with Nobel prizes at stake, unintentionally producing experimenter effects? We can no longer naïvely assume that we are just "discovering" subatomic particles using various elaborate machines without considering that in some cases we may just be creating the appearance of having found them (Barušs, 1986, 1996).

There is another problem with quantum theory, which is that "in a way, [it] still looks like a kind of formal deformation of classical physics" (Dürr, 2005, p. 13). This problem is not specific to quantum theory. Throughout all scientific disciplines, it seems that when a theory no longer fits the empirical data, instead of being thrown out, it just gets "patched" so that it works again. This process continues to be iterated until the constructs of the theory no longer match the original concepts, and it is not clear how to interpret the elements of the deformed theory. For instance, as we saw in Chapter 1, "particles" are not particles any more in the sense in which that concept was originally formulated. In fact, the further the deformation proceeds, the less able a theory may be to incorporate new elements that were never considered in the original version. So, in our case, how are deformed materialist theories to account for consciousness?

Consciousness exists in the physical universe. It does not show up anywhere in quantum theory. "Observers" show up in the metatheory and sometimes in the theory itself. For instance, in relational quantum mechanics, all of physics is relative to "observers" that are simply regarded as further quantum systems themselves (Laudisa & Rovelli, 2008). But consciousness is not necessary for any such observers. So, it is not clear how to incorporate consciousness into quantum theory or metatheory. Nonetheless, reasoning from quantum theory as a starting point, a number of postquantum theories have arisen to account for consciousness, of which the flicker-filter theory discussed next could be considered to be an example.

Another approach would be to start fresh and conceptualize a theory with consciousness as its centerpiece that also takes into account as many as possible of the known observations in science (cf. E. F. Kelly, Crabtree, & Marshall, 2015). Such an effort would be too much for this chapter. But let us look for a moment at theories of another type, the filter models.

FILTER MODELS

In Chapter 5, we noted that in some exceptional cases, the more the brain is compromised, the more likely it is for vivid mental experiences to occur. This is one way of getting at the notion that perhaps the brain acts as a reducing valve or filter for the contents of subjective experience rather than a generator of that experience.

This idea has been brought out explicitly in the context of research with psychedelic drugs. (All of the research with psychedelic drugs cited in this book, to our knowledge, was carried out legally and ethically.) Under the influence of mescaline, the American writer Aldous Huxley found that the focus of his awareness shifted from the ordinary relationships among objects in the room to one whereby those objects were imbued with rich significance. He subsequently conceptualized the human condition as one in which an expanded "Mind at Large has to be funnelled through the reducing valve of the brain and nervous system" (Huxley, 1977, p. 20). Most of the time, we can only know "what comes through the reducing valve," but under some conditions, such as under the influence of some drugs, there can be "by-passes" (Huxley, 1977, p. 20), which give access to "something more than, and above all something different from, the carefully selected utilitarian material which our narrowed, individual minds regard as a complete, or at least sufficient, picture of reality" (Huxley, 1977, p. 21). Similarly, in the context of research with dimethyltryptamine (DMT), "the brain is not the source of spiritual experience, but is instead the organ by which volunteers apprehended . . . a previously invisible level of existence that DMT-induced changes in brain chemistry made possible" (Strassman, 2014, p. 48). We usually assume that such attributions of reality to experiences in drug-induced states are delusions brought about by altered brain chemistry caused by the drugs. But let us leave the possibility open for a bit that there could be at least some truth to the ideas obtained with the use of psychedelics.

In a recent study in which 30 volunteers were each injected with 2 mg of psilocybin, brain imaging revealed decreased activity in areas of the brain that functionally connect regions of the brain that are thought to be associated with consciousness and "high-level functions linked to the self-construct" (Carhart-Harris et al., 2012, p. 2142). The authors interpreted these results to mean that the richly connected parts of the cortex that would normally regulate a maelstrom of impressions and ideas were quieted, releasing unusual experiences that were usually inhibited. Moreover, there was a dose effect in that the intensity of the subjective effects of the psychedelic drugs was proportional to the degree of deactivation of some of these neural circuits. "These results strongly imply that the subjective effects of psychedelic drugs are caused by decreased activity and connectivity in the brain's key connector hubs, enabling a state of unconstrained cognition" (Carhart-Harris et al., 2012, p. 2138). The authors specifically noted that "this finding is consistent with Aldous Huxley's 'reducing valve' metaphor" (Carhart-Harris et al., 2012, p. 2142). On the basis of the context of the rest of the article, the authors clearly meant that the connector hubs act as reducing valves, not that the brain itself acts globally as a reducing valve for a disembodied consciousness.

The notion of a filter theory has been supported by the experiences of John Wren-Lewis, who came close to death on being poisoned, apparently by morphine. Upon awakening, he found himself in a transcendent state of consciousness. It seemed to him that "some kind of brain-cataract [had been] removed, making unobscured perception possible for the first time" (Wren-Lewis, 1994, p. 109). He identified that "cataract" as the hyperactivity of a survival mechanism resulting from the fear of death. He felt that this hyperactive survival mechanism usually shuts out the expanded consciousness. When a person comes close to death, as she sometimes does in the course of a near-death experience, that mechanism is no longer necessary and relinquishes its grip. When a person resumes physical functioning, she does so without the hyperactivity of the survival mechanism, thereby allowing an expanded state of consciousness to be continuously available to her. In other words, the filter's activity has been attenuated (Wren-Lewis, 1988, 1991, 1994; cf. Ring, 1987).

In a filter model of consciousness, it is the unconstrained mind that is directly connected to other minds, probably outside the usual confines of space and apparent time. As we described in Chapter 2, the idea of such connection between minds can seem to go past the boggle thresholds for many of us. One way to make this idea more palatable, in addition to the empirical evidence already discussed, is to realize that our intuitions about the way that the physical world works need not carry over to the way that the mental world works. The nature of the mental world could be quite different from that of the physical world.

According to the filter model, experiences of anomalous information transfer and anomalous remote influencing could occur to the extent that there is information from the unconstrained or shared mental level that is sent through the filter, resulting in brain-based experiences. Timelessness, nonduality, bliss, and other features of transcendent states of consciousness could be explained as experiences that ensue when either the filter is removed or one's subjective point of reference somehow passes beyond the filter to the unconstrained mental level (cf. Pribram, 1982). Along this line of thinking, interactions with discarnate beings could become possible when we stop filtering them out of our experience, with the caveat that such permissivity could lead us to become overwhelmed with unwanted influences.

We need to be careful, however. Not all transcendent states of consciousness are alike. For instance, in a study that we discussed in Chapter 7 whose purpose was to explicitly seek to find the neural correlates of nondual states of consciousness experienced in some forms of Tibetan Buddhist meditation, there was no attenuation of connectivity between key self-referential areas of the cortex. In fact, functional connectivity was strengthened between anatomical systems that reference oneself versus referencing others (Josipovic, 2014). If self-referential structures in our brains are assumed to be equivalent to filters, these data do not support a filter model. However, what if the filter consists of any brain activity related to experiencing a distinction between self and objects? In nondual states of consciousness, our usual sense of self with its attendant subjective point of view and the objects present to it are both experienced within the greater context of nondual awareness. The coactivation of brain areas referencing self and task-based brain areas referencing objects could be interpreted as the embedding of the distinction between self and objects into a view in which such a distinction does not exist. In other words, there may be less of a differentiation between the functioning of the two brain areas when the subject–object distinction no longer acts as a filter.

As with any first-person account, experiences reported from psychedelic or transcendent states as subjective data must be rigorously examined, as discussed in Chapter 7. Keeping that caveat in mind, psychedelically induced transcendent states could well be different from meditative nondual states of consciousness. One possibility is that the former could perhaps correspond to an "elevation" and "dispersal" of a subjective point of view into the transcendent realm leaving the brain relatively quiet, whereas the latter could "embody" the transcendent mind so that the brain is functioning optimally to capture as much of the transcendent material as possible. Another way to consider the differences between studies of psychedelic drug intoxication and nonduality is to acknowledge that the notion of a passive filter is too simplistic. What we need to do is consider the more complex idea that there are ways of "tuning" the brain so as to create "openings" to transcendent abilities and contents. And "these 'openings' clearly must be tied, in ways we presently do not understand, to functional states of the brain" (E. F. Kelly & Presti, 2015, p. 121; emphases in original).

Finally, it is critical to take into account that the brain, or parts of the brain, can only act as a filter if the brain is actually functioning. In Chapter 5, we wondered how someone could speak in cases of terminal lucidity when the brain is compromised in such a way as to prohibit the ordinary processes of speech. One way to think about what could be happening in such cases is to speculate that memories are not in the brain in the first place but in an independently existing mental domain. As a person is dying, perhaps she disengages from the damaged brain so as to give her access, once again, to those memories (Grosso, 2015). But then, how is she able to speak? Motor actions, such as speech, are based on memory, but they are performed using some sort of causative force. To explain such motor movements observed in people who previously could not perform them, there needs to be a secondary mechanism through which such motor activity becomes possible. Although that mechanism could be some neural circuit that we do not currently understand, it could alternatively be similar to whatever mechanism enables stones to fly through the air in poltergeist cases. In other words, the mind could directly manipulate the body without the mediation of the brain. "The body itself is to some degree plastic, and . . . sufficiently intense and focused conscious imagery can somehow alter it *directly*—i.e., in ways that go beyond the reach of the physiological output mechanisms available to the unaided brain" (E. F. Kelly, 2015, p. 511; emphasis in original). So it is not just that the brain may normally function as a filter, but that it may not even be necessary for conscious experience in the body or outside of it.

THE BRAIN AS A BY-PRODUCT OF CONSCIOUSNESS

The materialist assumption is that consciousness is a by-product of the brain. What if we turn that around and consider the idea that the brain is a by-product of consciousness? In other words, what if consciousness of some sort is the fundamental substance of the universe and everything else is made out of consciousness? This is not a new position. In fact, *idealism*, the notion that mind is the fundamental reality from which the physical world is derived, was a prominent philosophical position before the rise of analytic philosophy at the turn of the 20th century. In particular, according to the British idealist tradition, the objects of the world are not discrete, but part of a single, indivisible whole that is fundamentally mental in nature, not physical. Objects do not exist in and of themselves but only insofar as they are part of a network of relations with other objects (Preston, 2015). However, rather than revisiting previous versions of idealism, let us see what we can do ourselves to address some obvious questions: How do we get a brain from consciousness? Why is brain activity correlated with conscious awareness? And what is the point of having a brain?

Bernardo Kastrup (2015) used the metaphor of whirlpools in water as an analogy for a brain formed of consciousness. Just as a whirlpool is nothing other than water in a particular pattern, so the brain and, by extension, one's entire body and all matter are nothing other than consciousness in a particular configuration. Neurons are what experience looks like from the outside, which is why brain activity is correlated with conscious awareness. In fact, for Kastrup (2015), "the entire organism is an *image of experiences*" (p. 75; emphases in original). The mental contents at the center of the whirlpool are those of which we are explicitly aware and are realized in the neural correlates of consciousness, whereas those at the periphery of the whirlpool are "obfuscated" and hence consist of nonconscious memories that are expressed in the rest of the body (Kastrup, 2014, 2015).

Another way to think of this is to think of consciousness as having a fractal nature. Larger patterns repeat themselves on smaller and smaller scales, with the brain being one instance of a self-similar structure (cf. Schmitt, 2007). Or if we iterate the filter metaphor, we can think of consciousness as being successively stepped down through layers from "the clear, unbroken Light of the Void" through levels with "multiple forms" at lower intensities (H. Smith, 2000, p. 11), with the brain being one of those forms. This does not answer the question about why we have a brain in the first place, but it places the brain in the context of a universal consciousness. And, anyway, it is difficult for those who put forward the idea that the brain creates consciousness to explain why we have consciousness in the first place, so the difficulty is at least symmetrical.

FLICKER-FILTER MODEL

Let us pursue this theory-making project just a bit further. A good theory is one that has good goodness-of-fit to the relevant data. In a filter model, we have a way of accounting for shared mind. What about precognition? How can we use what we know about precognition to improve our model (cf. E. F. Kelly, 2015)? Well, precognition is consistent with conventional deterministic versions of reality. If everything from the past to the future is completely determined, then whatever events are going to occur will occur, and there is no reason why there cannot be a secondary process that causally links intimations of future events to those events. However, precognition is incompatible with the stochastic nature of reality assumed in quantum theory, unless we propose that we are evaluating the probabilities of future events at a nonconscious level and getting lucky (G. Williams, 2013, p. 278). So what are we to make of precognition?

This raises the much-debated question of whether free will even exists (Libet, Freeman, & Sutherland, 1999). What we know is that whatever the answer to the philosophical question, as a practical matter, it is adaptive for a person to behave as though free will were to exist. Numerous psychological studies have shown that acting in a self-determining manner leads to healthier outcomes than acting as though one could not change the course of one's life (Ferrucci, 2014). Of course, if determinism were to be true, then whether one behaves as though one could change one's own destiny would itself already be determined. But, for practical purposes, that seems beside the point.

These considerations about free will take us back to our reexamination of the nature of time. The data from experiments testing precognition suggest that we live in a block universe. But if free will were to exist, then perhaps we are moving between block universes with different futures and, possibly, different pasts as we choose one course of action as opposed to another. Perhaps some variation of Julian Barbour's theory of time best fits the data. Perhaps we have a sequence of "nows" ordered in deep time, each of which consists of a block universe with implied apparent past and future events. If we live our lives without any effort to change anything, then the implied future events could become actual future events in future instances of "nows." But if we decide to change what is happening, in some effective way, whatever that might be, then we move to one of several block universes in which the precognized events do not occur (Baruss, 2007b).

The sequence of "nows" is discrete, so that, in effect, we can think of this as a *flicker theory* (Baruss, 2008b). The idea is that physical manifestation comes into existence and disappears, over and over again, producing the appearance of a continuous stream of consciousness from a series of discrete "nows." To where does physical manifestation disappear when a "now" disappears? One idea is based on Wren-Lewis's (1991) description of a "timeless, spaceless void which in some indescribable way [is] total aliveness" (p. 5) from which everything is brought into manifestation. "What I perceive with my eyes and other senses is a whole world that seems to be coming fresh-minted into existence *moment by moment*" (Wren-Lewis, 1988, p. 116; emphases in original). Perhaps that is an accurate perception of reality obtained in an altered state of consciousness, perhaps not. But it matches the basic idea of a flicker theory of consciousness that there is a deep consciousness from which physical manifestation emerges. And now, in keeping with the stochastic nature of quantum theory, there is ultimately nothing keeping one "now" from being radically different from its preceding "now" (Baruss, 1986, 2008b). Let us develop this idea a bit further.

The "void" from which everything emerges can be conceptualized as a *prephysical substrate* (Miller, 2012; cf. de Broglie, 1987) or *deep consciousness* from which both physical and mental events arise (Baruss, 2008b; cf. G. Williams, 2013). This would be a realm of nondual consciousness prior to the split into physical and mental forms of expression. We could posit that there are patterns or *deep structures* within deep consciousness that extrude into our experiences in the ordinary waking state. This could explain both apparently causal chains of events as well as complex synchronicities that appear to be beyond the capability of a single person to produce (Barušs, 2008b; cf. E. F. Kelly, 2015). At a deeper level of reality, events that appear to be unrelated are, in fact, integrated. This was the idea behind David Bohm's (1983) notion of an *implicate order*.

In other words, there is an underlying realm from which "nows" emerge along deep time. And to explain the continuity of everyday experience, we must also posit deep structures within that underlying realm that inform the manner in which deep consciousness is expressed at the level of physical manifestation and determining the order in which "nows" unfold (Barušs, 2008b, 2010). Of course, because we are talking about a flicker universe that can produce discrete events that may or may not follow our expectations, it may be that those structures that determine the substance of the "nows" that unfold can differ between "nows" as we experience them. In that case, it would appear to us that physical laws are changing over apparent time.

Of course, invoking deep structures that dictate our conscious waking experience of apparent time begs the question of the rules by which these structures usually "decide" that a coffee cup is whole before, and not after, it falls to the floor. The point is that according to this model, these deep structures can simulate a block universe, a universe in which everything that has ever happened and everything that will ever happen are all present, so that events follow apparently causal sequences. Precognition occurs when the deep structure produces sequences that match the projected events of an imagined future in a particular "now." But perhaps also the deep structure can be modified by deep consciousness in such a way that the coffee cup begins shattered on the floor and ends up reconstituted in one's hand.

We find that the notion that there are laws governing existence is a problem for all theories. So is the notion of laws that change over time (cf. Barrow & Webb, 2005), which must then require meta-laws to determine which laws are applicable to which situations and the nature in which laws change with deep time. These are profound problems that need to be addressed (cf. Smolin, 2013).

One way to think about modifying the deep structures that shape physical manifestation is to think of our experiences in the ordinary waking state as experiences whose origins lie in deep consciousness. We can propose that these origins are on the other side of a filter that constrains the contents of deep consciousness in such a way as to produce what we experience as the contents of our ordinary waking state. The more permeable the filter, the better able we are to access the material in deep consciousness—the same deep consciousness that is the prephysical substrate for physical manifestation. We can further suppose that we can change what happens in our experience by intending (or whatever it is that is the effective mechanism) what it is that we would like to experience. This would mean that such mental activity is already tied to the deep consciousness that now selects a different projection into physical manifestation that more closely matches our intentions.

This could explain psychokinesis, whereby objects are displaced in anomalous ways from their expected locations. It could also explain the formation of brass plate on a woman's skin or the accelerated biological development of unfertilized eggs into baby chicks within minutes. And such events could be just the beginning of what is possible, if the malleability of physical manifestation as proposed by this model can occur.

With the reintroduction of a filter aspect, we are now discussing an adapted flicker model, which we call a *flicker-filter model*. This model predicts that both the future and past can be changed, although it is not clear how one would obtain evidence that that had occurred given that one is always in a "now" with consonant past and future projections. Of course, there could be "nows" with multiple pasts and futures as well as "nows" whose pasts and futures are transparently fictional. And there could be states of deep consciousness from which our participation in different projected realities could be observed. But we can see that if this model were to be true, then a past or future that we do not like could be replaced by one that we like, with its consequent impact on the present. Of course, that also calls into question the source of our "likings."

So what happened to precognition? Precognition occurs at a present "now," revealing an event in a future "now." We can think of this as a block universe model, in which deep structures could carry a "drop" of "now" to that imagined future so that the precognized event occurs or, conversely, in which a "now" is actually at a later point in deep time that "follows" the "now" in which the precognized future event has already occurred in deep time. If we do not like an upcoming precognitive event, we could change the underlying deep structures through whatever is the instrumental means of doing so. Then a future "now" in apparent time could be changed to a different event in deep time. And the precognized event would not occur in apparent time for the person who anticipated it (Baruss, 2007b). This could explain why evidence for precognition is often easier to find in paradigms that measure nonconscious rather than conscious responses, as discussed in Chapter 3. In other words, consciously precognized experiences of future events could reflect awareness of "nows" that were going to occur but were changed through deep structures into other events.

So, we have "explained" shared mind, psychokinesis, and precognition with our flicker-filter model. Given its speculative nature, perhaps this is as far as we should go at the moment in working out the flicker-filter model. Once we have posited a prephysical reality that is primary with respect to our ordinary waking consciousness and physical manifestation, there is scope for accounting for a variety of phenomena. But, as always, it is necessary to test this theory empirically to determine its continued utility for understanding the nature of consciousness.

GUIDELINES FOR FUTURE RESEARCH IN CONSCIOUSNESS

The quantum mind, filter, consciousness-as-primary, and flicker-filter models, along with every other model of consciousness of which we are presently aware, are incomplete. Assuming the existence of something like what we have loosely identified as deep consciousness, extended mind, shared mind, the prephysical substrate, and so on, we are likely a long way from understanding consciousness. What is needed is a surge of creative research taking the investigation of consciousness in new directions. In this section, we present our best guesses for research ideas that we think could lead to innovative and potentially more satisfying models of consciousness. We think of this section as a compact field guide for consciousness researchers.

1. Learn and Teach Self-Observation and Reporting Skills.

As consciousness researchers, training in observation and reporting skills is essential. We discussed this in detail in Chapter 7, in which we noted that skills in self-observation are critical for consciousness researchers. For the scientifically inclined, the most accessible approach to developing self-observation skills may be by using the scientific method to train oneself in introspection and the pursuit of self-development (Barušs, 1996, 2007b; Mossbridge, 2002). Examining biases and taking steps to eliminate them; understanding flaws in human perception, cognition, and memory; and integrating observations of one's own conscious experiences with those of others with similar training—these practices could all be useful in any consciousness researcher's training.

2. Use Learning Paradigms to Examine Hypotheses.

A basic experimental approach that we think could be more widespread in consciousness research is to use learning paradigms to investigate potential relationships between mechanisms underlying conscious states. In a traditional learning paradigm, participants are trained in one task using one set of stimuli, and the generalization of learning to other conditions is examined as a way to gain insight into the mechanisms that underlie processing of the trained condition. If there is generalization of learning to an untrained condition, the implication is that the mechanisms influenced by training are also at least partially responsible for performance on the condition to which the learning generalized. This technique is used in psychophysics to examine relationships between mechanisms governing perceptual skills (e.g., Mossbridge, 2009; Mossbridge, Fitzgerald, O'Connor, & Wright, 2006; Mossbridge, Scissors, & Wright, 2008).

How could this approach benefit consciousness research? Well, for example, what if we wanted to understand whether the mechanisms underlying lucid dreaming were related to those underlying remote viewing, precognition, and telepathy? We could use a battery of tests to determine the accuracy with which each participant could perform these three psi tasks. Then we could train one group of participants in lucid dreaming, giving them practice until they could dream lucidly at a certain threshold level to consider them as having improved in their abilities. We could then have these trained participants perform the original battery of psi tests and compare their performance on each of these tests with their original performance. To determine whether any improvement on the psi battery was due to training in lucid dreaming, we could then compare the improvement of trained participants to the performance of a control group of participants who also performed the battery of tests twice but were trained on a sham task in between these tests. Such an experimental approach might allow us to uncover hidden connections between seemingly disparate aspects of consciousness, as well as to falsify hypotheses that propose connections between aspects of consciousness that are in fact unrelated.

3. Use Prescreened Skilled Participants.

Throughout this book we have underscored the importance of using prescreened participants to examine hypotheses related to consciousness. It appears that skills such as telepathy, precognition, mental influence on matter, apparent communication with discarnates, and access to transcendent states are similar to musical talent in that they are not evenly distributed in the population and are especially apparent in certain individuals. Just as investigating the characteristics of composers requires using composers as participants, examining the mechanisms underlying these skills and abilities requires participants who are proficient at them. Two exceptions to this general rule are when a learning paradigm is being used and therefore the experimenter will control the training of the participants during the experiment, and when the goal of an experimenter is to assess the distribution of a particular belief, experience, ability, or trait in a population.

4. Create Game-Like Tasks to Amplify Data Acquisition.

An excellent way to screen for skilled participants, determine the distribution of skills in a population, and train participants is to create online or app-based games that focus on the skill being studied and also send data to a research database. For instance, the ESP Trainer game, designed by Russell Targ, screens for precognition using a smartphone app (see http://www.espresearch.com/iphone/). The app rewards participants with encouragement as they score higher in their ability to predict which of four colorful buttons will produce an attractive image and a rewarding tone. According to Targ (2015), in a year-long study with 145 participants using the app, some participants showed significant improvements in precognition performance over time. Another possible approach would be to create a game that required precognition, telepathy, psychokinesis, introspection, or another consciousness-based skill without the user explicitly being made aware that the skill is necessary to play the game. Such an approach guards against hackers who are intrigued by the consciousness-related tasks and desire to "beat the system" (e.g., Radin, 2002). However, in such cases where implicit tests are embedded into games, users should still be made aware that their data are being saved in a database and analyzed.

5. Obtain Massive Online Single-Trial Data Sets.

Laboratory research costs time and money because participants must come to a laboratory to perform experiments. Partially as a result of these costs, researchers have often ensured that each participant performed multiple trials in an experimental session even when order effects and boredom could introduce noise into the data. Tens of participants are used, but each participant might be performing 20 to 500 trials. However, now that we can provide participants with experiments they can perform in their own homes over the Internet at a fraction of the cost of laboratory experiments, consciousness researchers could consider gathering single-trial data from hundreds or thousands of participants, creating massive data sets. The advantage of this approach is that fatigue, boredom, and expectation effects are virtually eliminated by having each participant perform only a single trial, or separately analyzing the first trial performed by each participant. One potential disadvantage is that participants might not be as committed to the performance of the task as they would be in the laboratory. The *Ganzfeld* experiments described in Chapter 2, which have been the most successfully replicated demonstrations of telepathy, used only a single trial per participant, yet they were performed in laboratories rather than online. It is possible that the feelings of importance and specialness that go along with gathering a single data point per participant contributed to the success of those experiments. We could attempt to mimic that effect online across hundreds to thousands of participants.

6. Perform Open-Ended Thought Experiments.

Performing a brief thought experiment on a topic related to consciousness can sometimes bring interesting questions and ideas to light. For example, what if we hypothesize that deep consciousness is primary, that it creates the brain and all other physical manifestation? To test this hypothesis, we would need to find ways to alter the process that deep consciousness uses to create matter. Of course, we do not know what this postulated process is, but we can think about what ways we might produce documented changes in matter that seem to arise from deep consciousness. In other words, if we think of deep consciousness as a projector and matter as the film that is being projected, it could be useful to do the thought experiment of trying to imagine ways in which we can make shadows in the projection.

We can go further and think about physics experiments bearing on the idea. Consider the phenomenon of *entanglement*, whereby particles that interacted at some point in time continue to share quantum properties even though they may end up being quite far apart. In particular, a measurement of the state of one particle instantly gives information about the state of the other particle (Law & Rennie, 2015). We can imagine that each of two such entangled particles are projections from a third source, and the process of entangling them is just a story that is told within the projection. Should we then be surprised that the behavior of each of these particles is linked to the other instantaneously over vast regions of space? No, because we can assume that they are controlled by a single projector, which has instructions on how to tell the story in the "film" (Bohm, 1983). But now a set of different questions arises, including: What is the purpose of deep consciousness providing information to produce a physical projection? Why should only certain particles in the physical projection appear to be entangled? Is there any form of feedback or communication between the projected particles and deep consciousness? And so on. Questions like these, derived from thought experiments and stories, can provide fruitful foundations for new experimental approaches.

7. Engage Dreams to Gather Insights.

It is apparent from empirical data that rapid eye movement (REM) sleep, which occurs during dreaming, supports creative solutions to problems. Awakening participants during REM sleep produces improved performance on difficult anagram tasks after awakening as compared to awakening participants during non-REM sleep (M. P. Walker, Liston, Hobson, & Stickgold, 2002), REM sleep deepens associations between loosely associated concepts (Cai, Mednick, Harrison, Kanady, & Mednick, 2009), and these improvements in associative ability seem to be specifically focused on associations between ideas that seem to be most difficult to make in the waking state (Sio, Monaghan, & Ormerod, 2013). In our case, we could consider drawing on the help of our dreams to gain insight into surprising connections between ideas about the mechanisms underlying consciousness.

Otto Loewi won the Nobel Prize in Physiology or Medicine for work that shed light on the chemistry underlying neural transmission, an experiment he carried out based on a dream.

> The night before Easter Sunday of that year I awoke, turned on the light, and jotted down a few notes on a tiny slip of paper. Then I fell asleep again. . . . It was the design of an experiment to determine whether or not the hypothesis of chemical transmission that I had uttered 17 years ago was correct. I got up immediately, went to the laboratory, and performed a single experiment on a frog's heart according to the nocturnal design. (Otto Loewi, 1960, p. 17)

Assuming deep consciousness exists, perhaps one direct form of communication with deep consciousness occurs during dreams, when we are not participating in discursive everyday thought processes that may limit the breadth of our ideas and experiences. Some neuroscientists would offer another explanation, which is that during dreaming our brain chemistry may support making associations between seemingly distant ideas (M. P. Walker et al., 2002). Regardless of the explanation for the creative problem-solving ability of dreams, we can consider actively engaging our dreams to incubate ideas for gathering insights. If an answer to a problem does not occur on the first night a question is posed, a dreamer can continue posing the question and look for answers on subsequent nights (Barrett, 1993, 2001; Baruss, 2003a).

8. Query the Extended Mind.

Assuming the reality of a shared mind, discussed in Chapter 2, that can respond to queries based on intention, drawing on the extended mind for insights into consciousness could be worthwhile. Such querying of the extended mind is likely to be a skill that can be developed with practice, as could be the case for the superforecasters we discussed in Chapter 7. Further, improving this capacity may be more efficient if we work in groups. Superforecasters working in groups of like-minded individuals improved their intuitive abilities more quickly than those who worked alone. If at least some of their abilities derived from being able to access the extended mind, it seems reasonable for consciousness researchers to mimic this procedure by working together with at least one other person to practice accessing verifiable information. As accuracy improves, then attention can be turned to addressing research questions related to consciousness. Again, we emphasize that keen self-observation as well as comparing notes with others can help inform a determination about whether information is being fabricated or accurately received.

9. Access Information at Different Points in Time.

Once we make the assumption of a shared mind that has access to information about future events, it seems reasonable to suppose that we can gain insight into research problems by accessing information about future solutions to those problems. We have seen, in Chapter 2, that querying the extended mind to gain information about the future is not entirely different from querying it to gain information about the past or present. Thus, training ourselves to access accurate information from the extended mind could include practicing the ability to access information from any point in time.

10. Examine Meaning in Transcendent States.

Not only is consciousness a requisite quality for our experience of meaning, but concerns about existential meaning could be resolved in transcendent states of consciousness (Barušs, 1996; Barušs, van Lier, & Ali, 2014). Currently, there are few studies that use transcendent states of consciousness to address questions about the purpose of life, death, and suffering. By carefully integrating first- and third-person research methods, we may be able to actually address these perennial concerns by finding common responses across multiple adept participants in transcendent states. Such an approach could lead to positive shifts in our understanding of who we are and the purposes of our lives.

IMPLICATIONS FOR CLINICAL PRACTICE

What implications does the material in this book have for those in clinical practice? Some are obvious. So let us start with those. Perhaps most obvious is that given that anomalous phenomena occur, they need to be properly taken into account in clinical practice.

Taking anomalous phenomena properly into account in clinical practice begins with diagnosis. Anomalous phenomena can occur in the context of evident psychopathology. We have seen examples of that in this book. But the mere occurrence or belief in the occurrence of anomalous phenomena should not be considered a symptom of a mental disorder, as it currently is. For instance, "odd beliefs . . . e.g., . . . belief in clairvoyance, telepathy, or 'sixth sense'" as well as "unusual perceptual experiences" are currently listed as symptoms of schizotypal personality disorder (American Psychiatric Association, 2013, p. 655). Such beliefs are widespread throughout the world (Watt & Tierney, 2014), so ostensibly the "odd beliefs" are "odd" not because they are uncommon but because mental health professionals do not believe that they have anything to do with reality. "Unusual perceptual experiences" could include many of the anomalous perceptual experiences described in this book. Although apparently associated with schizophrenia, only a "small proportion" of individuals with schizotypal personality disorder go on "to develop schizophrenia or another psychotic disorder" (American Psychiatric Association, 2013, p. 657). Also, there are *happy schizotypes* who report unusual perceptual and cognitive experiences, including anomalous experiences, without the "negative psychological characteristics" otherwise associated with schizotypy (Cardeña, Krippner, & Lynn, 2014, p. 413). In fact, psychometrically, the "positive symptom/unusual experiences part of schizotypy is its strongest, most face-valid, component" (Claridge, 1997, p. 306) identifying schizotypy for what it is. Yet that part of schizotypy is also present in people who are not "clinically insane" (Claridge, 1997, p. 306). So why should the anomalous-experience component be regarded as the identifying feature of a mental disorder?

What may be occurring is that schizotypy is a psychological condition in which nonconscious material arises in consciousness more easily than usual. If a person is unprepared for such irruption, then pathology ensues; if she is well-integrated, then access to such material can lead to exceptional functioning (Baruš, 1996; Claridge, 1997). At the least, diagnostic categories need to be cleaned up so that the occurrence of anomalous phenomena or belief in the occurrence of anomalous phenomena are not considered pathological in and of themselves.

The manner in which a mental health professional responds to someone who describes having had anomalous experiences is also important. Numerous times over his more than 30 years of teaching, students have come up to one of the authors of this book, Imants Baruš, and begun with the phrase "I've never told anyone about this because I didn't want them to think that I was crazy, but . . ." and then have gone on to describe anomalous experiences that they have had of the sort that have been described in this book. The other author, Julia Mossbridge, has had similar experiences with courses she has taught in which she has merely mentioned the possibility of psi. So there is already avoidance of consulting mental health professionals with questions about anomalous phenomena for fear of being considered to be "crazy."

Those receiving psychotherapy who have had anomalous experiences, at some point, might ask a psychotherapist if unusual experiences are possible.

> If the therapist prevaricates or is noncommittal about the possibility that such events can take place in the real, consensual world, the therapeutic relationship can suffer, often severely. The experient and therapist then find themselves in different universes of discourse. (Watt & Tierney, 2014, p. 259)

The net result is that, to seek help for whatever it is that is going on with them, people who believe that they have had anomalous experiences find resources outside the mental health profession and outside the few academic research centers specializing in the study of such experiences. There has been evidence that such people are turning instead to Internet sites that offer what might appear to be more relevant information and support (Watt & Tierney, 2014). It would be helpful if proper psychotherapeutic interventions could be worked out for responding to clients who believe that they have had unusual experiences (Cardeña, Krippner, & Lynn, 2014) and for evaluating any such protocols for their effectiveness.

There is another important matter that we need to take up. Anomalous phenomena can cause psychological distress and psychopathology. One example is that of some individuals who have had near-death experiences (NDEs). In spite of some clearly beneficial effects, a person who has had an NDE can experience "anger and depression at having been brought back to life, career interruptions, fear of ridicule and rejection, alienation from her relatives and acquaintances, and broken relationships, including divorce" (Baruš, 2003a, p. 11; Greyson, 2014). There is a need to effectively manage disruptions created by the occurrence of anomalous phenomena and to learn to integrate new abilities into one's lifestyle.

There will also be a developmental sequence as people learn to use anomalous abilities. For instance, a person who realizes that some of her spontaneous thoughts correspond to actual events occurring in consensus reality can become confused as to when such thoughts are just products of the imagination and when they are veridical (Baruš, 2007b). As one example, one of the authors of this book, Julia Mossbridge, has had at least one clear precognitive dream of a terrorism event that correlated strongly with events occurring the day after the dream. She dreamed of the June 26, 2015, bombing of a religious temple during prayers. She had a strongly negative feeling after rereading her dream in her dream journal, feeling helpless at having the ability to see something horrible with a specific date tied to it but not being able to do anything about it. In another case, suppose that someone who has been able to correctly identify physical pathology inside another person's body has an impression of a brain tumor in someone else's head (cf. Curry, 2008).

Is that a veridical impression or a product of the imagination? Does she say something to that person or not? Those are two separate issues—determining whether something is veridical or a product of the imagination, and what to do about it if one does not know or suspects that one is right. Research is necessary to determine best practices for learning these skills in such a way that one can distinguish veridical impressions from fictional ones. This is not a theoretical problem but a practical one with which some people struggle. And that is just the first, most obvious, problem that needs to be addressed (Baruš, 1996, 2007b, 2013a). As psychologists and mental health professionals, we need to step in to help people who are developing these skills.

This discussion leads to another obvious implication. If such anomalous abilities can be developed to the point of consistent accuracy, then they could be a useful adjunct to other resources in health care. In fact, they are already being used with varying levels of proficiency (e.g., Curry, 2008). The following is an example:

> For one particular patient an intuitive expert [NT] provided several exact laboratory values (for example, thyroid stimulating hormone) that were later verified in the laboratory. She also described the clinical course of another patient's depression over the previous five years with such detail that the psychiatrist [PG] had to check the dates and details from his own notes. The intuitively provided information was correct and accurate. (Grof & Kautz, 2010, p. 186)

Such abilities could be applied more generally to the improvement of mental health services. For instance, as we discussed in Chapter 7, information was gathered from six "intuitive experts" about the medical diagnosis and treatment of bipolar disorder (Grof & Kautz, 2010).

IMPLICATIONS FOR SCIENTIFIC DISCOVERY

Obviously, the use of "intuitive experts" is not limited to mental health research but can be used for advances in science more generally (Baruš, 2007b; cf. Harman & Rheingold, 1984). Psychologists could study how the resources of such experts could be used most effectively in research settings.

If discarnates do exist and communicate with the living, and those that had been human beings do retain the expert knowledge that they had when they were alive, then perhaps we, the living, could engage them in carrying forward research to which they could contribute their knowledge and skills. There have been claims that this has already occurred with regard to instrumental transcommunication research, for instance, by specifying the types of equipment that could be built to facilitate communication (e.g., Fuller, 1985; Keen, Ellison, & Fontana, 1999). And, in fact, there is a history of the deceased ostensibly having meddled in the affairs of the living (Brennan, 2013). Let us just give one suggestive example from our own experience.

At one point, Imants Barušs was reading a book by Richard Feynman, an influential 20th-century physicist who died in 1988 (Feynman, 1989). He asked a medium with whom he had done previous research, Angie Aristone, whether she could contact Feynman. This she apparently did, obtaining accurate information about his life. Julia Mossbridge suggested that Barušs ask the apparent Feynman some technical physics questions. Barušs met again with Aristone and, among other questions, asked her for the value of the "fine structure constant." This is a combination of physical constants that occurs in quantum electrodynamics and that has an approximate value of 1/137 (Daintith, 2005), something that Feynman would have known during his lifetime. Aristone did not know, prior to the session, that she would be asked about this. Barušs was expecting to hear the number "1/137" or just "137." Instead, Aristone said, "Zero. Eight." At that point, Barušs cut her off, saying something like "No. No. That's wrong. That's not the right number." (Only handwritten notes were taken of the sessions with the medium.) Then Aristone said that there is a "capital M piece of something; attached to something" to which Barušs replied that there was no capital M anywhere.

The following week, while on the phone with Mossbridge, whose name starts with a capital M, Barušs recounted this apparent miss. Mossbridge quickly brought up a website with information on it about the fine structure constant. On that website was a quotation by Richard Feynman, part of which Mossbridge read aloud to Barušs. Something about Feynman giving the value of the "coupling constant" as point zero eight something. Barušs still did not get it. At that point, the phone died. Barušs called Mossbridge back, and she said that when her phone had died, the number .08 had been left staring her in the face, a number that she had punched into the calculator on her phone earlier during the conversation, when she had been playing around with numbers related to the fine structure constant. The lightbulb finally went on for Barušs. He recognized Feynman's .08 as the square root of .007297, the approximate value of the fine structure constant. Here is the complete quotation from Feynman's (1985/2006) book:

> There is a most profound and beautiful question associated with the observed coupling constant, e—the amplitude for a real electron to emit or absorb a real photon. It is a simple number that has been experimentally determined to be close to 0.08542455. (My physicist friends won't recognize this number, because they like to remember it as the inverse of its square: about 137.03597 with an uncertainty of about 2 in the last decimal place. It has been a mystery ever since it was discovered more

than 50 years ago, and all good theoretical physicists put this number up on their wall and worry about it.) (p. 129)

So Aristone correctly got the first two digits, not of the value of the fine structure constant as a generic physicist would define it, but the first two digits of the value of the fine structure constant as Feynman himself would have defined it!

There are several interesting things to note about this story. First, the probability of guessing two digits of a number in sequence correctly is .01, so at a superficial level of analysis, the probability associated with this event is .01, which is below the level of .05 needed to regard it as a fact rather than a coincidence. Second is the specificity of the information to the alleged communicator. We saw this in the Géza Maróczy case, where the chess match proceeded in the manner in which Maróczy would have played it. Baruš expected to hear 1/137 or twaddle, thought he was hearing twaddle, and shut up the medium who said subsequently that she had had more digits to report. The information that the medium provided was unexpected but proved to be correct specifically for Feynman. Third, the coauthors talked on the phone usually once a week for over a year as they wrote this book, yet this was the only time that either can remember when the phone died in the middle of a conversation. It died at precisely the point at which Baruš was ready to permanently dismiss the possibility that the medium had received correct information about the fine structure constant. This is reminiscent of the timing in the Michael Shermer case in which the inoperative radio started playing precisely on his wedding day as his newly wed wife was missing her grandfather. Finally, we call this a story because it does not prove anything. But it is suggestive. If we actually have access to deceased scientists and other experts who are capable of communicating technical information through mediums, then perhaps we can exploit their knowledge and skills for solving problems that we face.

To summarize, we bring the discussion back to the implications of the material in this book. First, each person could already always be in contact with all other people and events in the past, present, and future and could obtain knowledge of those events as well as influence them simply by having access to them. Second, contact with discarnates could be helpful, not only for resolving grief, but also for acquiring knowledge about the afterlife and helping to solve problems that humanity faces on the planet today. Third, unwanted intrusions by discarnates could account for some forms of psychopathology and other unusual phenomena, such as poltergeist cases. Fourth, remote viewing could be used for obtaining useful information. Fifth, remote influencing could specifically be developed for healing purposes as an adjunct to other types of medical care. Finally, in all cases, care needs to be taken to develop ethical applications of any of these phenomena. We leave it to the reader to work out other implications and applications of the material in this book.

THE NATURE OF CONSCIOUSNESS

In Chapter 1, we noted that the extraordinarily transcendent position along the material-transcendent dimension of beliefs about consciousness and reality is characterized by the notion that consciousness is the ultimate reality, that physical manifestation is a by-product of the mental, that anomalous phenomena occur, that there are anomalous means of acquiring knowledge, and that it is important to undergo a process of self-development to understand consciousness. Interestingly enough, such a position ends up being largely supported by the evidence that we have discussed in this book, so that we can think of this book as incidentally presenting an extraordinarily transcendent view of consciousness and reality.

Okay, but what do we, the authors, really think consciousness is? Not just everyday waking consciousness, but all of it, all of these states of consciousness together? We think consciousness has an aspect that is a deep reality that we might only be able to partially know conceptually. On the basis of the evidence described in this book, we think it is likely to exist ontologically prior to space and time, at least as space and time are usually experienced. We speculate that consciousness creates physical manifestation through which it then expresses itself in stepped-down, accessible form. On the basis of this idea, in everyday waking consciousness, human beings are explicitly aware of only a fragment of the scope of consciousness. Self-development is necessary to deepen one's understanding of the nature of consciousness and reality. Deep consciousness offers an invitation to explore what it means to exist. Perhaps.

The job of science is not to reject this or any other hypothesis outright, but to determine how much, if any of it, is correct and how much is incorrect. As scientists, we make models, test them, and see the extent to which they hold up to empirical scrutiny. If we do our jobs right, then each model gives us greater understanding of reality. On the basis of what we have discussed in this book, such a process could lead beyond itself to states of mind in which we can more adequately comprehend what is happening mentally and physically, in time and space. That is the adventure that awaits us.

REFERENCES

Achterberg, J., Cooke, K., Richards, T., Standish, L. J., Kozak, L., & Lake, J. (2005). Evidence for correlations between distant intentionality and brain function in recipients: A functional magnetic resonance imaging analysis. *The Journal of Alternative and Complementary Medicine, 11*, 965–971. http://dx.doi.org/10.1089/acm.2005.11.965

Adriaanse, M. A., Weijers, J., De Ridder, D. T., De Witt Huberts, J., & Evers, C. (2014). Confabulating reasons for behaving bad: The psychological consequences of unconsciously activated behaviour that violates one's standards. *European Journal of Social Psychology, 44*, 255–266. http://dx.doi.org/10.1002/ejsp.2005

Aglioti, S. M., Cesari, P., Romani, M., & Urgesi, C. (2008). Action anticipation and motor resonance in elite basketball players. *Nature Neuroscience, 11*, 1109–1116. http://dx.doi.org/10.1038/nn.2182

Agrillo, C. (2011). Near-death experience: Out-of-body and out-of-brain? *Review of General Psychology, 15*, 1–10. http://dx.doi.org/10.1037/a0021992

Aharonov, Y., Bergmann, P. G., & Lebowitz, J. L. (1964). Time symmetry in the quantum process of measurement. *Physical Review, 134*(6B), B1410–B1416. http://dx.doi.org/10.1103/PhysRev.134.B1410

Aldrich, M. S. (1999). *Sleep medicine*. New York, NY: Oxford University Press.

Allison, R. (with Schwarz, T.). (1980). *Minds in many pieces: The making of a very special doctor*. New York, NY: Rawson, Wade.

Allman, M. J., Teki, S., Griffiths, T. D., & Meck, W. H. (2014). Properties of the internal clock: First- and second-order principles of subjective time. *Annual Review of Psychology, 65*, 743–771. http://dx.doi.org/10.1146/annurev-psych-010213-115117

Alsop, S. C. R. (1989). *Whispers of immortality: Electronic voices and images from the dead*. London, England: Regency Press.

Alvarado, C. S., & Zingrone, N. L. (2015). Features of out-of-body experiences: Relationships to frequency, willfulness of, and previous knowledge about the experience. *Journal of the Society for Psychical Research, 79*, 98–111.

American Psychiatric Association. (2013). *Diagnostic and statistical manual of mental disorders* (5th ed.). Washington, DC: Author.

Amorth, G. (1999). *An exorcist tells his story* (N. V. MacKenzie, Trans.). San Francisco, CA: Ignatius Press.

Arstila, V., & Lloyd, D. (Eds.). (2014). *Subjective time: The philosophy, psychology, and neuroscience of temporality*. Cambridge, MA: MIT Press.

Ashby, F. G., Turner, B. O., & Horvitz, J. C. (2010). Cortical and basal ganglia contributions to habit learning and automaticity. *Trends in Cognitive Sciences, 14*, 208–215. http://dx.doi.org/10.1016/j.tics.2010.02.001

Assagioli, R. (1965). *Psychosynthesis: A manual of principles and techniques*. New York, NY: Penguin.

Assagioli, R. (2007). *Transpersonal development*. Findhorn, Scotland: Inner Way Productions.

Assagioli, R., & Vargui, J. (1976). *The superconscious and the self*. London, England: The Psychosynthesis and Education Trust. Retrieved from http://www.psykosyntese.dk/a-172/

Assante, J. (2012). *The last frontier: Exploring the afterlife and transforming our fear of death*. Novato, CA: New World Library.

Atwater, P. M. H. (2007). *The big book of near-death experiences: The ultimate guide to what happens when we die*. Charlottesville, VA: Hampton Roads.

Atwater, P. M. H. (2011). *Near-death experiences, the rest of the story: What they teach us about living, dying, and our true purpose*. Charlottesville, VA: Hampton Roads.

Atwater, P. M. H. (2013). *Future memory*. Charlottesville, VA: Hampton Roads.

Baars, B. J. (2013). A scientific approach to silent consciousness. *Frontiers in Psychology*, 4, 678. http://dx.doi.org/10.3389/fpsyg.2013.00678

Bacon, F. (1842). The second book of Francis Bacon, of the proficience and advancement of learning, divine and human. In B. Mantagu (Ed. & Trans.), *The works of Francis Bacon, Lord Chancellor of England: A new edition, with a life of the author* (Vol. 1, pp. 184–254). Retrieved from https://books.google.com/books?id=hSnbMsCjTXEC&printsec=frontcover#v=onepage&q&f=false

Baker, D. M. (n.d.). *The techniques of astral projection*. Essendon, Hertfordshire, England: Author.

Baptista, J., & Derakhshani, M. (2014). Beyond the coin toss: Examining Wiseman's criticisms of parapsychology. *Journal of Parapsychology*, 78(1), 56–79.

Baptista, J., Derakhshani, M., & Tressoldi, P. (2015). Explicit anomalous cognition: A review of the best evidence in Ganzfeld, forced-choice, remote viewing and dream studies. In E. Cardeña, J. Palmer, & D. Marcusson-Clavertz (Eds.), *Parapsychology: A handbook for the 21st century* (pp. 192–214). Jefferson, NC: McFarland.

Barbato, M., Blunden, C., Reid, K., Irwin, H., & Rodriguez, P. (1999). Parapsychological phenomena near the time of death. *Journal of Palliative Care*, 15, 30–37.

Barbour, J. (2000). *The end of time: The next revolution in physics*. New York, NY: Oxford University Press.

Barrell, J. J., & Richards, A. C. (1982). Overcoming jealousy: An experiential analysis of common factors. *The Personnel and Guidance Journal*, 61, 40–47. http://dx.doi.org/10.1002/j.2164-4918.1982.tb00807.x

Barrett, D. (1993). The "committee of sleep": A study of dream incubation for problem solving. *Dreaming*, 3, 115–122. http://dx.doi.org/10.1037/h0094375

Barrett, D. (2001). *The committee of sleep: How artists, scientists, and athletes use dreams for creative problem-solving—and how you can too*. New York, NY: Crown.

Barrow, J. D., & Webb, J. K. (2005). Inconstant constants: Do the inner workings of nature change with time? *Scientific American, 292*(6), 56–63. http://dx.doi.org/10.1038/scientificamerican0605-56

Baruss, I. (1986). Quantum mechanics and human consciousness. *Physics in Canada/La Physique au Canada, 42*(1), 3–5.

Baruss, I. (1987). Metanalysis of definitions of consciousness. *Imagination, Cognition and Personality, 6,* 321–329. http://dx.doi.org/10.2190/39X2-HMUL-WB7B-B1A1

Baruss, I. (1990). *The personal nature of notions of consciousness: A theoretical and empirical examination of the role of the personal in the understanding of consciousness.* Lanham, MD: University Press of America.

Baruss, I. (1993). Can we consider matter as ultimate reality? Some fundamental problems with a materialist interpretation of reality. *Ultimate Reality and Meaning: Interdisciplinary Studies in the Philosophy of Understanding, 16*(3–4), 245–254.

Baruss, I. (1996). *Authentic knowing: The convergence of science and spiritual aspiration.* West Lafayette, IN: Purdue University Press.

Baruss, I. (2001). Failure to replicate electronic voice phenomenon. *Journal of Scientific Exploration, 15,* 355–367.

Baruss, I. (2003a). *Alterations of consciousness: An empirical analysis for social scientists.* http://dx.doi.org/10.1037/10562-000

Baruss, I. (2003b). *Saints and madmen: Psychiatry opens its doors to religion* by Russell Shorto and *Feet of clay: A study of gurus* by Anthony Storr [Book reviews]. *Journal of Scientific Exploration, 17,* 553–555.

Baruss, I. (2006). Quantum theories of consciousness. *Baltic Journal of Psychology, 7,* 39–45.

Baruss, I. (2007a). An experimental test of instrumental transcommunication. *Journal of Scientific Exploration, 21,* 89–98.

Baruss, I. (2007b). *Science as a spiritual practice.* Exeter, England: Imprint Academic.

Baruss, I. (2008a). Beliefs about consciousness and reality: Clarification of the confusion concerning consciousness. *Journal of Consciousness Studies, 15*(10–11), 277–292.

Baruss, I. (2008b). Characteristics of consciousness in collapse-type quantum mind theories. *Journal of Mind and Behavior, 29,* 255–265.

Baruss, I. (2008c). Quantum mind: Conscious intention in the context of quantum mechanics. *Dydaktyka Literatury, 28,* 31–40.

Baruss, I. (2009). Speculations about the direct effects of intention on physical manifestation. *Journal of Cosmology, 3,* 590–599.

Baruss, I. (2010). Beyond scientific materialism: Toward a transcendent theory of consciousness. *Journal of Consciousness Studies, 17*(7–8), 213–231.

Baruss, I. (2012). What we can learn about consciousness from altered states of consciousness. *Journal of Consciousness Exploration & Research, 3,* 805–819.

Baruss, I. (2013a). *The impossible happens: A scientist's personal discovery of the extraordinary nature of reality.* Alresford, Hampshire, England: Iff Books.

Barušs, I. (2013b). Learning to forget: Deprogramming as a precondition for the occurrence of non-dual states of consciousness. *Journal of Consciousness Exploration & Research, 4,* 816–832.

Barušs, I. (2014a). Questions about interacting with invisible intelligences. *EdgeScience, 18,* 18–19.

Barušs, I. (2014b). A vision for the Society for Consciousness Studies [Guest editorial]. *Journal of Consciousness Exploration & Research, 5,* 551–555.

Barušs, I., & Moore, R. J. (1989). Notions of consciousness and reality. In J. E. Shorr, P. Robin, J. A. Connella, & M. Wolpin (Eds.), *Imagery: Current perspectives* (pp. 87–92). http://dx.doi.org/10.1007/978-1-4899-0876-6_8

Barušs, I., & Moore, R. J. (1992). Measurement of beliefs about consciousness and reality. *Psychological Reports, 71*(1), 59–64. http://dx.doi.org/10.2466/pr0.1992.71.1.59

Barušs, I., & Moore, R. J. (1998). Beliefs about consciousness and reality of participants at 'Tucson II.' *Journal of Consciousness Studies, 5,* 483–496.

Barušs, I., & Rabier, V. (2014). Failure to replicate retrocausal recall. *Psychology of Consciousness: Theory, Research, and Practice, 1*(1), 82–91.

Barušs, I., van Lier, C., & Ali, D. (2014). Alterations of consciousness at a self-development seminar: A Matrix Energetics seminar survey. *Journal of Consciousness Exploration & Research, 5,* 1064–1086.

Beaman, L. A., Chattopadhyay, R., Duflo, E., Pande, R., & Topalova, P. (2008). *Powerful women: Does exposure reduce bias?* (Working Paper No. 14198). http://dx.doi.org/10.3386/w14198

Beaufort, F. (1858). *Notice of Rear-Admiral Sir Francis Beaufort, K. C. B.* London, England: J. D. Potter.

Beck, T. E., & Colli, J. E. (2003). A quantum biomechanical basis for near-death life reviews. *Journal of Near-Death Studies, 21,* 169–189. http://dx.doi.org/10.1023/A:1021292006371

Beischel, J. (2007). Contemporary methods used in laboratory-based mediumship research. *Journal of Parapsychology, 71,* 37–68.

Beischel, J. (2013). *Among mediums: A scientist's quest for answers.* Tucson, AZ: Windbridge Institute.

Beischel, J. (Ed.). (2014). *From the mouths of mediums. Vol. 1: Experiencing communication.* Tucson, AZ: Windbridge Institute.

Beischel, J., Boccuzzi, M., Biuso, M., & Rock, A. J. (2015). Anomalous information reception by research mediums under blinded conditions II: Replication and extension. *EXPLORE: The Journal of Science and Healing, 11,* 136–142. http://dx.doi.org/10.1016/j.explore.2015.01.001

Beischel, J., Mosher, C., & Boccuzzi, M. (2014–2015). The possible effects on bereavement of assisted after-death communication during readings with psychic mediums: A continuing bonds perspective. *Omega: Journal of Death and Dying, 70,* 169–194. http://dx.doi.org/10.2190/OM.70.2.b

Beischel, J., & Schwartz, G. E. (2007). Anomalous information reception by research mediums demonstrated using a novel triple-blind protocol. *EXPLORE: The Journal of Science and Healing, 3*, 23–27. http://dx.doi.org/10.1016/j.explore.2006.10.004

Bellamy, N., Buchanan, W. W., Goldsmith, C. H., Campbell, J., & Stitt, L. W. (1988). Validation study of WOMAC: A health status instrument for measuring clinically important patient relevant outcomes to antirheumatic drug therapy in patients with osteoarthritis of the hip or knee. *The Journal of Rheumatology, 15*, 1833–1840.

Bem, D. J. (2011). Feeling the future: Experimental evidence for anomalous retroactive influences on cognition and affect. *Journal of Personality and Social Psychology, 100*, 407–425. http://dx.doi.org/10.1037/a0021524

Bem, D. J., & Honorton, C. (1994). Does psi exist? Replicable evidence for an anomalous process of information transfer. *Psychological Bulletin, 115*, 4–18. http://dx.doi.org/10.1037/0033-2909.115.1.4

Bem, D. J., Tressoldi, P., Rabeyron, T., & Duggan, M. (2016). Feeling the future: A meta-analysis of 90 experiments on the anomalous anticipation of random future events (revised, version 2). *F1000Research, 4*, 1188. http://dx.doi.org/10.12688/f1000research.7177.2

Benson, H., Dusek, J. A., Sherwood, J. B., Lam, P., Bethea, C. F., Carpenter, W., . . . Hibberd, P. L. (2006). Study of the Therapeutic Effects of Intercessory Prayer (STEP) in cardiac bypass patients: A multicenter randomized trial of uncertainty and certainty of receiving intercessory prayer. *American Heart Journal, 151*, 934–942. http://dx.doi.org/10.1016/j.ahj.2005.05.028

Berenbaum, H., Kerns, J., & Raghavan, C. (2000). Anomalous experiences, peculiarity, and psychopathology. In E. Cardeña, S. J. Lynn, & S. Krippner (Eds.), *Varieties of anomalous experience: Examining the scientific evidence* (pp. 25–46). http://dx.doi.org/10.1037/10371-001

Berger, A. S. (1995). Quoth the raven: Bereavement and the paranormal. *Omega: Journal of Death and Dying, 31*, 1–10.

Berger, J. (1940). *Psyche*. Jena, Germany: Gustav Fischer.

Berger, P. L. (1970). *A rumor of angels: Modern society and the rediscovery of the supernatural*. Garden City, NY: Anchor Books.

Bergson, H. (1965). *Duration and simultaneity: With reference to Einstein's theory*. Indianapolis, IN: Bobbs-Merrill. (Original work published 1922)

Bergson, H. (2001). *Time and free will: An essay on the immediate data of consciousness* (F. L. Pogson, Trans.). Mineola, NY: Dover. (Original work published 1913)

Bering, J. (2014, November 25). One last goodbye: The strange case of terminal lucidity. *Scientific American*. Retrieved from http://blogs.scientificamerican.com/bering-in-mind/2014/11/25/one-last-goodbye-the-strange-case-of-terminal-lucidity/

Berman, P. (1996). *The journey home: What near-death experiences and mysticism teach us about the gift of life*. New York, NY: Simon and Schuster.

Bérubé, M. (2011, Winter). The science wars redux. *Democracy: A Journal of Ideas, 19,* 64–74. Retrieved from http://democracyjournal.org/magazine/19/the-science-wars-redux/

Bierman, D. J. (2001). On the nature of anomalous phenomena: Another reality between the world of subjective consciousness and the objective world of physics? In P. Van Loocke (Ed.), *The physical nature of consciousness* (pp. 269–292). http://dx.doi.org/10.1075/aicr.29.12bie

Bierman, D. J., & Houtkooper, J. M. (1975). Exploratory PK tests with a programmable high speed random number generator. *European Journal of Parapsychology, 1*(1), 3–14.

Bierman, D. J., Spottiswoode, J. P., & Bijl, A. (2015, July). *Can results in 'experimental parapsychology' be accounted for by 'questionable research practices?'* Paper presented at the 58th annual convention of the Parapsychological Association, Greenwich University, England.

Billington, J., Baron-Cohen, S., & Wheelwright, S. (2007). Cognitive style predicts entry into physical sciences and humanities: Questionnaire and performance tests of empathy and systemizing. *Learning and Individual Differences, 17,* 260–268. http://dx.doi.org/10.1016/j.lindif.2007.02.004

Blackmore, S. J. (1991). Near-death experiences: In or out of the body? *Skeptical Inquirer, 16,* 34–45.

Blackmore, S. J. (1993). *Dying to live: Near-death-experiences.* Buffalo, NY: Prometheus.

Blackmore, S. J. (1996). Near-death experiences. *Journal of the Royal Society of Medicine, 89,* 73–76.

Block, R. A. (1990). Models of psychological time. In R. A. Block (Ed.), *Cognitive models of psychological time* (pp. 1–35). Hillsdale, NJ: Erlbaum.

Bohm, D. (1983). *Wholeness and the implicate order.* London, England: Routledge.

Bond, K., Karkhaneh, M., Tjosvold, L., Vandermeer, B., Liang, Y., Bialy, L., & Klassen, T. P. (2007). *Meditation practices for health: State of the research.* Rockville, MD: Agency for Healthcare Research and Quality.

BonJour, L. (2010). Against materialism. In R. C. Koons & G. Bealer (Eds.), *The waning of materialism* (pp. 3–23). Oxford, England: Oxford University Press.

Bonta, I. L. (2004). Schizophrenia, dissociative anaesthesia and near-death experience; three events meeting at the NMDA receptor. *Medical Hypotheses, 62,* 23–28. http://dx.doi.org/10.1016/S0306-9877(03)00307-4

Borjigin, J., Lee, U., Liu, T., Pal, D., Huff, S., & Klarr, D., . . . Mashour, G. A. (2013). Surge of neurophysiological coherence and connectivity in the dying brain. *Proceedings of the National Academy of Sciences, USA, 110,* 14432–14437.

Botkin, A. L. (with Hogan, R. C.). (2014). *Induced after-death communication.* Charlottesville, VA: Hampton Roads.

Bowden, E. M., Jung-Beeman, M., Fleck, J., & Kounios, J. (2005). New approaches to demystifying insight. *Trends in Cognitive Sciences, 9,* 322–328.

Bowie, F. (2013). Building bridges, dissolving boundaries: Toward a methodology for the ethnographic study of the afterlife, mediumship, and spiritual beings. *Journal of the American Academy of Religion, 81,* 698–733. http://dx.doi.org/10.1093/jaarel/lft023

Bowie, F. (2014). Believing impossible things: Scepticism and ethnographic enquiry. In J. Hunter & D. Luke (Eds.), *Talking with the spirits: Ethnographies from between the worlds* (pp. 19–55). Brisbane, Australia: Daily Grail.

Bowman, C. (2001). *Return from heaven: Beloved relatives reincarnated within your family.* New York, NY: HarperCollins.

Braude, S. E. (2003). *Immortal remains: The evidence for life after death.* Lanham, MD: Rowman & Littlefield.

Braude, S. E. (2007). *The gold leaf lady and other parapsychological investigations.* http://dx.doi.org/10.7208/chicago/9780226071534.001.0001

Braude, S. E. (2014). Editorial. *Journal of Scientific Exploration, 28,* 579–584.

Brennan, J. H. (2013). *Whisperers: The secret history of the spirit world.* New York, NY: Overlook Press.

Broderick, D. (2015). *Knowing the unknowable: Putting psi to work.* Creede, CO: Ramble House.

Broderick, D., & Goertzel, B. (Eds.). (2015a). *Evidence for psi: Thirteen empirical research reports.* Jefferson, NC: McFarland.

Broderick, D., & Goertzel, B. (2015b). Introduction. In D. Broderick & B. Goertzel (Eds.), *Evidence for psi: Thirteen empirical research reports* (pp. 3–30). Jefferson, NC: McFarland.

Broughton, R. (2010, April). *An evolutionary approach to anomalous intuition.* Paper presented at the 8th symposium of the Bial Foundation: Beyond and Behind the Brain, Porto, Portugal.

Brown, D., & Sheldrake, R. (2001). The anticipation of telephone calls: A survey in California. *Journal of Parapsychology, 65,* 145–156.

Bynum, W. F., & Porter, R. (Eds.). (2005). *Oxford dictionary of scientific quotations.* Oxford, England: Oxford University Press.

Byrd, R. C. (1988). Positive therapeutic effects of intercessory prayer in a coronary care unit population. *Southern Medical Journal, 81,* 826–829. http://dx.doi.org/10.1097/00007611-198807000-00005

Cahn, B. R., & Polich, J. (2006). Meditation states and traits: EEG, ERP, and neuro-imaging studies. *Psychological Bulletin, 132,* 180–211.

Cai, D. J., Mednick, S. A., Harrison, E. M., Kanady, J. C., & Mednick, S. C. (2009). REM, not incubation, improves creativity by priming associative networks. *Proceedings of the National Academy of Sciences, USA, 106,* 10130–10134. http://dx.doi.org/10.1073/pnas.0900271106

Callender, C. (2010). Is time an illusion? *Scientific American, 302*(6), 58–65. http://dx.doi.org/10.1038/scientificamerican0610-58

Čapek, M. (1966). Time in relativity theory: Arguments for a philosophy of becoming. In J. T. Fraser (Ed.), *The voices of time: A cooperative survey of man's views of time as expressed by the sciences and by the humanities* (pp. 434–454). New York, NY: George Braziller.

Cardeña, E. (2014). A call for an open, informed study of all aspects of consciousness. *Frontiers in Human Neuroscience, 8*(17), 1–4. http://dx.doi.org/10.3389/fnhum.2014.00017

Cardeña, E., Krippner, S., & Lynn, S. J. (2014). Anomalous experiences: An integrative summary. In E. Cardeña, S. J. Lynn, & S. Krippner (Eds.), *Varieties of anomalous experience: Examining the scientific evidence* (2nd ed., pp. 409–426). http://dx.doi.org/10.1037/14258-014

Carhart-Harris, R. L., Erritzoe, D., Williams, T., Stone, J. M., Reed, L. J., Colasanti, A., . . . Nutt, D. J. (2012). Neural correlates of the psychedelic state as determined by fMRI studies with psilocybin. *Proceedings of the National Academy of Sciences, 109*(6), 2138–2143.

Carmack, B. J., & Packman, W. (2011). Pet loss: The interface of continuing bonds research and practice. In R. A. Neimeyer, D. L. Harris, H. R. Winokuer, & G. F. Thornton (Eds.), *Grief and bereavement in contemporary society: Bridging research and practice* (pp. 273–284). New York, NY: Routledge.

Carpenter, J. C. (1991). Prediction of forced-choice ESP performance: III. Three attempts to retrieve coded information using mood reports and a repeated-guessing technique. *Journal of Parapsychology, 55,* 227–280.

Carpenter, J. C. (2002). The intrusion of anomalous communication in group and individual psychotherapy: Clinical observations and a research project. *Proceedings of the Symposium of the Bial Foundation, 4,* 255–274.

Carpenter, J. C. (2005). First sight: Part two, elaboration of a model of psi and the mind. *Journal of Parapsychology, 69,* 63–112.

Carpenter, J. (2012). *First sight: ESP and parapsychology in everyday life.* Lanham, MD: Rowman & Littlefield.

Carpenter, J. C. (2014, August). *Psi in psychotherapy from a first sight perspective: Integration and prospectus.* President's address presented at the 57th Annual Parapsychology Association Conference, Concord, CA.

Carskadon, M. A., & Rechtschaffen, A. (2000). Monitoring and staging human sleep. In M. H. Kryger, T. Roth, & W. C. Dement (Eds.), *Principles and practice of sleep medicine* (3rd ed., pp. 1197–1215). Philadelphia, PA: W. B. Saunders.

Carter, C. (2012a). *Science and psychic phenomena: The fall of the house of skeptics.* Rochester, VT: Inner Traditions. (Original work published 2007)

Carter, C. (2012b). *Science and the afterlife experience: Evidence for the immortality of consciousness.* Rochester, VT: Inner Traditions.

Chalmers, A. (2008, Fall). Atomism from the 17th to the 20th century. In E. N. Zalta (Ed.), *The Stanford encyclopedia of philosophy.* Retrieved from http://plato.stanford.edu/entries/atomism-modern/

Chalmers, D. J. (1995). Facing up to the problem of consciousness. *Journal of Consciousness Studies, 2*, 200–219.

Chargaff, E. (1977). *Voices in the labyrinth: Nature, man and science*. New York, NY: Seabury Press.

Cheyne, J. A. (2005). Sleep paralysis episode frequency and number, types, and structure of associated hallucinations. *Journal of Sleep Research, 14*, 319–324. http://dx.doi.org/10.1111/j.1365-2869.2005.00477.x

Child, I. L. (1985). Psychology and anomalous observations: The question of ESP in dreams. *American Psychologist, 40*, 1219–1230. http://dx.doi.org/10.1037/0003-066X.40.11.1219

Churchland, P. S. (1980). A perspective on mind-brain research. *The Journal of Philosophy, 77*, 185–207. http://dx.doi.org/10.2307/2025588

Claridge, G. (1997). Final remarks and future directions. In G. Claridge (Ed.), *Schizotypy: Implications for illness and health* (pp. 301–313). http://dx.doi.org/10.1093/med:psych/9780198523536.003.0014

Clark, J. (1992). Contemplating nature with Arthur Zajonc. *Noetic Sciences Review, 23*, 19–28.

Clemence, G. M. (1966). Time measurement for scientific use. In J. T. Fraser (Ed.), *The voices of time: A cooperative survey of man's views of time as expressed by the sciences and by the humanities* (pp. 401–414). New York, NY: George Braziller.

Clifton, S. (2014). The dark side of prayer for healing: Toward a theology of well-being. *Pneuma, 36*, 204–225. http://dx.doi.org/10.1163/15700747-03602003

Coecke, B., & Pavlovic, D. (2009). *Quantum measurements without sums*. Retrieved from http://www.comlab.ox.ac.uk//files/674/RR-06-02.pdf

Cohen, M. X. (2014). *Analyzing neural time series data: Theory and practice*. Cambridge, MA: MIT Press.

Connelly, G. (2001). *Electronic voice phenomenon: The Cinderella science*. Corby, England: Domra.

Crispino, L. C. B., Higuchi, A., & Matsas, G. E. A. (2008). The Unruh effect and its applications. *Reviews of Modern Physics, 80*, 787–838. http://dx.doi.org/10.1103/RevModPhys.80.787

Cummins, G. (2012). *The road to immortality: Being a description of the afterlife purporting to be communicated by the late F. W. H. Myers*. Guildford, England: White Crow Books. (Original work published 1932)

Cuneo, M. W. (2001). *American exorcism: Expelling demons in the land of plenty*. New York, NY: Broadway Books.

Cunningham, P. F. (2012). The content-source problem in modern mediumship research. *Journal of Parapsychology, 76*, 295–319.

Cunningham, W. A., Preacher, K. J., & Banaji, M. R. (2001). Implicit attitude measures: Consistency, stability, and convergent validity. *Psychological Science, 12*, 163–170. http://dx.doi.org/10.1111/1467-9280.00328

Curry, L. E. (2008). *The doctor and the psychic*. Charleston, SC: BookSurge.

Czopp, A. M., Monteith, M. J., & Mark, A. Y. (2006). Standing up for a change: Reducing bias through interpersonal confrontation. *Journal of Personality and Social Psychology, 90*, 784–803. http://dx.doi.org/10.1037/0022-3514.90.5.784

Dai, H., & Wright, B. A. (1995). Detecting signals of unexpected or uncertain durations. *The Journal of the Acoustical Society of America, 98*, 798–806. http://dx.doi.org/10.1121/1.413572

Daintith, J. (Ed.). (2005). *A dictionary of physics* (5th ed.). Oxford, England: Oxford University Press.

Daintith, J. (Ed.). (2014). *A dictionary of physics* (6th ed.). Oxford, England: Oxford University Press.

Darghawth, R. (2013). Contemporary mediumship: Anthropological perspectives on the Long Island Medium. *Totem: The University of Western Ontario Journal of Anthropology, 21*(1), 83–90. Retrieved from http://ir.lib.uwo.ca/totem/vol21/iss1/9

Datson, S. L., & Marwit, S. J. (1997). Personality constructs and perceived presence of deceased loved ones. *Death Studies, 21*, 131–146. http://dx.doi.org/10.1080/074811897202047

Davies, P. (2002). *How to build a time machine*. New York, NY: Penguin Books.

de Broglie, L. (1987). Interpretation of quantum mechanics by the double solution theory. *Annales de la Fondation Louis de Broglie, 12*(4), 1–23.

De Pablos, F. (2011). Incorporation of future events into dream content: An experimental study. *Australian Journal of Parapsychology, 11*, 138–153.

de Peyer, J. (2014). Telepathic entanglements: Where are we today? Commentary on paper by Claudie Massicotte. *Psychoanalytic Dialogues, 24*, 109–121. http://dx.doi.org/10.1080/10481885.2014.870842

De Quincey, T. (1866). *Confessions of an English opium-eater, and suspiria de profundis*. Boston, MA: Ticknor and Fields.

Dein, S., & Littlewood, R. (2008). The psychology of prayer and the development of the Prayer Experience Questionnaire. *Mental Health, Religion & Culture, 11*, 39–52. http://dx.doi.org/10.1080/13674670701384396

Delgado-Romero, E. A., & Howard, G. S. (2005). Finding and correcting flawed research literatures. *The Humanistic Psychologist, 33*, 293–303. http://dx.doi.org/10.1207/s15473333thp3304_5

Della Negra, M., Jenni, P., & Virdee, T. S. (2012). Journey in the search for the Higgs boson: The ATLAS and CMS experiments at the Large Hadron Collider. *Science, 338*, 1560–1568. http://dx.doi.org/10.1126/science.1230827

Denkmayr, T., Geppert, H., Sponar, S., Lemmel, H., Matzkin, A., Tollaksen, J., & Hasegawa, Y. (2014, July). Observation of a quantum Cheshire cat in a matter wave interferometer experiment. *Nature Communications*. Retrieved from http://www.nature.com/ncomms/archive/date/2014/07/index.html

Dennett, D. C. (1978). *Brainstorms: Philosophical essays on mind and psychology*. Montgomery, VT: Bradford.

Dennett, D. C. (1982). How to study human consciousness empirically or nothing comes to mind. *Synthese, 53*, 159–180. http://dx.doi.org/10.1007/BF00484895

Dennett, D. C. (1988). Quining qualia. In A. J. Marcel & E. Bisiach (Eds.), *Consciousness in contemporary science* (pp. 42–77). Oxford, England: Oxford University Press.

Dennett, D., & Kinsbourne, M. (1992). Time and the observer: The where and when of consciousness in the brain. *Behavioral and Brain Sciences, 15*, 183–201. http://dx.doi.org/10.1017/S0140525X00068229

Desbordes, G., & Negi, L. T. (2013). A new era for mind studies: Training investigators in both scientific and contemplative methods of inquiry. *Frontiers in Human Neuroscience, 7*, 741. http://dx.doi.org/10.3389/fnhum.2013.00741

Dijksterhuis, A., Bos, M. W., Nordgren, L. F., & van Baaren, R. B. (2006). On making the right choice: The deliberation-without-attention effect. *Science, 311*, 1005–1007. http://dx.doi.org/10.1126/science.1121629

Dobyns, Y. (2015). The PEAR laboratory: Explorations and observations. In D. Broderick & B. Goertzel (Eds.), *Evidence for psi: Thirteen empirical research reports* (pp. 213–236). Jefferson, NC: McFarland.

Dossey, L. (1997). *Be careful what you pray for . . . you just might get it: What we can do about the unintentional effects of our thoughts, prayers, and wishes.* New York, NY: HarperSanFrancisco.

Draaisma, D. (2004). *Why life speeds up as you get older: How memory shapes our past* (A. Pomerans & E. Pomerans, Trans.). (Original work published 2001) http://dx.doi.org/10.1017/CBO9780511489945

Dunne, B. J., & Jahn, R. G. (2003). Information and uncertainty in remote perception research. *Journal of Scientific Exploration, 17*, 207–241.

Dunne, B. J., Nelson, R. D., & Jahn, R. G. (1988). Operator-related anomalies in a random mechanical cascade. *Journal of Scientific Exploration, 2*, 155–179.

Dürr, H.-P. (2005). Radically quantum: Liberation and purification from classical prejudice. In A. Elitzur, S. Dolev, & N. Kolenda (Eds.), *Quo vadis quantum mechanics?* (pp. 7–45). http://dx.doi.org/10.1007/3-540-26669-0_2

Eagleman, D. M. (2008). Human time perception and its illusions. *Current Opinion in Neurobiology, 18*, 131–136. http://dx.doi.org/10.1016/j.conb.2008.06.002

Eagleman, D. M. (2011, October 27). Your brain knows a lot more than you realize. *Discover.* Retrieved from http://discovermagazine.com/2011/sep/18-your-brain-knows-lot-more-than-you-realize

Eccles, J. C. (1976). How dogmatic can materialism be? In G. G. Globus, G. Maxwell, & I. Savodnik (Eds.), *Consciousness and the brain—A scientific and philosophical inquiry* (pp. 155–160). New York, NY: Plenum.

835850 Ontario Limited. (Producer). (1974). *Philip: The imaginary ghost* [DVD]. Available from Visual Education Centre Limited, 30 MacIntosh Blvd., Unit 7, Vaughan, Ontario, Canada L4K 4P1.

Eisenbeiss, W., & Hassler, D. (2006). An assessment of ostensible communications with a deceased grandmaster as evidence for survival. *Journal of the Society for Psychical Research, 70.2*(883), 65–97.

Eisler, A. D. (2003). The human sense of time: Biological, cognitive, and cultural considerations. In R. Buccheri, M. Saniga, & W. Stucky (Eds.), *The nature of time: Geometry, physics and perception* (pp. 5–18). http://dx.doi.org/10.1007/978-94-010-0155-7_2

Eisler, H. (2003). The parallel-clock model: A tool for quantification of experienced duration. In R. Buccheri, M. Saniga, & W. Stucky (Eds.), *The nature of time: Geometry, physics and perception* (pp. 19–26). http://dx.doi.org/10.1007/978-94-010-0155-7_3

Elitzur, A. (2006). What's the mind–body problem with you anyway? Prolegomena to any scientific discussion of consciousness. In A. Batthyany & A. Elitzur, (Eds.), *Mind and its place in the world: Non-reductionist approaches to the ontology of consciousness* (pp. 15–22). Frankfurt, Germany: Ontos Verlag.

Elitzur, A., Dolev, S., & Kolenda, N. (Eds.). (2005). *Quo vadis quantum mechanics?* Berlin, Germany: Springer. http://dx.doi.org/10.1007/b137897

Elliott, J. C., Wallace, B. A., & Giesbrecht, B. (2014). A week-long meditation retreat decouples behavioral measures of the alerting and executive attention networks. *Frontiers in Human Neuroscience, 8,* 1–9. http://dx.doi.org/10.3389/fnhum.2014.00069

Engel, A. K., & Singer, W. (2001). Temporal binding and the neural correlates of sensory awareness. *Trends in Cognitive Sciences, 5,* 16–25. http://dx.doi.org/10.1016/S1364-6613(00)01568-0

Epstein, M. (1990). Psychodynamics of meditation: Pitfalls on the spiritual path. *Journal of Transpersonal Psychology, 22,* 17–34.

Fenwick, P., & Fenwick, E. (1995). *The truth in the light: An investigation of over 300 near-death experiences.* New York, NY: Berkeley.

Fenwick, P., & Fenwick, E. (2013). *The art of dying.* London, England: Bloomsbury Academic.

Ferracuti, S., & Sacco, R. (1996). Dissociative trance disorder: Clinical and Rorschach findings in ten persons reporting demon possession and treated by exorcism. *Journal of Personality Assessment, 66,* 525–539. http://dx.doi.org/10.1207/s15327752jpa6603_4

Ferrucci, P. (2014). *Your inner will: Finding personal strength in critical times* (V. R. Ferrucci, Trans.). New York, NY: Tarcher/Penguin.

Feynman, R. P. (1989). *"What do you care what other people think?" Further adventures of a curious character.* New York, NY: Bantam Books.

Feynman, R. P. (2006). *QED: The strange theory of light and matter.* Princeton, NJ: Princeton University Press. (Original work published 1985)

Field, N. P., & Wogrin, C. (2011). The changing bond in therapy for unresolved loss: An attachment theory perspective. In R. A. Neimeyer, D. L. Harris, H. R. Winokuer, & G. F. Thornton (Eds.), *Grief and bereavement in contemporary society: Bridging research and practice* (pp. 37–46). New York, NY: Routledge.

Fisher, S. (2014, Spring). Pierre Gassendi. In E. N. Zalta (Ed.), *The Stanford encyclopedia of philosophy*. Retrieved from http://plato.stanford.edu/archives/spr2014/entries/gassendi/

Fisk, G. W., & West, D. J. (1957). Towards accurate predictions from ESP data. *Journal of the Society for Psychical Research, 39,* 157–162.

Fodor, J. (2000). *The mind doesn't work that way: The scope and limits of computational psychology*. Cambridge, MA: MIT Press.

Fontana, D. (2005). *Is there an afterlife? A comprehensive overview of the evidence*. Winchester, England: O-Books.

Foy, R. P. (2008). *Witnessing the impossible*. Diss, England: Torcal.

Franklin, M. S., Baumgart, S. L., & Schooler, J. W. (2014). Future directions in precognition research: More research can bridge the gap between skeptics and proponents. *Frontiers in Psychology, 5,* 907. http://dx.doi.org/10.3389/fpsyg.2014.00907

Freud, E. L. (Ed.). (1961). *Letters of Sigmund Freud: 1873–1939*. London, England: Hogarth Press.

Freud, S. (1961). The occult significance of dreams. In J. Strachey & A. Freud (Eds.), *Standard edition of the complete psychological works of Sigmund Freud* (Vol. 19, pp. 135–138). London, England: Hogarth Press. (Original work published 1925)

Freud, S. (1962a). Dreams and telepathy. In J. Strachey & A. Freud (Eds.), *Standard edition of the complete psychological works of Sigmund Freud* (Vol. 18, pp. 195–220). London, England: Hogarth Press. (Original work published 1922)

Freud, S. (1962b). Psychoanalysis and telepathy. In J. Strachey & A. Freud (Eds.), *Standard edition of the complete psychological works of Sigmund Freud* (Vol. 18, pp. 171–193). London, England: Hogarth Press. (Original work published 1921)

Friedman, H. L., & Krippner, S. (2010). Is it time for a détente? In S. Krippner & H. L. Friedman (Eds.), *Debating psychic experience: Human potential or human illusion?* (pp. 195–204). Santa Barbara, CA: Praeger.

Friedman, W. J. (1990). *About time: Inventing the fourth dimension*. Boston, MA: MIT Press.

Fuller, J. G. (1985). *The ghost of 29 megacycles: A new breakthrough in life after death?* London, England: Souvenir Press.

Fuster, J. M. (2001). The prefrontal cortex—an update: Time is of the essence. *Neuron, 30,* 319–333. http://dx.doi.org/10.1016/S0896-6273(01)00285-9

Gabora, L. (2002). Amplifying phenomenal information: Toward a fundamental theory of consciousness. *Journal of Consciousness Studies, 9*(8), 3–29.

Gale, R. M. (Ed.). (1967). *The philosophy of time: A collection of essays*. Garden City, NY: Anchor Books.

Gawande, A. (2014). *Being mortal: Medicine and what matters in the end*. Toronto, Ontario, Canada: Doubleday Canada.

Goertzel, T., & Goertzel, B. (2015). Skeptical responses to psi research. In D. Broderick & B. Goertzel (Eds.), *Evidence for psi: Thirteen empirical research reports* (pp. 291–301). Jefferson, NC: McFarland.

Gooch, S. (2007). *The origins of psychic phenomena: Poltergeists, incubi, succubi, and the unconscious mind*. Rochester, VT: Inner Traditions. (Original work published 1984)

Goswami, A., Reed, R. E., & Goswami, M. (1993). *The self-aware universe: How consciousness creates the material world*. New York, NY: Tarcher.

Greeley, A. (1987). The "impossible": It's happening. *Noetic Sciences Review, 2*, 7–9.

Green, D. M., & Swets, J. A. (1966). *Signal detection theory and psychophysics*. New York, NY: Wiley.

Greenwald, A. G. (1975). Consequences of prejudice against the null hypothesis. *Psychological Bulletin, 82*, 1–20. http://dx.doi.org/10.1037/h0076157

Greyson, B. (1985). A typology of near-death experiences. *The American Journal of Psychiatry, 142*, 967–969. http://dx.doi.org/10.1176/ajp.142.8.967

Greyson, B. (2010). Implications of near-death experiences for a postmaterialist psychology. *Psychology of Religion and Spirituality, 2*, 37–45. http://dx.doi.org/10.1037/a0018548

Greyson, B. (2013). Is consciousness produced by the brain? In G. Lhakdor & B. E. Johnson (Eds.), *Cosmology & consciousness: Mind & matter: Exchanges between Buddhist scholars and Indian and Western scientists* (pp. 61–81). Dharamsala, India: Library of Tibetan Works and Archives.

Greyson, B. (2014). Near-death experiences. In E. Cardeña, S. J. Lynn, & S. Krippner (Eds.), *Varieties of anomalous experience: Examining the scientific evidence* (2nd ed., pp. 333–367). http://dx.doi.org/10.1037/14258-012

Greyson, B., & Bush, N. E. (1992). Distressing near-death experiences. *Psychiatry, 55*, 95–110.

Greyson, B., Holden, J. M., & Mounsey, P. (2006). Failure to elicit near-death experiences in induced cardiac arrest. *Journal of Near-Death Studies, 25*, 85–98.

Grinspoon, L., & Bakalar, J. B. (1979). *Psychedelic drugs reconsidered*. New York, NY: Basic Books.

Gröblacher, S., Paterek, T., Kaltenbaek, R., Brukner, C., Żukowski, M., Aspelmeyer, M., & Zeilinger, A. (2007). An experimental test of non-local realism. *Nature, 446*, 871–875. http://dx.doi.org/10.1038/nature05677

Grof, P., & Kautz, W. H. (2010). Bipolar disorder: Verification of insights obtained by intuitive consensus. *Journal of Transpersonal Psychology, 42*, 171–191.

Grosso, M. (1994, Winter). The status of survival research: Evidence, problems, paradigms. *Noetic Sciences Review, 32*, 12–20.

Grosso, M. (2014). Two perspectives on possession. *Journal of Scientific Exploration, 28*, 509–517.

Grosso, M. (2015). The "transmission" model of mind and body: A brief history. In E. F. Kelly, A. Crabtree, & P. Marshall (Eds.), *Beyond physicalism: Toward reconciliation of science and spirituality* (pp. 79–113). Lanham, MD: Rowman & Littlefield.

Guggenheim, B., & Guggenheim, J. (1996). *Hello from heaven! A new field of research—after-death communication—confirms that life and love are eternal.* New York, NY: Bantam.

Guiley, R. E. (1991). *Harper's encyclopedia of mystical & paranormal experience.* New York, NY: HarperSanFrancisco.

Guirdham, A. (1982). *The psychic dimensions of mental health.* Wellingborough, Northamptonshire, England: Turnstone.

Hafele, J. C., & Keating, R. E. (1972). Around-the-world atomic clocks: Observed relativistic time gains. *Science, 177,* 168–170. http://dx.doi.org/10.1126/science.177.4044.168

Haisch, B. (2007). Reductionism and consciousness. In T. Pfeiffer, J. E. Mack, & P. Devereux (Eds.), *Mind before matter: Visions of a new science of consciousness* (pp. 51–63). Ropley, Hampshire, England: O Books.

Hall, C. (2014). Bereavement theory: Recent developments in our understanding of grief and bereavement. *Bereavement Care, 33,* 7–12. http://dx.doi.org/10.1080/02682621.2014.902610

Hallett, E. (2002). *Stories of the unborn soul: The mystery and delight of pre-birth communication.* San Jose, CA: Writers Club Press.

Hamilton-Parker, C. (2001). *What to do when you are dead: Living better in the afterlife.* New York, NY: Sterling.

Haraldsson, E. (2012). *The departed among the living: An investigative study of afterlife encounters.* Guildford, England: White Crow.

Harman, W., & Rheingold, H. (1984). *Higher creativity: Liberating the unconscious for breakthrough insights.* Los Angeles, CA: Tarcher.

Harnad, S. (1987). Methodological epiphenomenalism vs. methodological behaviorism. *Psychnet Newsletter, 2*(7). [Machine-readable data file]. Retrieved from EPSYNET@UHUPVM1

Harris, W. S., Gowda, M., Kolb, J. W., Strychacz, C. P., Vacek, J. L., Jones, P. G., . . . McCallister, B. D. (1999). A randomized, controlled trial of the effects of remote, intercessory prayer on outcomes in patients admitted to the coronary care unit. *Archives of Internal Medicine, 159,* 2273–2278. http://dx.doi.org/10.1001/archinte.159.19.2273

Hassin, R. R. (2013). Yes it can: On the functional abilities of the human unconscious. *Perspectives on Psychological Science, 8*(2), 195–207. http://dx.doi.org/10.1177/1745691612460684

Healy, T., & Cropper, P. (2014). *Australian poltergeist.* Sydney, Australia: Strange Nation.

Heavey, C. L., & Hurlburt, R. T. (2008). The phenomena of inner experience. *Consciousness and Cognition, 17,* 798–810. http://dx.doi.org/10.1016/j.concog.2007.12.006

Helminiak, D. A. (1984). Consciousness as a subject matter. *Journal for the Theory of Social Behaviour, 14,* 211–230. http://dx.doi.org/10.1111/j.1468-5914.1984.tb00495.x

Hempel, C. G. (1980). Comments on Goodman's *Ways of Worldmaking. Synthese, 45,* 193–199. http://dx.doi.org/10.1007/BF00413558

Henderson, J. (1982). Exorcism and possession in psychotherapy practice. *Canadian Journal of Psychiatry, 27,* 129–134.

Herzog, S. M., & Hertwig, R. (2014). Harnessing the wisdom of the inner crowd. *Trends in Cognitive Sciences, 18,* 504–506. http://dx.doi.org/10.1016/j.tics.2014.06.009

Hess, D. J. (1992). Disciplining heterodoxy, circumventing discipline: Parapsychology, anthropologically. *Knowledge and society: The anthropology of science and technology, 9,* 223–252.

Hewitt, M. A. (2014). Freud and the psychoanalysis of telepathy: Commentary on Claudie Massicotte's "psychical transmissions." *Psychoanalytic Dialogues, 24*(1), 103–108. http://dx.doi.org/10.1080/10481885.2014.870841

Hinterberger, T., Schmidt, S., Kamei, T., & Walach, H. (2014). Decreased electrophysiological activity represents the conscious state of emptiness in meditation. *Frontiers in Psychology, 5,* 99. http://dx.doi.org/10.3389/fpsyg.2014.00099

Hinze, S. (1997). *Coming from the light: Spiritual accounts of life before life.* New York, NY: Pocket Books.

Hirsch, H. V. B., & Spinelli, D. N. (1971). Modification of the distribution of receptive field orientation in cats by selective visual exposure during development. *Experimental Brain Research, 12,* 509–527. http://dx.doi.org/10.1007/BF00234246

Hoffer, A. (Ed.). (2015). *Freud and the Buddha: The couch and the cushion.* London, England: Karnac Books.

Hoffman, D. D. (1998). *Visual intelligence: How we create what we see.* New York, NY: W. W. Norton.

Holden, J., & Joesten, L. (1990). Near-death veridicality research in the hospital setting: Problems and promise. *Journal of Near-Death Studies, 9,* 45–54. http://dx.doi.org/10.1007/BF01074101

Holden, M., McKeon, D. G. C., & Sherry, T. N. (2011). The double slit experiment with polarizers. *Canadian Journal of Physics, 89,* 1079–1081. http://dx.doi.org/10.1139/p11-122

Honorton, C. (2015). A moving experience. *Journal of Scientific Exploration, 29,* 62–74. (Original work published 1993)

Honorton, C., & Ferrari, D. (1989). Future telling: A meta-analysis of forced-choice precognition experiments, 1935–1987. *Journal of Parapsychology, 53,* 281–308.

Horst, S. (2011, Spring). The computational theory of mind. In E. N. Zalta (Ed.), *The Stanford encyclopedia of philosophy.* Retrieved from http://plato.stanford.edu/archives/spr2011/entries/computational-mind/

Hu, X., Antony, J. W., Creery, J. D., Vargas, I. M., Bodenhausen, G. V., & Paller, K. A. (2015). Unlearning implicit social biases during sleep. *Science, 348,* 1013–1015. http://dx.doi.org/10.1126/science.aaa3841

Hufford, D. J. (1982). *The terror that comes in the night: An experience-centered study of supernatural assault traditions.* Philadelphia: University of Pennsylvania Press.

Hufford, D. J. (1994). Awakening paralyzed in the presence of a strange "visitor." In A. Pritchard, D. E. Pritchard, J. E. Mack, P. Kasey, & C. Yapp (Eds.), *Alien discussions: Proceedings of the abduction study conference held at MIT, Cambridge, MA* (pp. 348–354). Cambridge, MA: North Cambridge Press.

Hufford, D. J. (2005). Sleep paralysis as spiritual experience. *Transcultural Psychiatry, 42,* 11–45. http://dx.doi.org/10.1177/1363461505050709

Hufford, D. (2014). The healing power of extraordinary spiritual experiences. *Journal of Near-Death Studies, 32,* 137–156.

Hume, D. (1993). An enquiry concerning human understanding. In E. Steinberg (Ed.), *Philosophical essays concerning human understanding* (2nd ed., pp. 1–114). Indianapolis, IN: Hackett. (Original work published 1748)

Hurlburt, R. T., & Heavey, C. L. (2001). Telling what we know: Describing inner experience. *Trends in Cognitive Sciences, 5,* 400–403. http://dx.doi.org/10.1016/S1364-6613(00)01724-1

Husserl, E. (1990). *On the phenomenology of the consciousness of internal time (1893–1917)* (T. J. B. Brough, Trans.). Dordrecht, The Netherlands: Kluwer.

Hutchinson, E. D. (1939). Varieties of insight in humans. *Psychiatry, 2,* 323–332.

Huxley, A. (1977). *The doors of perception and heaven and hell.* London, England: Grafton Books.

Hyman, R. (2010). What's wrong with materialism? In S. Krippner & H. L. Friedman (Eds.), *Debating psychic experience: Human potential or human illusion?* (pp. 133–148). Santa Barbara, CA: Praeger.

Hyman, R., & Honorton, C. (1986). A joint communiqué: The psi Ganzfeld controversy. *Journal of Parapsychology, 50,* 351–364.

Ioannidis, J. P. A. (2005). Why most published research findings are false. *PLoS Medicine, 2*(8), e124. http://dx.doi.org/10.1371/journal.pmed.0020124

Irwin, H. J. (1994). *An introduction to parapsychology* (2nd ed.). Jefferson, NC: McFarland.

Irwin, H. J. (2014). Aberrant salience and motivation as factors in the formation of belief in scientifically unaccepted phenomena. *Journal of Scientific Exploration, 28,* 633–645.

Isaacs, T. C. (1987). The possessive states disorder: The diagnosis of demonic possession. *Pastoral Psychology, 35,* 263–273. http://dx.doi.org/10.1007/BF01760734

Jackson, D. N. (1999). *Personality research form manual* (3rd ed.). Port Huron, MI: Sigma Assessment Systems.

Jahn, R. G. (2001). 20th and 21st century science: Reflections and projections. *Journal of Scientific Exploration, 15,* 21–31.

Jahn, R. G., Dunne, B. J., Bradish, G. J., Dobyns, Y. H., Lettieri, A., Nelson, R. D., . . . Walter, B. (2000). Mind/Machine Interaction Consortium: PortREG replication experiments. *Journal of Scientific Exploration, 14,* 499–555.

Jahn, R. G., Dunne, B. J., Nelson, R. D., Dobyns, Y. H., & Bradish, G. J. (1997). Correlations of random binary sequences with pre-stated operator intention: A review of a 12-year program. *Journal of Scientific Exploration, 11,* 345–367.

James, W. (1909). Confidences of a psychical researcher. *The American Magazine, 68,* 580–589.

James, W. (1981). *The principles of psychology* (Vol. 1). Cambridge, MA: Harvard University Press. (Original work published 1890)

Janis, I. L. (1971, November). Groupthink. *Psychology Today, 5,* 43–46, 74–76.

Jansen, K. L. R. (1997). The ketamine model of the near-death experience: A central role for the N-methyl-D-aspartate receptor. *Journal of Near-Death Studies, 16,* 5–26. http://dx.doi.org/10.1023/A:1025055109480

Jensen, C. G., & Cardeña, E. (2009). A controlled long-distance test of a professional medium. *European Journal of Parapsychology, 24,* 53–67.

Jewkes, S., & Baruš, I. (2000). Personality correlates of beliefs about consciousness and reality. *Advanced Development: A Journal on Adult Giftedness, 9,* 91-103.

John, L. K., Loewenstein, G., & Prelec, D. (2012). Measuring the prevalence of questionable research practices with incentives for truth telling. *Psychological Science, 23,* 524–532. http://dx.doi.org/10.1177/0956797611430953

Josephson, B. D. (2012). Coupled superconductors and beyond. *Low Temperature Physics, 38,* 260–262. http://dx.doi.org/10.1063/1.3697974

Josipovic, Z. (2014). Neural correlates of nondual awareness in meditation. *Annals of the New York Academy of Sciences, 1307,* 9–18. http://dx.doi.org/10.1111/nyas.12261

Jung, C. G. (1969). *The archetypes and the collective unconscious: Vol. 9. The collected works of C. G. Jung.* Princeton, NJ: Princeton University Press. (Original work published 1936)

Jung, C. G. (1989). *Memories, dreams, reflections* (A. Jaffé, Ed.; R. Winston & C. Winston, Trans.). New York, NY: Vintage Books. (Original work published 1961)

Kafatos, M., & Nadeau, R. (1990). *The conscious universe: Part and whole in modern physical theory.* http://dx.doi.org/10.1007/978-1-4684-0360-2

Kardec, A. (1874). *Experimental spiritism: Book on mediums; Or, guide for mediums and invocators* (E. A. Wood, Trans.). Boston, MA: Colby and Rich.

Karni, A., Tanne, D., Rubenstein, B. S., Askenasy, J. J., & Sagi, D. (1994). Dependence on REM sleep of overnight improvement of a perceptual skill. *Science, 265,* 679–682. http://dx.doi.org/10.1126/science.8036518

Kastrup, B. (2014). *Why materialism is baloney: How true skeptics know there is no death and fathom answers to life, the universe and everything.* Winchester, England: Iff Books.

Kastrup, B. (2015). *Brief peeks beyond: Critical essays on metaphysics, neuroscience, free will, skepticism and culture.* Winchester, England: Iff Books.

Keen, M. (2001). The Scole investigation: A study in critical analysis of paranormal physical phenomena. *Journal of Scientific Exploration, 15,* 167–182.

Keen, M., Ellison, A., & Fontana, D. (1999). The Scole report: An account of an investigation into the genuineness of a range of physical phenomena associated with a mediumistic group in Norfolk, England. *Proceedings of the Society for Psychical Research, 58*(Pt. 220), 149–392.

Kelly, E. F. (2015). Toward a worldview grounded in science and spirituality. In E. F. Kelly, A. Crabtree, & P. Marshall (Eds.), *Beyond physicalism: Toward reconciliation of science and spirituality* (pp. 493–551). Lanham, MD: Rowman & Littlefield.

Kelly, E. F., Crabtree, A., & Marshall, P. (Eds.). (2015). *Beyond physicalism: Toward reconciliation of science and spirituality.* Lanham, MD: Rowman & Littlefield.

Kelly, E. F., & Grosso, M. (2010a). Genius. In E. F. Kelly, E. W. Kelly, A. Crabtree, A. Gauld, M. Grosso, & B. Greyson (Ed.), *Irreducible mind: Toward a psychology for the 21st century* (pp. 423–493). Lanham, MD: Rowman & Littlefield.

Kelly, E. F., & Grosso, M. (2010b). Mystical experience. In E. F. Kelly, E. W. Kelly, A. Crabtree, A. Gauld, M. Grosso, & B. Greyson (Eds.), *Irreducible mind: Toward a psychology for the 21st century* (pp. 495–575). Lanham, MD: Rowman & Littlefield.

Kelly, E. F., & Presti, D. E. (2015). A psychobiological perspective on "transmission" models. In E. F. Kelly, A. Crabtree, & P. Marshall (Eds.), *Beyond physicalism: Toward reconciliation of science and spirituality* (pp. 115–155). Lanham, MD: Rowman & Littlefield.

Kelly, E. W., & Arcangel, D. (2011). An investigation of mediums who claim to give information about deceased persons. *Journal of Nervous and Mental Disease, 199,* 11–17. http://dx.doi.org/10.1097/NMD.0b013e31820439da

Kelly, E. W., Greyson, B., & Kelly, E. F. (2010). Unusual experiences near death and related phenomena. In E. F. Kelly, E. W. Kelly, A. Crabtree, A. Gauld, M. Grosso, & B. Greyson (Eds.), *Irreducible mind: Toward a psychology for the 21st century* (pp. 367–421). Lanham, MD: Rowman & Littlefield.

Kennedy, J. B. (2003). *Space, time and Einstein: An introduction.* Montreal & Kingston, Canada: McGill-Queen's University Press.

Kerr, N. H. (2000). Dreaming, imagery, and perception. In M. H. Kryger, T. Roth, & W. C. Dement (Eds.), *Principles and practice of sleep medicine* (3rd ed., pp. 482–490). Philadelphia, PA: W. B. Saunders.

Kihlstrom, J. F., Barnhardt, T. M., & Tataryn, D. J. (1992). The psychological unconscious. Found, lost, and regained. *American Psychologist, 47,* 788–791. http://dx.doi.org/10.1037/0003-066X.47.6.788

Klemenc-Ketis, Z. (2013). Life changes in patients after out-of-hospital cardiac arrest: The effect of near-death experiences. *International Journal of Behavioral Medicine, 20*, 7–12. http://dx.doi.org/10.1007/s12529-011-9209-y

Klemenc-Ketis, Z., Kersnik, J., & Grmec, S. (2010). The effect of carbon dioxide on near-death experiences in out-of-hospital cardiac arrest survivors: A prospective observational study. *Critical Care, 14*, R56. http://dx.doi.org/10.1186/cc8952

Koch, C. (2012). *Consciousness: Confessions of a romantic reductionist.* Cambridge, MA: MIT Press.

Kochen, S., & Specker, E. P. (1967). The problem of hidden variables in quantum mechanics. *Journal of Mathematics and Mechanics, 17*, 59–87.

Koltko-Rivera, M. E. (2004). The psychology of worldviews. *Review of General Psychology, 8*, 3–58.

Koons, R. C., & Bealer, G. (2010). Introduction. In R. C. Koons & G. Bealer (Eds.), *The waning of materialism* (pp. ix–xxxi). http://dx.doi.org/10.1093/acprof:oso/9780199556182.001.0001

Korf, J. (2015). Quantum and multidimensional explanations in a neurobiological context of mind. *The Neuroscientist, 21*, 345–355. http://dx.doi.org/10.1177/1073858414542250

Kornmeier, J., & Mayer, G. (2014). The alien in the forest OR when temporal context dominates perception. *Perception, 43*, 1270–1274. http://dx.doi.org/10.1068/p7844

Kounios, J., Frymiare, J. L., Bowden, E. M., Fleck, J. I., Subramaniam, K., Parrish, T. B., & Jung-Beeman, M. (2006). The prepared mind: Neural activity prior to problem presentation predicts subsequent solution by sudden insight. *Psychological Science, 17*, 882–890. http://dx.doi.org/10.1111/j.1467-9280.2006.01798.x

Krippner, S., Honorton, C., & Ullman, M. (1972). A second precognitive dream study with Malcolm Bessent. *Journal of the American Society for Psychical Research, 66*, 269–279.

Krippner, S., Ullman, M., & Honorton, C. (1971). A precognitive dream study with a single subject. *Journal of the American Society for Psychical Research, 65*, 192–203.

Krucoff, M. W., Crater, S. W., Gallup, D., Blankenship, J. C., Cuffe, M., Guarneri, M., . . . Lee, K. L. (2005). Music, imagery, touch, and prayer as adjuncts to interventional cardiac care: The Monitoring and Actualisation of Noetic Trainings (MANTRA) II randomised study. *The Lancet, 366*, 211–217. http://dx.doi.org/10.1016/S0140-6736(05)66910-3

Kübler-Ross, E. (1977, Summer). Death does not exist. *CoEvolution Quarterly.* Retrieved from http://www.wholeearth.com/issue/2014/article/379/death.doea.not.exist

Kübler-Ross, E. (1997). *The wheel of life: A memoir of living and dying.* New York, NY: Touchstone.

Kuhlmann, M. (2013). What is real? *Scientific American, 309*(2), 40–47. http://dx.doi.org/10.1038/scientificamerican0813-40

Kuhn, T. S. (1970). *The structure of scientific revolutions* (2nd ed.). Chicago, IL: University of Chicago Press.

Kwilecki, S. (2014). The soul contract theodicy: New Age understandings of the death of a child. *Journal of Contemporary Religion, 29*, 411–424. http://dx.doi.org/10.1080/13537903.2014.945724

Ladd, K. L., & Spilka, B. (2014). Prayer and health research: Proxies, missed targets, and opportunities. *Revista Pistis e Práxis: Teologia e Pastoral, 6*(1), 33–50. http://dx.doi.org/10.7213/revistapistispraxis.06.001.DS02

Lamotte, M., Izaute, M., & Droit-Volet, S. (2012). Awareness of time distortions and its relation with time judgment: A metacognitive approach. *Consciousness and Cognition, 21*(2), 835–842. http://dx.doi.org/10.1016/j.concog.2012.02.012

Lange, R., Schredl, M., & Houran, J. (2000). What precognitive dreams are made of: The nonlinear dynamics of tolerance of ambiguity, dream recall, and paranormal belief. *Dynamic Psychology: An International Interdisciplinary Journal of Complex Mental Processes.* Retrieved from http://www.goertzel.org/dynapsyc/dynacon.html

Laplace, P.-S. (1951). *A philosophical essay on probabilities.* New York, NY: Dover. (Original work published 1814)

Larson, C. S. (2012). *Reality shifts: When consciousness changes the physical world.* Berkeley, CA: RealityShifters.

Laudisa, F., & Rovelli, C. (2008, Summer). Relational quantum mechanics. In E. N. Zalta (Ed.), *The Stanford encyclopedia of philosophy.* Retrieved from http://stanford.library.usyd.edu.au/archives/sum2008/entries/qm-relational/

Law, J., & Rennie, R. (Eds.). (2015). *A dictionary of physics* (7th ed.). http://dx.doi.org/10.1093/acref/9780198714743.001.0001

Le Poidevin, R. (2011, Fall). The experience and perception of time. In E. N. Zalta (Ed.), *The Stanford encyclopedia of philosophy.* Retrieved from http://plato.stanford.edu/archives/fall2011/entries/time-experience/

Lethbridge, T. C. (1961). *Ghost and ghoul.* London, England: Routledge and Kegan Paul.

Lévy-Leblond, J.-M. (1988). Neither waves, nor particles, but quantons. *Nature, 334*, 19–20. http://dx.doi.org/10.1038/334019c0

Lewis, L. (1994). *The assassination of Lincoln: History and myth.* Lincoln: University of Nebraska Press.

Libet, B., Freeman, A., & Sutherland, K. (1999). Editors' introduction: The volitional brain: Towards a neuroscience of free will. *Journal of Consciousness Studies, 6*(8–9), ix–xxii.

Lindström, T. C. (1995). Experiencing the presence of the dead: Discrepancies in "the sensing experience" and their psychological concomitants. *Omega: Journal of Death and Dying, 31*, 11–21. http://dx.doi.org/10.2190/FRWJ-U2WM-V689-H30K

Lipson, M. (1987). Objective experience. *Noûs*, *21*, 319–343. http://dx.doi.org/10.2307/2215185

Lloyd, P. B. (2006). Mental monism considered as a solution to the mind–body problem. In A. Batthyany & A. Elitzur (Eds.), *Mind and its place in the world: Non-reductionist approaches to the ontology of consciousness* (pp. 101–144). http://dx.doi.org/10.1515/9783110325683.101

Loewi, O. (1960). An autobiographical sketch. *Perspectives in Biology and Medicine*, *4*(1), 3–25. http://dx.doi.org/10.1353/pbm.1960.0006

Luke, D., Zychowicz, K., Richterova, O., Tjurina, I., & Polonnikova, J. (2012). A sideways look at the neurobiology of psi: Precognition and circadian rhythms. *NeuroQuantology*, *10*, 580–590. http://dx.doi.org/10.14704/nq.2012.10.3.614

Lukey, N., & Barušs, I. (2005). Intelligence correlates of transcendent beliefs: A preliminary study. *Imagination, Cognition and Personality*, *24*, 259–270. http://dx.doi.org/10.2190/5H80-2PCY-02YB-F7HN

Lutz, A., Slagter, H. A., Dunne, J. D., & Davidson, R. J. (2008). Attention regulation and monitoring in meditation. *Trends in Cognitive Sciences*, *12*, 163–169. http://dx.doi.org/10.1016/j.tics.2008.01.005

Lycan, W. G. (1987). *Consciousness*. Cambridge, MA: MIT Press.

Lyons, W. (1986). *The disappearance of introspection*. Cambridge, MA: MIT Press.

Manford, M., & Andermann, F. (1998). Complex visual hallucinations: Clinical and neurobiological insights. *Brain: A Journal of Neurology*, *121*, 1819–1840. http://dx.doi.org/10.1093/brain/121.10.1819

Markosian, N. (2014, Spring). Time. In E. N. Zalta (Ed.), *The Stanford encyclopedia of philosophy*. Retrieved from http://plato.stanford.edu/archives/spr2014/entries/time/

Masayuki, O., & Akira, I. (2014). Children with life-between-life memories. *Journal of Scientific Exploration*, *28*, 477–490.

Maslow, A. H. (1969). The farther reaches of human nature. *Journal of Transpersonal Psychology*, *1*(1), 1–9.

Massicotte, C. (2014). Psychical transmissions: Freud, spiritualism, and the occult. *Psychoanalytic Dialogues: The International Journal of Relational Perspectives*, *24*(1), 88–102. http://dx.doi.org/10.1080/10481885.2014.870840

Masson, M. M. (1985). *The assault on truth: Freud's suppression of the seduction theory*. New York, NY: Penguin.

Mathewson, K. E., Gratton, G., Fabiani, M., Beck, D. M., & Ro, T. (2009). To see or not to see: Prestimulus alpha phase predicts visual awareness. *The Journal of Neuroscience*, *29*, 2725–2732. http://dx.doi.org/10.1523/JNEUROSCI.3963-08.2009

May, E. C. (2013). *A test of thermodynamic entropy effects in anomalous cognition* (Progress Report for the Bial Foundation, Bursary Identification 28/12). Coronado, Portugal: Bial Foundation.

May, E. C. (2014). Advances in anomalous cognition analysis: A judge-free and accurate confidence-calling technique. In E. C. May & S. B. Marwaha (Eds.),

Anomalous cognition: Remote viewing research and theory (pp. 80–88). Jefferson, NC: McFarland.

May, E. C., & Lantz, N. D. (2010). Anomalous cognition technical trials: Inspiration for the target entropy concept. *Journal of the Society for Psychical Research, 74,* 224–243.

May, E. C., & Marwaha, S. B. (Eds.). (2014). *Anomalous cognition: Remote viewing research and theory.* Jefferson, NC: McFarland.

May, E. C., & Spottiswoode, S. (2014). Shannon entropy: A possible intrinsic target property. In E. C. May & S. B. Marwaha (Eds.), *Anomalous cognition: Remote viewing research and theory* (pp. 299–313). Jefferson, NC: McFarland.

Mayer, E. L. (2001). On "telepathic dreams?": An unpublished paper by Robert J. Stoller. *Journal of the American Psychoanalytic Association, 49,* 629–652.

Mayhew, C. (1965). ". . . All the events in my drawing room between one-thirty and four existed together at the same time . . ." In D. Ebin (Ed.), *The drug experience: First-person accounts of addicts, writers, scientists, and others* (First Evergreen Black Cat ed., pp. 293–300). New York, NY: Grove Press.

McNamara, P. (2011). *Spirit possession and exorcism: History, psychology, and neurobiology* (Vols. 1 & 2). Santa Barbara, CA: Praeger.

McTaggart, J. M. E. (1967). Time. In R. M. Gale (Ed.), *The philosophy of time: A collection of essays* (pp. 86–97). Garden City, NY: Anchor Books. (Original work published 1927)

McTaggart, J. M. E. (1993). The unreality of time. In R. Le Poidevin & M. MacBeath (Eds.), *The philosophy of time* (pp. 23–34). Oxford, England: Oxford University Press. (Original work published 1908)

McTaggart, L. M. (2007). *The intention experiment: Using your thoughts to change your life and the world.* New York, NY: Free Press.

Meijer, D. K. F. (2014). The extended brain: Cyclic information flow in a quantum physical realm. *NeuroQuantology, 12,* 180–200. http://dx.doi.org/10.14704/nq.2014.12.2.754

Mellers, B., Stone, E., Murray, T., Minster, A., Rohrbaugh, N., Bishop, M., . . . Tetlock, P. (2015). Identifying and cultivating superforecasters as a method of improving probabilistic predictions. *Perspectives on Psychological Science, 10,* 267–281. http://dx.doi.org/10.1177/1745691615577794

Merrell-Wolff, F. (1966). *Mathematics, philosophy and yoga: Lecture #5* [Audio cassette recording]. Phoenix, AZ: Phoenix Philosophical Press.

Merrell-Wolff, F. (1995). *Transformations in consciousness: The metaphysics and epistemology.* Albany: State University of New York Press.

Merz, R. J. (2010). *Transformations of bereavement in a psychomanteum process: Qualities of meaning and paths of change* (Doctoral dissertation). Available from ProQuest Dissertations and Theses database. (UMI No. 3407974)

Meyer zu Erpen, W. (2013). Canadian psychical research experiments with table tilting and ectoplasm phenomena in the séance room. In M. Moreman (Ed.), *The spiritualist movement: Speaking with the dead in America and around the world: Vol. 2. Belief, practice, and evidence for life after death* (pp. 205–228). Santa Barbara, CA: Praeger.

Milburn, G. J., & Poulin, D. (2006). Relational time for systems of oscillators. *International Journal of Quantum Information, 4*(1), 151–159.

Miller, I. (2012). The nonlocal mind paradigm: A transdisciplinary revision of mind–body in philosophy, art, and science. *Journal of Consciousness Exploration & Research, 3,* 260–277.

Millett, D. (2001). Hans Berger: From psychic energy to the EEG. *Perspectives in Biology and Medicine, 44,* 522–542. http://dx.doi.org/10.1353/pbm.2001.0070

Milton, J., & Wiseman, R. (1999). Does psi exist? Lack of replication of an anomalous process of information transfer. *Psychological Bulletin, 125,* 387–391. http://dx.doi.org/10.1037/0033-2909.125.4.387

Mishlove, J. (1993). *Roots of consciousness: The classic encyclopedia of consciousness studies* (Rev. ed.). Tulsa, OK: Council Oak Books. (Original work published 1975)

Mitrani, L., Shekerdjiiski, S., & Yakimoff, N. (1986). Mechanisms and asymmetries in visual perception of simultaneity and temporal order. *Biological Cybernetics, 54,* 159–165. http://dx.doi.org/10.1007/BF00356854

Mobbs, D., & Watt, C. (2011). There is nothing paranormal about near-death experiences: How neuroscience can explain seeing bright lights, meeting the dead, or being convinced you are one of them. *Trends in Cognitive Sciences, 15,* 447–449. http://dx.doi.org/10.1016/j.tics.2011.07.010

Monroe, R. A. (1972). *Journeys out of the body.* London, England: Corgi Books.

Monroe, R. A. (1994). *Ultimate journey.* New York, NY: Doubleday.

Moody, R. (1975). *Life after life: The investigation of a phenomenon—Survival of bodily death.* Covington, GA: Mockingbird Books.

Moody, R. (with Perry, P.). (1993). *Reunions: Visionary encounters with departed loved ones.* New York, NY: Villard.

Moore, B. C. (2012). *An introduction to the psychology of hearing* (6th ed.). Bingley, England: Emerald.

Moorjani, A. (2012). *Dying to be me: My journey from cancer, to near death, to true healing.* Carlsbad, CA: Hay House.

Mossbridge, J. A. (2002). *Unfolding: The perpetual science of your soul's work.* Novato, CA: New World Library.

Mossbridge, J. A. (2003). *Grief relief: Visiting the dead.* Retrieved from http://www.induced-adc.com/experiences/

Mossbridge, J. A. (2009). Brain shaping at work: Wiring our brains for integrity, leadership, creativity and [insert your favorite trait or skill here]. In J. Marques (Ed.), *The workplace and spirituality: New perspectives in research and practice* (pp. 45–56). Woodstock, VT: Skylight Paths.

Mossbridge, J. A. (2015). *Time and the unconscious mind.* Retrieved from http://arxiv.org/abs/1503.01368

Mossbridge, J. A., Fitzgerald, M. B., O'Connor, E. S., & Wright, B. A. (2006). Perceptual-learning evidence for separate processing of asynchrony and order tasks. *The Journal of Neuroscience, 26,* 12708–12716. http://dx.doi.org/10.1523/JNEUROSCI.2254-06.2006

Mossbridge, J. A., Scissors, B. N., & Wright, B. A. (2008). Learning and generalization on asynchrony and order tasks at sound offset: Implications for underlying neural circuitry. *Learning & Memory, 15*(1), 13–20. http://dx.doi.org/10.1101/lm.573608

Mossbridge, J. A., Tressoldi, P., & Utts, J. (2012). Predictive physiological anticipation preceding seemingly unpredictable stimuli: A meta-analysis. *Frontiers in Psychology, 3,* 390. http://dx.doi.org/10.3389/fpsyg.2012.00390

Muldoon, S. J., & Carrington, H. (1929). *The projection of the astral body.* London, England: Rider Books.

Murphy, M., & White, R. A. (1978). *The psychic side of sports.* Reading, MA: Addison Wesley.

Nadin, M. (2013). Quantifying anticipatory characteristics: The Anticipation-Scope and the AnticipatoryProfile. In B. Iantovics & R. Kountchev (Eds.), *Advanced intelligent computational technologies and decision support systems* (Vol. 486, pp. 143–160). http://dx.doi.org/10.1007/978-3-319-00467-9_13

Nagel, T. (2012). *Mind and cosmos: Why the materialist neo-Darwinian conception of nature is almost certainly false.* http://dx.doi.org/10.1093/acprof:oso/9780199919758.001.0001

Nahm, M. (2009). Terminal lucidity in people with mental illness and other mental disability: An overview and implications for possible explanatory models. *Journal of Near-Death Studies, 28,* 87–106.

Nahm, M., & Greyson, B. (2009). Terminal lucidity in patients with chronic schizophrenia and dementia: A survey of the literature. *Journal of Nervous and Mental Disease, 197,* 942–944. http://dx.doi.org/10.1097/NMD.0b013e3181c22583

Nahm, M., Greyson, B., Kelly, E. W., & Haraldsson, E. (2012). Terminal lucidity: A review and a case collection. *Archives of Gerontology and Geriatrics, 55,* 138–142. http://dx.doi.org/10.1016/j.archger.2011.06.031

Neimeyer, R. A. (Ed.). (2001). *Meaning reconstruction and the experience of loss.* http://dx.doi.org/10.1037/10397-000

Neimeyer, R. A. (2014). The changing face of grief: Contemporary directions in theory, research, and practice. *Progress in Palliative Care, 22,* 125–130. http://dx.doi.org/10.1179/1743291X13Y.0000000075

Neppe, V. M. (2007). A detailed analysis of an important chess game: Revisiting Maróczy versus Korchnoi. *Journal of the Society for Psychical Research, 71,* 129–147.

Newton, M. (Ed.). (2009). *Memories of the afterlife: Life-between-lives: Stories of personal transformation.* Woodbury, MN: Llewellyn.

Ney, A. (2008). Defining physicalism. *Philosophy Compass, 3,* 1033–1048. http://dx.doi.org/10.1111/j.1747-9991.2008.00163.x

Nickerson, R. S. (1998). Confirmation bias: A ubiquitous phenomenon in many guises. *Review of General Psychology, 2,* 175–220. http://dx.doi.org/10.1037/1089-2680.2.2.175

Nisbett, R. E., & Wilson, T. D. (1977). Telling more than we can know: Verbal reports on mental processes. *Psychological Review, 84,* 231–259. http://dx.doi.org/10.1037/0033-295X.84.3.231

Noreika, V., Falter, C. M., & Wagner, T. M. (2014). Variability of duration perception: From natural and induced alterations to psychiatric disorders. In V. L. Arstila & D. Lloyd (Eds.), *Subjective time: The philosophy, psychology, and neuroscience of temporality* (pp. 529–555). Cambridge, MA: MIT Press.

Normann, H. K., Asplund, K., Karlsson, S., Sandman, P.-O., & Norberg, A. (2006). People with severe dementia exhibit episodes of lucidity: A population-based study. *Journal of Clinical Nursing, 15,* 1413–1417. http://dx.doi.org/10.1111/j.1365-2702.2005.01505.x

Noyes, R., & Kletti, R. (1977). Panoramic memory: A response to the threat of death. *Omega: Journal of Death and Dying, 8,* 181–194.

O'Keeffe, C., & Wiseman, R. (2005). Testing alleged mediumship: Methods and results. *British Journal of Psychology, 96,* 165–179. http://dx.doi.org/10.1348/000712605X36361

Orme, J. (1974). Precognition and time. *Journal of the Society for Psychical Research, 47,* 351–365.

Osis, K., & Haraldsson, E. (1997). *At the hour of death* (3rd ed.). Norwalk, CT: Hastings House.

Otis, L. P., & Alcock, J. E. (1982). Factors affecting extraordinary belief. *The Journal of Social Psychology, 118,* 77–85. http://dx.doi.org/10.1080/00224545.1982.9924420

Owen, I. M. (with Sparrow, M.). (1976). *Conjuring up Philip: An adventure in psychokinesis.* Toronto, Ontario, Canada: Fitzhenry & Whiteside.

Padfield, S. (1980). Mind–matter interaction in the psychokinetic experience. In B. S. Josephson & V. S. Ramachandran (Eds.), *Consciousness and the physical world: Edited proceedings of an interdisciplinary symposium on consciousness held at the University of Cambridge in January 1978* (pp. 165–175). Oxford, England: Pergamon Press.

Palmieri, A., Calvo, V., Kleinbub, J. R., Meconi, F., Marangoni, M., Barilaro, P., . . . Sessa, P. (2014). "Reality" of near-death-experience memories: Evidence from a psychodynamic and electrophysiological integrated study. *Frontiers in Human Neuroscience, 8,* 429.

Parnia, S., Spearpoint, K., de Vos, G., Fenwick, P., Goldberg, D., Yang, J., . . . Schoenfeld, E. R. (2014). AWARE—AWAreness during REsuscitation—A prospective study. *Resuscitation, 85,* 1799–1805. http://dx.doi.org/10.1016/j.resuscitation.2014.09.004

Parnia, S., Waller, D. G., Yeates, R., & Fenwick, P. (2001). A qualitative and quantitative study of the incidence, features and aetiology of near death experiences in cardiac arrest survivors. *Resuscitation, 48,* 149–156. http://dx.doi.org/10.1016/S0300-9572(00)00328-2

Parra, A. (2013). Phenomenological examination of premonition experiences in dreams and waking states: A survey study. *Australian Journal of Parapsychology, 13,* 187–212.

Pearson, P. (2014). *Opening heaven's door: What the dying may be trying to tell us about where they're going.* Toronto, Ontario, Canada: Random House Canada.

Peierls, R. E. (1960). Wolfgang Ernst Pauli: 1900–1958. *Biographical Memoirs of Fellows of the Royal Society, 5,* 174–192. http://dx.doi.org/10.1098/rsbm.1960.0014

Pekala, R. J., & Cardeña, E. (2000). Methodological issues in the study of altered states of consciousness and anomalous experiences. In E. Cardeña, S. J. Lynn, & S. Krippner (Eds.), *Varieties of anomalous experience: Examining the scientific evidence* (pp. 47–82). Washington, DC: American Psychological Association.

Penfield, W. (1975). *The mystery of the mind: A critical study of consciousness and the human brain.* Princeton, NJ: Princeton University Press.

Peng, T., Chen, H., Shih, Y., & Scully, M. O. (2014). Delayed-choice quantum eraser with thermal light. *Physical Review Letters, 112,* 180401–180405. http://dx.doi.org/10.1103/PhysRevLett.112.180401

Petro, A. (2011). *Remembering the light through prosetry*: (*Integrating prose and poetry).* Denver, CO: Outskirts Press.

Pfeiffer, T., Mack, J. E., & Devereux, P. (Eds.). (2007). *Mind before matter: Visions of a new science of consciousness.* Ropley, Hampshire, England: O Books.

Pilkington, R. (2015). Interview with Felicia Parise, August 6, 2013. *Journal of Scientific Exploration, 29*(1), 75–108.

Polkinghorne, J. (2002). *Quantum theory: A very short introduction.* http://dx.doi.org/10.1093/actrade/9780192802521.001.0001

Pommé, S. (2015). Typical uncertainties in alpha-particle spectrometry. *Metrologia, 52,* S146–S155. http://dx.doi.org/10.1088/0026-1394/52/3/S146

Popper, K. R., & Eccles, J. C. (1981). *The self and its brain.* Berlin, Germany: Springer International.

Poulin, D. (2005). *Toy model for a relational formulation of quantum theory.* Retrieved from arXiv:quant-ph/0505081v2

Pratt, J. G., & Roll, W. G. (1958). The Seaford disturbances. *Journal of Parapsychology, 22,* 79–124.

Preston, A. (2015). Analytic philosophy. *Internet encyclopedia of philosophy.* Retrieved from http://www.iep.utm.edu/analytic/

Pribram, K. H. (1976). Problems concerning the structure of consciousness. In G. G. Globus, G. Maxwell, & I. Savodnik (Eds.), *Consciousness and the brain: A scientific and philosophical inquiry* (pp. 297–313). http://dx.doi.org/10.1007/978-1-4684-2196-5_11

Pribram, K. H. (1982). What the fuss is all about. In K. Wilber (Ed.), *The holographic paradigm and other paradoxes: Exploring the leading edge of science* (pp. 27–34). Boulder, CO: Shambhala.

Price, D. D., & Barrell, J. J. (2012). *Inner experience and neuroscience: Merging both perspectives.* Cambridge, MA: MIT Press.

Prince, W. F. (1927). *The case of Patience Worth: A critical study of certain unusual phenomena.* Boston, MA: Boston Society for Psychic Research.

Pronin, E., & Schmidt, K. (2013). Claims and denials of bias and their implications for policy. In E. Shafir (Ed.), *The biological foundations of public policy* (pp. 195–216). Princeton, NJ: Princeton University Press.

Pulos, L. (1995). From egg to chick in 14 minutes. *MISAHA Newsletter, 10,* 4–5.

Pulos, L., & Richman, G. (1990). *Miracles and other realities.* Vancouver, British Columbia, Canada: Omega Press.

Puthoff, H. E. (1996). CIA-initiated remote viewing program at Stanford Research Institute. *Journal of Scientific Exploration, 10*(1), 63–76.

Puthoff, H. E., & Targ, R. (1976). A perceptual channel for information transfer over kilometer distances: Historical perspective and recent research. *Proceedings of the IEEE, 64,* 329–354. http://dx.doi.org/10.1109/PROC.1976.10113

Radin, D. I. (1997a). *The conscious universe: The scientific truth of psychic phenomena.* New York, NY: HarperEdge.

Radin, D. I. (1997b). Unconscious perception of future emotions: An experiment in presentiment. *Journal of Scientific Exploration, 11*(2), 163–180.

Radin, D. I. (2002). *Preliminary analysis of a suite of informal web-based psi experiments.* Retrieved from https://www.researchgate.net/profile/Dean_Radin/publication/254423666_Preliminary_Analysis_of_a_Suite_of_Informal_Web-Based_Psi_Experiments/links/548f23b80cf2d1800d862226.pdf

Radin, D. I. (2007). Finding or imagining flawed research? *The Humanistic Psychologist, 35,* 297–299. http://dx.doi.org/10.1080/08873260701578384

Radin, D. I. (2013). *Supernormal: Science, yoga, and the evidence for extraordinary psychic abilities.* New York, NY: Deepak Chopra Books.

Radin, D. I., Michel, L., & Delorme, A. (2015). Psychophysical interactions with a single photon double-slit optical system. *Quantum Biosystems, 6*(1), 82–98.

Radin, D. I., Michel, L., Johnston, J., & Delorme, A. (2013). Psychophysical interactions with a double-slit interference pattern. *Physics Essays, 26,* 553–566. http://dx.doi.org/10.4006/0836-1398-26.4.553

Rae, A. I. M. (2004). *Quantum physics: Illusion or reality?* (2nd ed.). Cambridge, England: Cambridge University Press. http://dx.doi.org/10.1017/CBO9780511535284

Reinhardt, S., Saathoff, G., Buhr, H., Carlson, L. A., Wolf, A., Schwalm, D., . . . Gwinner, G. (2007). Test of relativistic time dilation with fast optical atomic clocks at different velocities. *Nature Physics, 3,* 861–864. http://dx.doi.org/10.1038/nphys778

Revonsuo, A. (1999). Binding and the phenomenal unity of consciousness. *Consciousness and Cognition, 8*, 173–185. http://dx.doi.org/10.1006/ccog.1999.0384

Rhine, J. B. (1934). *Extra-sensory perception.* Boston, MA: Bruce Humphries. http://dx.doi.org/10.1037/13314-000

Richards, T. A., & Folkman, S. (1997). Spiritual aspects of loss at the time of a partner's death from AIDS. *Death Studies, 21*, 527–552. http://dx.doi.org/10.1080/074811897201769

Richards, T. L., Kozak, L., Johnson, L. C., & Standish, L. J. (2005). Replicable functional magnetic resonance imaging evidence of correlated brain signals between physically and sensory isolated subjects. *The Journal of Alternative and Complementary Medicine, 11*, 955–963. http://dx.doi.org/10.1089/acm.2005.11.955

Ring, K. (1987). Near-death experiences: Intimations of immortality? In J. S. Spong (Ed.), *Consciousness and survival: An interdisciplinary inquiry into the possibility of life beyond biological death* (pp. 165–176). Sausalito, CA: Institute of Noetic Sciences.

Ring, K., & Cooper, S. (1997). Near-death and out-of-body experiences in the blind: A study of apparent eyeless vision. *Journal of Near-Death Studies, 16*, 101–147. http://dx.doi.org/10.1023/A:1025010015662

Ring, K., & Valarino, E. E. (1998). *Lessons from the light: What we can learn from the near-death experience.* Portsmouth, NH: Moment Point.

Ringbauer, M., Duffus, B., Branciard, C., Cavalcanti, E. G., White, A. G., & Fedrizzi, A. (2015). Measurements on the reality of the wavefunction. *Nature Physics, 11*, 249–254. http://dx.doi.org/10.1038/nphys3233

Rivas, T., & Smit, R. H. (2013). A near-death experience with veridical perception described by a famous heart surgeon and confirmed by his assistant surgeon. *Journal of Near-Death Studies, 31*, 179–186.

Roach, M. (2005). *Spook: Science tackles the afterlife.* New York, NY: W. W. Norton.

Robertson, T. J., & Roy, A. E. (2004). Results of the application of the Robertson-Roy protocol to a series of experiments with mediums and participants. *Journal of the Society for Psychical Research, 68*, 18–34.

Rock, A. J., Beischel, J., Boccuzzi, M., & Biuso, M. (2014). Discarnate readings by claimant mediums: Assessing phenomenology and accuracy under beyond double-blind conditions. *Journal of Parapsychology, 78*, 183–194.

Roe, C. A., Davey, R., & Stevens, P. (2006). Experimenter effects in laboratory tests of ESP and PK using a common protocol. *Journal of Scientific Exploration, 20*, 239–253.

Roe, C. A., Sonnex, C., & Roxburgh, E. C. (2015). Two meta-analyses of noncontact healing studies. *EXPLORE: The Journal of Science and Healing, 11*, 11–23. http://dx.doi.org/10.1016/j.explore.2014.10.001

Roll, W. G. (2008). Psi and the long body. *Australian Journal of Parapsychology, 8*(1), 6–28.

Roney-Dougal, S. M., Solfvin, J., & Fox, J. (2008). An exploration of degree of meditation attainment in relation to psychic awareness with Tibetan Buddhists. *Journal of Scientific Exploration, 22*, 161–178.

Rosenbaum, R. (2011). Exploring the other dark continent: Parallels between psi phenomena and the psychotherapeutic process. *Psychoanalytic Review, 98*(1), 57–90. http://dx.doi.org/10.1521/prev.2011.98.1.57

Rosenberg, G. (2004). *A place for consciousness: Probing the deep structure of the natural world*. Oxford, England: Oxford University Press. http://dx.doi.org/10.1093/acprof:oso/9780195168143.001.0001

Ross, C. A., Norton, G. R., & Wozney, K. (1989). Multiple personality disorder: An analysis of 236 cases. *Canadian Journal of Psychiatry, 34,* 413–418.

Rossman, A., & Utts, J. (2014). Interview with Jessica Utts. *Journal of Statistics Education, 22*(2), 1–25.

Ruhnau, E. (1994). The now—The missing link between matter and mind. In M. Bitbol & E. Ruhnau (Eds.), *Now, time and quantum mechanics* (pp. 101–130). Gif-sur-Yvette, France: Editions Frontières.

Ruhnau, E., & Pöppel, E. (1991). Adirectional temporal zones in quantum physics and brain physiology. *International Journal of Theoretical Physics, 30,* 1083–1090. http://dx.doi.org/10.1007/BF00671487

Ryzl, M. (1966). A model of parapsychological communication. *Journal of Parapsychology, 30,* 18–30.

Sabom, M. B. (1982). *Recollections of death: A medical investigation.* New York, NY: Harper & Row.

Sabom, M. B. (1998). *Light and death: One doctor's fascinating account of near-death experiences.* Grand Rapids, MI: Zondervan.

Sandelands, L. E. (2006). Evolution's lost souls. *Behavioral and Brain Sciences, 29,* 484–485. http://dx.doi.org/10.1017/S0140525X06479103

Sangster, L. T. (2004). *Characterizing feelings of reality* (Unpublished bachelor's thesis). University of Western Ontario, London, Ontario, Canada.

Sartori, P. (2008). *The near-death experiences of hospitalized intensive care patients: A five-year clinical study.* Lewiston, NY: Edwin Mellen Press.

Scarborough, D. L., Cortese, C., & Scarborough, H. S. (1977). Frequency and repetition effects in lexical memory. *Journal of Experimental Psychology: Human Perception and Performance, 3*(1), 1–17. http://dx.doi.org/10.1037/0096-1523.3.1.1

Schlegel, R. (1966). Time and thermodynamics. In J. T. Fraser (Ed.), *The voices of time: A cooperative survey of man's views of time as expressed by the sciences and by the humanities* (pp. 500–523). New York, NY: George Braziller.

Schlitz, M. (2014). Transpersonal healing: Assessing the evidence from laboratory and clinical trials. *International Journal of Transpersonal Studies, 33*(1), 97–101.

Schmidt, H. (1971). Mental influence on random events. *New Scientist and Science Journal, 50*(757), 757–758.

Schmitt, M. F. (2007). If all is consciousness, what then is my body? In T. Pfeiffer, J. E. Mack, & P. Devereux (Eds.), *Mind before matter: Visions of a new science of consciousness* (pp. 64–69). Ropley, Hampshire, England: O Books.

Schneider, J. (1994). The now, relativity theory and quantum mechanics. In M. Bitbol & E. Ruhnau (Eds.), *Now, time and quantum mechanics* (pp. 131–153). Gif-sur-Yvette, France: Editions Frontières.

Schooler, J. (2015). Bridging the objective/subjective divide: Towards a meta-perspective of science and experience. In T. Metzinger & J. M. Windt (Eds.), *Open MIND: 34(T)* (pp. 1–40). Frankfurt am Main, Germany: MIND Group.

Schouten, S. (1993). Are we making progress? In L. Coly & J. McMahon (Eds.), *Psi research methodology: A re-examination. Proceedings of an international conference, Oct 29–30, 1988* (pp. 295–322). New York, NY: Parapsychology Foundation.

Schutte, N. S., & Malouff, J. M. (2014). A meta-analytic review of the effects of mindfulness meditation on telomerase activity. *Psychoneuroendocrinology, 42,* 45–48. http://dx.doi.org/10.1016/j.psyneuen.2013.12.017

Schwaninger, J., Eisenberg, P. R., Schechtman, K. B., & Weiss, A. N. (2002). A prospective analysis of near-death experiences in cardiac arrest patients. *Journal of Near-Death Studies, 20,* 215–232. http://dx.doi.org/10.1023/A:1015258818660

Schwartz, G. E. R., Russek, L. G. S., Nelson, L. A., & Barentsen, C. (2001). Accuracy and replicability of anomalous after-death communication across highly skilled mediums. *Journal of the Society for Psychical Research, 65,* 1–25.

Schwartz, S. A. (2010). The antique roadshow: How denier movements critique evolution, climate change, and nonlocal consciousness. In S. Krippner & H. L. Friedman (Eds.), *Debating psychic experience: Human potential or human illusion?* (pp. 179–194). Santa Barbara, CA: Praeger.

Schwartz, S. A. (2015). Through time and space: The evidence for remote viewing. In D. Broderick & B. Goertzel (Eds.), *Evidence for psi: Thirteen empirical research reports* (pp. 168–212). Jefferson, NC: McFarland.

Schwarzkopf, D. S. (2014). We should have seen this coming. *Frontiers in Human Neuroscience, 8,* 332. http://dx.doi.org/10.3389/fnhum.2014.00332

Scott, D. (1997). Leibniz and the two clocks. *Journal of the History of Ideas, 58,* 445–463. http://dx.doi.org/10.1353/jhi.1997.0030

Seager, W., & Allen-Hermanson, S. (2013, Fall). Panpsychism. In E. N. Zalta (Ed.), *The Stanford encyclopedia of philosophy.* Retrieved from http://plato.stanford.edu/archives/fall2013/entries/panpsychism/

Searle, J. R. (1983). *Intentionality: An essay in the philosophy of mind.* http://dx.doi.org/10.1017/CBO9781139173452

Segal, S. (1996). *Collision with the infinite: A life beyond the personal self.* San Diego, CA: Blue Dove Press.

Shanon, B. (2001). Altered temporality. *Journal of Consciousness Studies, 8(1),* 35–58.

Shanon, B. (2002). *The antipodes of the mind: Charting the phenomenology of the ayahuasca experience.* Oxford, England: Oxford University Press.

Shapin, S. (1981). Of gods and kings: Natural philosophy and politics in the Leibniz-Clarke disputes. *Isis, 72,* 187–215. http://dx.doi.org/10.1086/352718

Sheldrake, R. (2000). Telepathic telephone calls: Two surveys. *Journal of the Society for Psychical Research, 64,* 224–232.

Sheldrake, R. (2012). *Science set free: 10 paths to new discovery.* New York, NY: Deepak Chopra Books.

Sheldrake, R., Godwin, H., & Rockell, S. (2004). A filmed experiment on telephone telepathy with the Nolan sisters. *Journal of the Society for Psychical Research, 68,* 168–172.

Sheldrake, R., & Smart, P. (2003). Videotaped experiments on telephone telepathy. *Journal of Parapsychology, 67,* 187–206.

Shepard, R. N., & Metzler, J. (1971). Mental rotation of three-dimensional objects. *Science, 171,* 701–703. http://dx.doi.org/10.1126/science.171.3972.701

Shermer, M. (2014, October). Infrequencies. *Scientific American, 311*(4), 97. http://dx.doi.org/10.1038/scientificamerican1014-97

Sherwood, S., & Roe, C. (2003). A review of dream ESP studies conducted since the Maimonides dream ESP programme. *Journal of Consciousness Studies, 10,* 85–109.

Sherwood, S., Roe, C., Simmons, C., & Biles, C. (2002). An exploratory investigation of dream precognition using consensus judging and static targets. *Journal of the Society for Psychical Research, 66,* 22–28.

Shushan, G. (2009). *Conceptions of the afterlife in early civilizations: Universalism, constructivism, and near-death experience.* London, England: Continuum.

Siewert, C. (2010). Saving appearances: A dilemma for physicalists. In R. C. Koons & G. Bealer (Eds.), *The waning of materialism* (pp. 67–88). http://dx.doi.org/10.1093/acprof:oso/9780199556182.003.0003

Siler, K., Lee, K., & Bero, L. (2015). Measuring the effectiveness of scientific gatekeeping. *Proceedings of the National Academy of Sciences, USA, 112,* 360–365. http://dx.doi.org/10.1073/pnas.1418218112

Sio, U. N., Monaghan, P., & Ormerod, T. (2013). Sleep on it, but only if it is difficult: Effects of sleep on problem solving. *Memory & Cognition, 41,* 159–166. http://dx.doi.org/10.3758/s13421-012-0256-7

Skrbina, D. (2005). *Panpsychism in the West.* Cambridge, MA: MIT Press.

Skrbina, D. (2009). Introduction. In D. Skrbina (Ed.), *Mind that abides: Panpsychism in the new millennium* (pp. xi–xiv). http://dx.doi.org/10.1075/aicr.75

Smart, J. J. C. (1967). Spatialising time. In R. M. Gale (Ed.), *The philosophy of time: A collection of essays* (pp. 163–167). Garden City, NY: Anchor Books.

Smith, D. W. (2013, Winter). Phenomenology. In E. N. Zalta (Ed.), *The Stanford encyclopedia of philosophy.* Retrieved from http://plato.stanford.edu/archives/win2013/entries/phenomenology/

Smith, H. (2000). *Cleansing the doors of perception: The religious significance of entheogenic plants and chemicals.* New York, NY: Tarcher/Putnam.

Smith, M. D. (2003). The role of the experimenter in parapsychological research. *Journal of Consciousness Studies, 10*(6–7), 69–84.

Smolin, L. (2006). *The trouble with physics: The rise of string theory, the fall of a science, and what comes next*. Boston, MA: Houghton Mifflin.

Smolin, L. (2013). *Time reborn: From the crisis in physics to the future of the universe*. Toronto, Ontario, Canada: Alfred A. Knopf Canada.

Sokal, A. D. (1996a). A physicist experiments with cultural studies. *Lingua Franca*, 6(4), 62–64.

Sokal, A. D. (1996b). Transgressing the boundaries: Toward a transformative hermeneutics of quantum gravity. *Social Text*, 14(46/47), 217–252. http://dx.doi.org/10.2307/466856

Sokal, A. (2008). *Beyond the hoax: Science, philosophy and culture*. Oxford, England: Oxford University Press.

Sommer, A. (2014). Psychical research in the history and philosophy of science. An introduction and review. *Studies in History and Philosophy of Biological and Biomedical Sciences*, 48, 38–45. http://dx.doi.org/10.1016/j.shpsc.2014.08.004

Sondow, N. (1988). The decline of precognized events with the passage of time: Evidence from spontaneous dreams. *Journal of the American Society for Psychical Research*, 82, 33–51.

Srednicki, M. (2007). *Quantum field theory*. http://dx.doi.org/10.1017/CBO9780511813917

Stace, W. T. (1960). *Mysticism and philosophy*. London, England: Macmillan.

Standish, L. J., Johnson, L. C., Kozak, L., & Richards, T. (2003). Evidence of correlated functional magnetic resonance imaging signals between distant human brains. *Alternative Therapies in Health and Medicine*, 9(1), 122–125.

Standish, L. J., Kozak, L., Johnson, L. C., & Richards, T. (2004). Electroencephalographic evidence of correlated event-related signals between the brains of spatially and sensory isolated human subjects. *Journal of Alternative and Complementary Medicine*, 10, 307–314. http://dx.doi.org/10.1089/107555304323062293

Stapp, H. P. (2001). Quantum theory and the role of mind in nature. *Foundations of Physics*, 31, 1465–1499. http://dx.doi.org/10.1023/A:1012682413597

Stapp, H. P. (2004). *Mind, matter and quantum mechanics* (2nd ed.). http://dx.doi.org/10.1007/978-3-662-05369-0

Stapp, H. P. (2007). *The mindful universe*. Berlin, Germany: Springer.

Stevenson, I. (1997a). *Reincarnation and biology: A contribution to the etiology of birthmarks and birth defects*. Westport, CT: Praeger.

Stevenson, I. (1997b). *Where reincarnation and biology intersect*. Westport, CT: Praeger.

Stevenson, I., & Cook, E. W. (1995). Involuntary memories during severe physical illness or injury. *Journal of Nervous and Mental Disease*, 183, 452–458. http://dx.doi.org/10.1097/00005053-199507000-00005

Storm, L., Tressoldi, P. E., & Di Risio, L. (2010). Meta-analysis of free-response studies, 1992–2008: Assessing the noise reduction model in parapsychology. *Psychological Bulletin*, 136, 471–485. http://dx.doi.org/10.1037/a0019457

Storr, W. (2014, December 9). James Randi: Debunking the king of the debunkers. *The Telegraph*. Retrieved from http://www.telegraph.co.uk/culture/film/film-news/11270453/James-Randi-debunking-the-king-of-the-debunkers.html

Strassman, R. (2014). *DMT and the soul of prophecy: A new science of spiritual revelation in the Hebrew Bible*. Rochester, VT: Park Street Press.

Tallis, R. (2010, Fall). What neuroscience cannot tell us about ourselves. *The New Atlantis, 29*, 3–25. Retrieved from http://www.thenewatlantis.com/publications/what-neuroscience-cannot-tell-us-about-ourselves

Targ, R. (2004). *Limitless mind*. Novato, CA: New World Library.

Targ, R. (2012). *The reality of ESP: A physicist's proof of psychic abilities*. Wheaton, IL: Theosophical Publishing House.

Targ, R. (2015). *ESP Trainer by Russell Targ support page*. Retrieved from http://www.espresearch.com/iphone/

Targ, R., & Puthoff, H. E. (1974). Information transmission under conditions of sensory shielding. *Nature, 251*, 602–607. http://dx.doi.org/10.1038/251602a0

Tarlaci, S. (2010). A historical view of the relation between quantum mechanics and the brain: A neuroquantologic perspective. *NeuroQuantology, 8*, 120–136. http://dx.doi.org/10.14704/nq.2010.8.2.278

Tart, C. T. (1972). States of consciousness and state-specific sciences. *Science, 176*, 1203–1210. http://dx.doi.org/10.1126/science.176.4040.1203

Tart, C. T. (1998). Six studies of out-of-body experiences. *Journal of Near-Death Studies, 17*, 73–99. http://dx.doi.org/10.1023/A:1022932505993

Tart, C. T. (2009). *The end of materialism: How evidence of the paranormal is bringing science and spirit together*. Oakland, CA: New Harbinger.

Taylor, E. (1984). *William James on exceptional mental states: The 1896 Lowell lectures*. Amherst: University of Massachusetts Press.

Tegmark, M. (2014). *Consciousness as a state of matter*. Retrieved from http://arxiv.org/abs/1405.0493v1

Terhune, D. B., & Smith, M. D. (2006). The induction of anomalous experiences in a mirror-gazing facility: Suggestion, cognitive perceptual personality traits and phenomenological state effects. *Journal of Nervous and Mental Disease, 194*, 415–421. http://dx.doi.org/10.1097/01.nmd.0000221318.30692.a5

Thompson, E. (2015). *Waking, dreaming, being: Self and consciousness in neuroscience, meditation, and philosophy*. New York, NY: Columbia University Press.

Thonnard, M., Charland-Verville, V., Brédart, S., Dehon, H., Ledoux, D., Laureys, S., & Vanhaudenhuyse, A. (2013). Characteristics of near-death experiences memories as compared to real and imagined memories. *PLoS ONE, 8*(3), e57620, 1–5.

Toulmin, S. (1982). The genealogy of "consciousness." In P. F. Secord (Ed.), *Explaining human behaviour* (pp. 53–70). London, England: Sage.

Trent-von Haesler, N., & Beauregard, M. (2013). Near-death experiences in cardiac arrest: Implications for the concept of non-local mind. *Revista de Psiquiatria Clinica, 40*(5), 197–202. http://dx.doi.org/10.1590/S0101-60832013000500005

Trethowan, W. H. (1976). Exorcism: A psychiatric viewpoint. *Journal of Medical Ethics, 2*, 127–137.

Tuana, N. (1988). The weaker seed: The sexist bias of reproductive theory. *Hypatia, 3*, 35–59. http://dx.doi.org/10.1111/j.1527-2001.1988.tb00055.x

Turing, A. M. (1950). Computing machinery and intelligence. *Mind, 59*, 433–460. http://dx.doi.org/10.1093/mind/LIX.236.433

Tyrrell, G. (1947). The "modus operandi" of paranormal cognition. *Proceedings of the Society for Psychical Research, 48*, 65–120.

Utts, J. (1996). An assessment of the evidence for psychic functioning. *Journal of Scientific Exploration, 10*(1), 3–30.

Van Dusen, W. (1974). Hallucinations as the world of spirits. In J. White (Ed.), *Frontiers of consciousness: The meeting ground between inner and outer reality* (pp. 53–71). New York, NY: Julian Press.

van Lommel, P. (2006). Near-death experience, consciousness, and the brain. *World Futures, 62*, 134–151. http://dx.doi.org/10.1080/02604020500412808

van Lommel, P. (2013). Non-local consciousness: A concept based on scientific research on near-death experiences during cardiac arrest. *Journal of Consciousness Studies, 20*, 7–48.

van Lommel, P., van Wees, R., Meyers, V., & Elfferich, I. (2001). Near-death experience in survivors of cardiac arrest: A prospective study in the Netherlands. *The Lancet, 358*, 2039–2045. http://dx.doi.org/10.1016/S0140-6736(01)07100-8

Varela, F. J. (1996). Neurophenomenology: A methodological remedy for the hard problem. *Journal of Consciousness Studies, 3*, 330–349.

Varela, F. J. (1999). Present-time consciousness. *Journal of Consciousness Studies, 6*(2–3), 111–140.

Varvoglis, M., & Bancel, P. (2015). *Micro-psychokinesis*. Retrieved from http://www.researchgate.net/publication/273889027_Micro-psychokinesis

Velmans, M. (2009). *Understanding consciousness* (2nd ed.). New York, NY: Routledge.

Vernon, D. J. (2015). Exploring precognition using a repetition priming paradigm. *Journal of the Society for Psychical Research, 79*(2), 65–79.

Viemeister, N. F., & Wakefield, G. H. (1991). Temporal integration and multiple looks. *The Journal of the Acoustical Society of America, 90*(2), 858–865. http://dx.doi.org/10.1121/1.401953

Voss, J. L., Baym, C. L., & Paller, K. A. (2008). Accurate forced-choice recognition without awareness of memory retrieval. *Learning & Memory, 15*, 454–459. http://dx.doi.org/10.1101/lm.971208

Voss, J. L., Lucas, H. D., & Paller, K. A. (2012). More than a feeling: Pervasive influences of memory without awareness of retrieval. *Cognitive Neuroscience, 3*, 193–207. http://dx.doi.org/10.1080/17588928.2012.674935

Wagner, M. W., & Monnet, M. (1979). Attitudes of college professors toward extrasensory perception. *Zetetic Scholar, 5*, 7–17.

Walker, E. H. (1970). The nature of consciousness. *Mathematical Biosciences, 7,* 131–178. http://dx.doi.org/10.1016/0025-5564(70)90046-5

Walker, E. H. (1975). Foundations of paraphysical and parapsychological phenomena. In L. Oteri (Ed.), *Quantum physics and parapsychology* (pp. 1–53). New York, NY: Parapsychology Foundation.

Walker, E. H. (1977). Quantum mechanical tunneling in synaptic and ephaptic transmission. *International Journal of Quantum Chemistry, 11,* 103–127. http://dx.doi.org/10.1002/qua.560110109

Walker, E. H. (2000). *The physics of consciousness: Quantum minds and the meaning of life.* Cambridge, MA: Perseus.

Walker, E. H. (2001). The natural philosophy and physics of consciousness. In P. van Loocke (Ed.), *The physical nature of consciousness* (pp. 63–82). http://dx.doi.org/10.1075/aicr.29.03wal

Walker, M. P., Liston, C., Hobson, J. A., & Stickgold, R. (2002). Cognitive flexibility across the sleep-wake cycle: REM-sleep enhancement of anagram problem solving. *Cognitive Brain Research, 14,* 317–324. http://dx.doi.org/10.1016/S0926-6410(02)00134-9

Wallace, B. A. (2007). *Hidden dimensions: The unification of physics and consciousness.* New York, NY: Columbia University Press.

Wallas, G. (1926). *The art of thought.* New York, NY: Harcourt & Brace.

Watson, D. E., & Williams, B. O. (2003). Eccles' model of the self controlling its brain: The irrelevance of dualist-interactionism. *NeuroQuantology, 1,* 119–128.

Watson, J. B. (1913). Psychology as the behaviorist views it. *Psychological Review, 20,* 158–177. http://dx.doi.org/10.1037/h0074428

Watt, C. (2014). Precognitive dreaming: Investigating anomalous cognition and psychological factors. *Journal of Parapsychology, 78*(1), 115–125.

Watt, C., & Tierney, I. (2014). Psi-related experiences. In E. Cardeña, S. J. Lynn, & S. Krippner (Eds.), *Varieties of anomalous experience: Examining the scientific evidence* (2nd ed., pp. 241–272). Washington, DC: American Psychological Association.

Watt, C., & Vuillaume, L. (2015). Dream precognition and sensory incorporation: A controlled sleep laboratory study. *Journal of Consciousness Studies, 22*(5–6), 172–190.

Watts, A. W. (1965). *The joyous cosmology: Adventures in the chemistry of consciousness.* New York, NY: Vintage Books.

Weisberg, D. S., Keil, F. C., Goodstein, J., Rawson, E., & Gray, J. R. (2008). The seductive allure of neuroscience explanations. *Journal of Cognitive Neuroscience, 20,* 470–477. http://dx.doi.org/10.1162/jocn.2008.20040

Wheeler, J. A. (1983). Law without law. In J. A. Wheeler & W. H. Zurek (Eds.), *Quantum theory measurement* (pp. 182–213). http://dx.doi.org/10.1515/9781400854554

Wheeler, J. A., & Feynman, R. P. (1949). Classical electrodynamics in terms of direct interparticle action. *Reviews of Modern Physics, 21,* 425–433. http://dx.doi.org/10.1103/RevModPhys.21.425

Whinnery, J. E., & Whinnery, A. M. (1990). Acceleration-induced loss of consciousness: A review of 500 episodes. *Archives of Neurology, 47*, 764–776. http://dx.doi.org/10.1001/archneur.1990.00530070058012

Whyte, W. H., Jr. (2012, July 22). Groupthink. *Fortune.* (Original work published 1952) Retrieved from http://fortune.com/2012/07/22/groupthink-fortune-1952/

Wickland, C. A. (1924). *Thirty years among the dead.* London, England: Spiritualist Press.

Williams, B. J. (2015). Empirical examinations of the reported abilities of a psychic claimant: A review of experiments and explorations with Sean Harribance. In D. Broderick & B. Goertzel (Eds.), *Evidence for psi: Thirteen empirical research reports* (pp. 102–137). Jefferson, NC: McFarland.

Williams, B. J., & Ventola, A. (2011). *Poltergeist phenomena: A primer on parapsychological research and perspectives.* Retrieved from http://www.publicparapsychology.org/Public%20Parapsych/Poltergeist%20Phenomena%20Primer%20Final.pdf

Williams, G. (2013). Psi and the problem of consciousness. *Journal of Mind and Behaviour, 34*(3–4), 259–283.

Williams, K. (2014). *Time and the near-death experience.* Retrieved from http://www.near-death.com/experiences/research13.html

Wilson, K. (2013). A skeptic's view of mediumship. In A. J. Rock (Ed.), *The survival hypothesis: Essays on mediumship* (pp. 79–89). Jefferson, NC: McFarland.

Wittmann, M. (2009). The inner experience of time. *Philosophical Transactions of the Royal Society B: Biological Sciences, 364*, 1955–1967. http://dx.doi.org/10.1098/rstb.2009.0003

Wittmann, M., & Paulus, M. P. (2008). Decision making, impulsivity and time perception. *Trends in Cognitive Sciences, 12*(1), 7–12. http://dx.doi.org/10.1016/j.tics.2007.10.004

Wren-Lewis, J. (1988). The darkness of God: A personal report on consciousness transformation through an encounter with death. *Journal of Humanistic Psychology, 28*, 105–122. http://dx.doi.org/10.1177/0022167888282011

Wren-Lewis, J. (1991). A reluctant mystic: God-consciousness not guru worship. *Self and Society, 19*(2), 4–11.

Wren-Lewis, J. (1994). Aftereffects of near-death experiences: A survival mechanism hypothesis. *Journal of Transpersonal Psychology, 26*, 107–115.

Wright, B. A., & Dai, H. (1998). Detection of sinusoidal amplitude modulation at unexpected rates. *The Journal of the Acoustical Society of America, 104*(5), 2991–2996. http://dx.doi.org/10.1121/1.423881

Wulff, D. M. (2014). Mystical experiences. In E. Cardeña, S. J. Lynn, & S. Krippner (Eds.), *Varieties of anomalous experience: Examining the scientific evidence* (2nd ed., pp. 369–408). http://dx.doi.org/10.1037/14258-013

Zackay, D. (1990). The evasive art of subjective time measurement: Some methodological dilemmas. In R. A. Block (Ed.), *Cognitive models of psychological time* (pp. 59–84). Hillsdale, NJ: Erlbaum.

Zanesco, A. P., King, B. G., MacLean, K. A., & Saron, C. D. (2013). Executive control and felt concentrative engagement following intensive meditation training. *Frontiers in Human Neuroscience, 7*, 566. http://dx.doi.org/10.3389/fnhum.2013.00566

Zee, A. (2003). *Quantum field theory in a nutshell*. Princeton, NJ: Princeton University Press.

Zee, A. (2007). *Fearful symmetry: The search for beauty in modern physics*. Princeton, NJ: Princeton University Press. (Original work published 1986)

Zimmerman, E. J. (1966). Time and quantum theory. In J. T. Fraser (Ed.), *The voices of time: A cooperative survey of man's views of time as expressed by the sciences and by the humanities* (pp. 479–499). New York, NY: George Braziller.

Zohar, D. (1982). *Through the time barrier: A study in precognition and modern physics*. London, England: Paladin Books.

INDEX

Exorcism, 97–98
Expectancy effects, 134–135
Experience(s)
    of anomalous phenomena, 21
    of contact with deceased persons, 86
    contemplating, 162
    continuity of, 182
    distortions of, 153–154
    ignoring, 149–150
    image of, 180
    independent verification of, 152–154
    of life reviews, 72, 73
    mystical, 79
    ordinary vs. transcendent, 79–80
    origins of, 182
    state-specific memories of, 153
    of time, 56
    of timelessness, 78–80
    valuing of, 149, 150
Experience sampling method
        (phenomenology), 155–156
Experimenter effect, 131–133, 175
Explanatory gap, 15, 18, 19
Extended mind. *See* Shared mind
Extraordinary evidence, 23
Extraordinary transcendence, 27
Eye movement desensitization and
        reprocessing (EMDR), 89–90

Feelings of reality, in life reviews, 75
Fenwick Peter, 101
Ferrari, D., 157
Feynman, Richard, v, 193–194
Fictitious ghost, collective hallucination
        of, 139–140
File-drawer problem, 39, 41, 45
Filter models, 176–179
First-person methods in psychology,
        154–164
    development of first-person
        observation skills, 159–164
    integrating third-person approach
        with, 158–159, 166
    phenomenology, 154–156
    psychophysics, 156–157
    psychophysiology, 157–158
First-person observation
    developing skills in, 159–164
    flaws in, 147

interpreting, 152
    lack of training in, 146
    in science, 147–150
Flicker-filter model, 180–184
Flicker theory, 181–183
Flow, of time, 60–61, 63
Focused awareness meditation, 163–164
Fodor, Jerry, 18
Fontana, David, 118–119
Forgetting, unintentional, 153
Fox, J., 167–168
Fraud
    in poltergeist activity, 136
    in research, 22, 86
Free will, 180–181
Freud, Sigmund, 30–33
Friedman, W. J., 62
Future memory episodes, 76–77

Gamma activity (brain), 158
Ganzfeld (term), 43
Ganzfeld state, 42
Ganzfeld telepathy experiments,
        44–47, 49, 186
Gassendi, Pierre, 7–8
Genius, mechanisms underlying, 49–50
Ghosts
    fictitious, collective hallucination of,
        139–140
    hungry, 123
Goertzel, B., 22
Goertzel, T., 22
"Gold leaf lady," 142
Graf, Jennifer, 86–87
Gravity, quantum, 173
Greyson, B., 49–50, 104–105
Grief, contact with deceased during, 88
Grof, P., 192
Grosso, Michael, 84
Groupthink, 24, 173

Haisch, B., 7, 24
Hallucinations, 98–99
    collective, of fictitious ghost, 139–140
    NDEs as, 107
Happy schizotypes, 190
Haraldsson, E., 85, 87
Hard problem of consciousness, 15
Harnad, S., 16
Harribance, Sean, 37, 49

Lutz, A., 163–164
Lycan, W. G., 16, 19

Machine intelligence, 16–17
Macro-pk, 140–143
Maimonides Medical Center studies,
    42–43
Manifestation, physical, 181–183, 195
Maróczy, Géza, 93–94, 117, 118, 194
Marwit, S. J., 88
Maslow A. H., 164–165
Maslow's hierarchy of needs, 164–165
Materialism, 3–4, 7–28
    and anomalous phenomena, 20–24
    and beliefs about consciousness and
        reality, 26–28
    and computationalism, 17–20
    and dissociation, 11–12
    as dogma, 24–26
    and emergentism, 15–20
    history of, 7–8
    and neuroscientism, 13–15
    and physicalism, 12–13
    promissory, 19
    and quantum theories, 8–11
    and time, 10
Material-transcendent dimension, 27
Mathematics, in quantum theories,
    172–173
Mature valuation, 150, 163
May, Ed, 69
Mayhew, Christopher, 79
McTaggart, John, 54
Meaning, 189
Measurement
    implicit attitude measures, 160
    neuroscientific, 39
    observation and, 9–10
Mechanism studies, 129
Meditation
    brainwave activity during, 158, 162,
        178
    focused awareness, 163–164
    introspection in, 161–162
    open monitoring, 164
    and peace with oneself, 165
    and precognition, 167–168
    training in, 164
Mediums, 85, 91. *See also specific individuals*
    control of unwanted intrusions by, 98
    in existence studies, 129

expert behaviors demonstrated by,
    96–97
and information about nonphysical
    world, 116
on mediumship, 94–95
who allow discarnates to take over
    their bodies, 96
Mediumship, 91–92
    evidence for, 92
    mediums on, 94–95
Meitner, Lise, 171
Memory(-ies)
    in afterlife, 121–122
    future, 76
    location of, 179
    of NDEs, 110
    state-specific, 153
Mental illness. *See also* Psychopathology;
    specific disorders
    anomalous phenomena labeled as,
        22–23
    and belief in anomalous phenomena,
        190
    stability over time of, 151
Merrell-Wolff, Franklin, 79–80
Mescaline, 176
Meta-analyses, 41–46, 64–65, 66, 68,
    134–135, 157
Micro-pk, 140
Milton, J., 44, 45
Mind. *See also* Shared mind; Transcendent
    mind
    defined, 15
    as fundamental reality, 179
    influencing physical processes
        through. *See* Direct mental
        influence
    nonconscious, 168. *See also* Non-
        conscious processing
    quantum, 171–176
    separated from brain. *See* Separation
        of mind from brain
    and superconscious, 168
Mind and Life Institute, 164
Mirror gazing, 89
Mobbs, Dean, 108
Models of consciousness
    filter models, 176–179
    flicker-filter model, 180–184
    quantum mind, 172–176

Moore, Robert, 26–27
Moorjani, Anita, 142–143
Morphine, 177
Mossbridge, Julia, 90, 190, 191, 193
Murphy, 126–128
Myers, Frederic, 119, 121
Mystical experiences, 79
Mysticism, 158–159

Nature. *See also* Reality
    absurdity of, v, 174
    time and, 56
Near-death experiences (NDEs)
    altered time in, 76
    of the blind, visual elements in,
        105–106
    explanations of, 107–111
    feelings of reality in, 75
    life reviews with, 72–75
    mental clarity in, 105
    of Moorjani, 143
    new body experienced in, 120
    out-of-body experiences with,
        112–116
    Pauli-type effects following, 135
    psychological distress/psychopathology
        caused by, 191
    and survival mechanism, 177
Needs, hierarchy of, 164–165
Neurons
    computation in, 17–20
    existential qualia produced by,
        15–18
Neurophenomenology, 158
Neurophysiological measures (telepathy),
    39–41
Neuroscientism, 13–15, 17, 24
Neutrons, separating mass and spin of, 9
Newton, Isaac, 55
Newton, Michael, 118
Ney, A., 12
Nonconscious bias, 160–161
Nonconscious processing, 168
    and altered state of consciousness, 81
    of events in time, 63–66, 70–72
    implicit recognition, 68–69
    potential mechanisms of, 70–72
    precognitive dreaming, 66–68
    precognitive remote viewing, 69–70

Nondual consciousness, 178, 181–182
Nondual meditation, 162, 178
Nonphysical entities. *See* Discarnate
    beings
Nonwhole human biological systems
    studies, 134

Objective apparent time, 58–59
Objective deep time, 59
Objectivity, 11
    in billiard-ball version of reality, 8
    and properties of particles, 9–10
    pseudo-objective observation, 159
Observation
    of causally unrelated events, 55
    developing first-person skills in,
        159–164
    first-person, in psychology. *See* First-
        person methods in psychology
    first-person, in science, 147–150
    measurement and, 9–10
    pseudo-objective, 159
    in research, 146. *See also* Subjectivity
        in consciousness research
"Observers," 8, 10, 55–56, 93, 132, 136,
    140–141, 146–147, 151, 158,
    159, 165, 174–175
Online games, 186
Online single-trial data sets, 186–187
Open-ended thought experiments, 187
Open monitoring meditation, 164
Order (time), 60, 62
Osmond, Humphry, 79
Outliers, excluding, 45
Outlook shifts, following NDEs, 108–111
Out-of-body experiences
    double in, 120
    with NDEs, 112–116
Owen, I. M., 139–140

Padfield, Susan, 140–141
Panpsychism, 19–20
Parnia, S., 114–115
Particles, 9, 175
    and acceleration through space, 10
    quantum properties of, 9–10
Pauli effect, 135
Pauli, Wolfgang, 125, 135–137
PEAR (Princeton Engineering
    Anomalies Research), 126–131

Reynolds, Pam, 107–108
Rhine, J. B., 33
Richards, A. C., 154–155
Richman, Gary, 141
Ring, K., 72–73, 105, 106, 135
Rock, A. J., 92
Rodriguez, P., 88
Rogers, Carl, 149–150
Rollans, Robbert, 93, 94, 117
Romi/Romih, 117
Roney-Dougal, S. M., 167–168
Rosenbaum, Ruth, 24–25
Rückert, Friedrich, 93
Rudy, Lloyd William, Jr., 114–115

Sabom, Michael, 114–115
SAIC (Science Applications International Corporation), 36–37
Sartori, Penny, 83, 115
Sauchie case, 135–138
Scalability, 10
    in billiard-ball version of reality, 8
    in understanding reality, 9
Scenic dilation, in life reviews, 72
Schizotypal personality disorder, 23, 29, 190
Schizotypy, 190
Schmidt, Helmut, 128, 130
Schooler, Jonathan, 60
Science. See also Physics; Psychology
    as empirical investigation, 21
    first-person observation in, 147–150
    job of, 195
    politics of, 24
    similarities of mysticism and, 158–159
    subjectivity in, 150–151
Science Applications International Corporation (SAIC), 36–37
Science as a Spiritual Practice (Barušs), 158–159
Scientific discovery
    implications of transcendent mind for, 192–194
    by physicists, 175
Scientism, 24
Scientists
    expectations of, 175
    experiences of, 148

judgmental heuristics of, 23–24
    persecution for studying anomalous phenomena, 25–26
Scole experiment, 93
Searle, John, 17
Second law of thermodynamics, 57
Segal, Suzanne, 165
Self
    escalating, 80
    losing the experience of having, 165
    synthesizing aspects of, 168–169
Self-development, 195
    for consciousness researchers, 164–166
    for scientists, 24
Self-examination, 162–166
Self-observation skills, 184
Sense of reality, in life reviews, 75
Sensorimotor functions
    border between external world and, 71
    and brain when dying, 179
    nonconscious processing of, 63–64
    in sports, 64
Sensory leakage, 91–92
Sensory systems, time in, 61–62
Separation of mind from brain, 103–123
    mind in compromised brains, 104–106
    mind in silent brains, 112–116
    mind in the afterlife, 118–123
    mind without a brain, 116–118
    near-death experiences, 107–111
Shanon, B., 75, 79
Shared mind, 29–51
    concepts underlying phenomena of, 47–49
    and creativity, 49–50
    in filter model, 177–178
    Freud's position on, 30–33
    information about past or present from, 189
    laboratory evidence of, 33–35
    neurophysiological measures of telepathy, 39–41
    in psychology, 30–33
    querying, 188–189

ABOUT THE AUTHORS

Imants Baruss, PhD, is a professor of psychology at King's University College at Western University Canada, where he has been teaching undergraduate courses about consciousness for 29 years. His research has focused on the fundamental nature of consciousness, and he has had academic papers published not only in consciousness journals but also in psychology, philosophy, physics, mathematics, anthropology, and other science journals. He is the author of five previous books, including *Authentic Knowing: The Convergence of Science and Spiritual Aspiration* and *Alterations of Consciousness: An Empirical Analysis for Social Scientists.*

Julia Mossbridge, PhD, is an experimental psychologist and cognitive neuroscientist at the Institute of Noetic Sciences and a Visiting Scholar in Psychology at Northwestern University. She pursues an understanding of time, especially in terms of the relationships between conscious and nonconscious processing of events. In 2014, she received the Charles Honorton Integrative Contributions award for her work in bringing the phenomenon of presentiment to the mainstream. Dr. Mossbridge is the author of *Unfolding: The Science of Your Soul's Work* and the upcoming mystical/philosophical adventure *The Garden: An Inside Experiment.*